# Assembling Women

# Assembling Women

## THE FEMINIZATION OF GLOBAL MANUFACTURING

## TERI L. CARAWAY

**ILR PRESS** an imprint of
CORNELL UNIVERSITY PRESS
ITHACA AND LONDON

First published 2007 by Cornell University Press
First printing, Cornell Paperbacks, 2007

Printed in the United States of America

*Library of Congress Cataloging-in-Publication Data*
Caraway, Teri L.
   Assembling women : the feminization of global manufacturing /
Teri L. Caraway.
     p.  cm.
   Includes bibliographical references and index.
   ISBN-13: 978-0-8014-4548-4 (cloth : alk. paper)
   ISBN-13: 978-0-8014-7365-4 (paperback)
    1. Women—Employment.   2. Manufacturing industries—Employees.
3. Sexual division of labor.   4. Women—Employment—Indonesia.
5. Manufacturing industries—Indonesia—Employees.   6. Sexual
division of labor—Indonesia.   I. Title.
   HD6068.C37  2007
   331.4—dc22                              2006035551

Cornell University Press strives to use environmentally responsible suppliers and materials to the fullest extent possible in the publishing of its books. Such materials include vegetable-based, low-VOC inks and acid-free papers that are recycled, totally chlorine-free, or partly composed of nonwood fibers. For further information, visit our website at www.cornellpress.cornell.edu.

Cloth printing    10 9 8 7 6 5 4 3 2 1
Paperback printing    10 9 8 7 6 5 4 3 2 1

*For Ari, Cicih, Lilis, and Yatini*

# Contents

# Acknowledgments

After participating in the comparative politics program at Northwestern University, which permitted students to pursue interdisciplinary projects, I was lucky to land my first job in the Department of Political Science at the University of Minnesota, where many colleagues share a similar respect for research that pushes the boundaries of the discipline. The department supported this book in many ways, most importantly by giving me time off from teaching during my first four years of employment.

A number of advisers, friends, and colleagues have been helpful at various stages of the writing process. I thank Jeffrey Winters, Edward Gibson, and Kathleen Thelen for their faith in this project and for never discouraging me from pursuing an unusual topic. Ben Ross Schneider and Michael Hanchard gave helpful comments on chapters in early drafts. Sidney Tarrow read the entire manuscript and provided not only suggestions for revision but also moral support at a tough time in my career. Lauren Morris MacLean, Tulia Faletti, Michele Ford, Tamara Loos, and Christa van Wijnbergen read an assortment of chapters and offered vital feedback. I could not have done the statistical analyses without the advice and assistance of my statistics guru and dear friend, Ernesto Calvo. Participants in the Minnesota International Relations Colloquium gave me extremely useful input early in the preparation of the cross-national analysis presented in Chapter 6.

Countless individuals in Indonesia made my research possible. I thank the Lembaga Ilmu Pengetahuan Indonesia and Nelly Polhaupessy at the American Indonesian Exchange Foundation (AMINEF) for assisting with the logistics of conducting research there. The letters of introduction provided by the Asosiasi Apparel Manufaktur Indonesia, the Asosiasi Pertekstilan Indonesia, the Association of Indonesian Automotive Industries, and the Asosiasi Produsen Panel Kayu Indonesia were instrumental in persuading numerous establishments to open their factory gates to me. The interviews and factory data supplied by managers and supervisors in these factories are at the heart of the book, and I would thank them all individually if I had not promised to protect their identity. Bapak Rifa Rufiadi at the Biro Pusat Statistik kindly provided the firm-level data from the industrial survey, and he responded with good humor to my frequent queries.

Gadis Arivia befriended me early in the research process, and her friendship (and Rick's martinis) helped me to recover from the long hours of fieldwork. Lilis M. not only assisted with the research in Tangerang but also became a close friend. My host families, Nana Nurliana Soeyono in Depok, and Irna and Hadi Soewito in Jakarta, made me feel at home and helped me in too many ways to recount. Emi and Fitri became my adopted little sisters and made sure that I never felt homesick. The fortuitous presence of Robin Bush, Jennifer Gaynor, Douglas Kammen, and Mary McCoy in Jakarta during my fieldwork contributed to many good times. Douglas Kammen generously shared his strike database, and Yamamoto Nobuto facilitated my visits to Japanese factories and cheerfully translated for me in the interviews with Japanese managers.

In the United States, I thank my friends and family for their moral support during the years between the beginning and end of this project. After working on it on and off for ten years, both I and they are ecstatic (and relieved) that I no longer have to dwell on getting my book published.

I also thank the numerous institutions that funded the research for this book. The Social Science Research Council supported my work with both an International Predissertation Fellowship in 1996–1997 and the International Dissertation Research Fellowship in 1998–1999. A Fulbright grant funded the fieldwork in 1998–1999, and a Woodrow Wilson Grant in Women's Studies helped with the purchase of equipment needed for the field research.

The publication of this book would not have been possible without the support of Maria Lorena Cook, who put me in touch with Frances Benson at ILR Press of Cornell University Press. Frances Benson and Nancy Ferguson shepherded the book smoothly to publication, and two anonymous reviewers provided valuable comments that resulted in a stronger book. Thanks to Michael Brehm for the preparation of the figures. Some of the material in Chapters 1, 2, 4, and 5 first appeared in two journal articles: "The Political Economy of Feminization: From 'Cheap Labor' to Gendered Discourses of Work," *Politics & Gender* 1, no. 3 (2005), and "Gendered Paths of Industrialization: A Cross-Regional Comparative Analysis," *Studies in Comparative International Development* 41, no. 1 (2006).

The book is dedicated to Ari Sunarijati, Cicih Sukaesih, Lilis M., and Yatini Sulistyowati. Although only Lilis participated directly in the research, all four women were participants in the process of feminization in Indonesia. Cicih, Lilis, and Yatini began as production workers and later became labor activists. Cicih was fired by a Nike subcontractor for joining in a strike and has continued her activism in worker communities. Lilis and Yatini became union organizers and have climbed the ranks in two of the country's most important unions, Serikat Pekerja Nasional and Serikat Buruh Sejahtera Indonesia. Ari, unlike the others, was not a production worker; it was her experience in the personnel department of a factory that led to her involvement in the labor movement. All four have been tireless advocates for Indonesian workers and have pushed for a strong role for women in trade unions—which have historically impeded feminization in part because they are male dominated. I dedicate this book to these amazing women in the hope that they will succeed in their endeavor to empower both women and workers in Indonesia.

TERI L. CARAWAY

*Minneapolis*

# Assembling Women

# Introduction

One of the greatest social and economic transformations in industrializing parts of the world has been the dramatic entry of women into paid work in the formal sector. The influx of women into manufacturing work has been especially notable (Economic and Social Commission for Asia and the Pacific 1987; Heyzer 1988; Joekes 1987; Lim 1985; Nash and Fernandez-Kelly 1983; Tomoda 1995; Ward 1990). During the last decades of the twentieth century, industrialization generated millions of new factory jobs in developing countries. Although men historically outnumbered women in formal-sector work in manufacturing, women reached near parity or beyond in many countries in the short space of just one to two decades. Women now constitute a significant share of the working class in much of the developing world, especially in countries that have experienced dramatic industrial expansion. Yet despite this impressive wave of feminization in manufacturing, employers in numerous countries have eschewed female labor and continue to employ primarily men. Moreover, even in countries that did feminize, although some employers hired women with alacrity, others resisted. Their aversion to hiring women is puzzling, as scholars have enumerated an array of attributes that make women the ideal workforce in today's global capitalist economy: women are cheaper to employ than men, docile, and willing to work long hours in dead-end jobs. Most employers, not just those in traditionally female sectors of employment, should find these attributes exceedingly attractive. Explaining the varied topography and timing of women's entry into formal-sector employment in manufacturing is the empirical puzzle at the heart of this book.

The feminization of factory labor has consequences not only for women's access to work but also for gender inequality. Women's incorporation into manufacturing work has been highly selective, with women flowing primarily into low-paid jobs in a few industries. Even in countries that have undergone massive feminization, work in the highest-paying sectors of manufacturing continues to elude women. Men still work across a wider range of industries and hold the most remunerative jobs. Consequently, feminization has had only a modest impact on reducing gender inequalities in labor markets. Indeed, gender has proved to be a particularly resilient dividing line between workers. Massive inflows of women into the workforce result rarely in a seamless integration of women into men's jobs but rather in a redrawing or reconfiguration of the gender divisions of labor that separate men's work from women's work.

My fundamental contention is that understanding either feminization or the persistent gender inequalities in labor markets requires scholars to grapple with the tenacity of gender divisions in labor markets. Why do employers segregate men and women into distinct realms of work, and how are divisions between men and women perpetuated, redrawn, and reconfigured rather than overturned? And how do shop-floor practices of gender segregation cascade through economies and interact with the wider political economy to produce distinctly gendered patterns of manufacturing employment?

The answers to these questions are of vital importance. A necessary condition for improving women's social status is undoubtedly greater access to work, and feminization opens the door of job opportunity to women. A greater understanding of what prompts feminization thus helps to identify the constellation of forces that combine to kick open the door of opportunity. Yet if women flow into feminized ghettos of the workforce, new opportunities may not succeed in undermining gender inequalities in the labor market. Escaping this quandary requires a better understanding of the processes that collectively conspire to reproduce or reconfigure— rather than obliterate—gender divisions at work. Once we comprehend these processes, it becomes possible to change them.

## The Argument in Brief

First, how are the doors of opportunity kicked open? How do women gain access to manufacturing work? I show that employment growth in labor-intensive industries is the primary stimulus for feminization. Employment growth has two effects. First, it creates higher demand for labor, including female labor; second, it gives employers the opportunity to dismantle established gender divisions of labor without firing male workers. In contrast to scholars who have argued that export-oriented industrialization (EOI) compels employers to seek out the cheapest labor possible— women—in order to compete in international markets (Chapkis and Enloe 1983; Elson and Pearson 1981a; Fernandez-Kelly 1983a; Fox 1993; Fuentes and Ehrenreich 1983; Joekes 1987; Lim 1983; Safa 1986; Tiano 1994), I argue that EOI is important only insofar as it generates employment growth in labor-intensive industries, which it does only during its initial stages. Moreover, as shown in the analysis that follows, the shift of work from men to women which takes place during the early stages of EOI is far more contingent than is portrayed by most scholars, with some employers eagerly feminizing and others sticking with men. As EOI matures, moreover, manufacturing becomes more capital intensive; employment growth slows; and masculinization usually ensues. EOI's positive impact on women's integration into manufacturing work is thus temporary; as countries shift to the production of more highly value-added goods, women are expelled from industrial jobs.

In addition to employment growth in labor-intensive industries, two additional factors, the supply characteristics of female labor and mediating institutions, help to explain the differences between countries in women's share of manufacturing employment. Most existing analyses of feminization assume that women are available to work in factories, that women are attractive potential employees, and that employers can hire them. But an ensemble of political factors both determines women's availability for employment and facilitates or obstructs their entry into the workforce. Government policy, through its effects on women's fertility, education levels, and labor force participation rates, affects the availability of women to work in factories and their attractiveness as potential employees. Likewise, institutions such as unions and protective legislation affect the capacity and willingness of employers to hire women. Perhaps the most controversial finding of this book is that strong unions negatively affect women's share of employment in manufacturing. Strong unions allow male workers to oppose employer efforts to replace them with women, and centralized bargaining institutions that set wages throughout the economy prevent employers from cutting wages by hiring women. The repression of labor in Asia is therefore an inseparable part of the explanation for women's impressive presence in manufacturing work in the region. Docile unions, not supposedly docile women, have been key determinants of the gendered contours of industrialization.

Finally, why does feminization have such a limited impact on gender inequalities in labor markets? Both Marxist and neoclassical political economists would expect feminization, which represents an increase in demand for female labor, to erode gender inequalities (Blau and Ferber 1992; Lim 1983; Marx 1977). Initially, feminists believed that it was women's exclusion from formal-sector work that prevented them from enjoying the fruits of development (Boserup 1970). After feminization began to sweep across the globe and women's presence in manufacturing work expanded, however, feminists began to argue that access to work had disappointing results because women flowed into feminized ghettos in the labor market (Elson and Pearson 1981a; Joekes 1987). Continued segregation is an important piece of the puzzle in explaining the limited impact of feminization on reducing gender inequality, but the dynamics of segregation and how it is reconfigured during the course of feminization is still poorly understood. The book contributes to this debate by highlighting a range of unexplored processes that produce this outcome.

A crucial component of the explanation lies in the resistance of high-paying employers in capital-intensive sectors to the siren call of "cheap female labor." Some scholars have insinuated that this defiance is part of a patriarchal conspiracy to perpetuate women's subordination to men (Hartmann 1979), while others have simply noted that since wages are a smaller share of costs in less-competitive, capital-intensive sectors, these employers do not need to cut wages by hiring women (Cohn 2000; Joekes 1982). Dual labor market theorists have emphasized women's instability as workers, noting that capital-intensive firms that invest in training are loath to hire women because they have short work tenures (Doeringer and Piore 1971). I argue that patriarchal conspiracies, indifference to reducing wage costs, and the alleged instability of women workers are insufficient to explain the resistance of employers to hiring women. The continued closure of many lines of work to women is intimately related to gendered discourses of work—ideas that managers hold about the qualities of male and female labor. Feminization involves both the definition of new jobs as realms of women's activity and the *re*definition as women's work of jobs previously held by men. Employers feminize their workforces only if they imagine that women will be more productive workers than men. Gendered discourses of work and the gendered logic of production in capital-intensive sectors have combined in a toxic mix that provides work opportunities for women but closes off most of the high-paying jobs to them. This outcome is not inevitable, but the workings of capitalism reproduce rather than undermine the processes that create it. Only political intervention in markets will undo it. Illuminating the forces that generate gendered outcomes relies on two crucial components that distinguish this book from other analyses of feminization: a gendered and multilevel methodology, and the use of gender as a category of political economic analysis.

## A Gendered and Multilevel Methodology

What does it mean to say that a methodology is gendered? Perhaps the simplest statement comes from Terrell Carver (1996), who has noted that gender is not a synonym for women. A gendered methodology thus requires the selection of some employers that employ primarily men and others that prefer to hire women. Theorists of feminization and studies of women factory workers in developing countries unfortunately rarely examine men or male-dominated industries; rather, they focus almost exclusively on export-oriented, labor-intensive, and female-dominated industries.[1] By studying only export-oriented, labor-intensive, and female-dominated industries, scholars not only have selected on the dependent variable but have also eliminated variation on the independent variables. Consequently, it is impossible to assess whether labor intensity and export orientation are driving the tendency to use female labor. Making this assessment requires that male-dominated sectors be included in the analysis as well. In addition, since the sectors studied are not only female-intensive but also labor-intensive and export-oriented, current accounts cannot confidently make the claim that these factors are important, since they cannot show that capital-intensive and inward-oriented sectors generate different gendered outcomes. Thus, although such studies produce valuable insights, they are a weak foundation for formulating a theory of feminization.

In order to overcome these methodological problems, I have adopted a multisectoral approach in which both male- and female-intensive sectors are selected and in which market orientation varies. For the sectoral case studies in Indonesia, I selected four industries—garments, textiles, plywood, and automobiles—that vary in terms of female shares of employment, changes in female employment over time, market orientation, and labor intensity. All four were major employers in Indonesia, and all underwent significant growth between 1970 and 1997. I visited more than fifty factories in these four sectors and interviewed some two hundred managers between September 1998 and June 1999. I also utilized a firm-level database from the Indonesian Central Bureau of Statistics (BPS), which includes data from approximately 23,000 medium- and large-scale firms throughout Indonesia.[2]

The analysis relies as well on two cross-national data sets, each of which covered a wide range of sectors of manufacturing. The first is the United Nations Industrial Development Organization's Industrial Statistics Database, which includes gendered employment and sectoral data for forty-nine countries from 1981 to the early 1990s. I also compiled a second data set comprising sectoral data gathered from the publications of national statistical offices in ten countries—Argentina, Brazil, Mexico, South Korea, Taiwan, Singapore, Indonesia, Malaysia, the Philippines, and Thailand—and spanning the 1950s to the mid-1990s (see the Statistical Appendix for sources). These cross-national data sets contain data for most sectors of manufacturing, which allows for the inclusion of both male- and female-intensive sectors.

The research design for this study incorporates different levels of analysis. Mapping the varied gendered processes that produce feminization requires a multilevel analysis that demonstrates the links between local, national, and global outcomes. Although there are scores of books about the women who have entered factory work in developing countries, most are ethnographies that document the daily lives of women both at work and at home (Cravey 1998; Fernandes 1997; Fernandez-Kelly 1983a; Kim 1997; Kung 1994; Lee 1998; Ong 1987; Pun 2005; Safa 1995; Salaff 1981; Salzinger 2003; Wolf 1992; Yelvington 1995). This book endeavors to connect different levels of analysis. It combines microlevel observations from the shop floor in a variety of sectors and an in-depth analysis of feminization in the one case of Indonesia with cross-national analyses of gendered patterns of industrialization. Each of these vantage points provides a different window on how gender shapes industrialization and each offers an empirical check on the claims advanced. The first component that guides the analysis in this book, a gendered methodology, is combined with the second, a gendered theoretical apparatus.

## A Gendered Theoretical Apparatus

Just as a gendered and comparative methodology is required to develop an explanation of feminization, so is moving beyond the dominant view of markets as gender-neutral institutions. Scholars agree that gender segregation is a pervasive phenomenon in labor markets (Anker 1998; Charles and Grusky 2004), but most scholars explain the existence and the persistence of these gender divisions through reference to nonmarket forces, in particular to women's role in reproduction and its consequences for their investment in education and their commitment to work. The prevailing view is that labor markets are in principle gender neutral, and premarket differences between men and women determine gender disparities in labor market outcomes (Humphrey 1987; Scott 1986).

The assumed gender neutrality of markets is perhaps most evident in the categories of analysis deployed to study them. On the surface, these categories are gender neutral, but since power relations based on gender are such a salient aspect of lived social relations, allegedly gender-neutral categories generally contain gender bias. In neoclassical political economy, for example, the individual acting in a world of scarcity is the bedrock of all analysis. This sexless individual appears to be free of gender bias, but theorists have shown that the individual in liberal theory, and hence in neoclassical economic theory, is not an abstract individual but conforms to characteristics of (white) men (Fraser 1989; Hanchard 1999; Mehta 1997; Pateman 1988). One of the crowning glories of neoclassical economics, human capital theory, therefore best explains labor market outcomes for white men and performs relatively poorly in accounting for the situations of African American men and of women, regardless of race (Tomaskovic-Devey 1993). Marxist political economy similarly treats the category of labor as a genderless entity that is "free" to sell its labor on the market, even though men and women are rarely equally free to sell their labor, since women bear the burdens of reproduction in most societies.

The theoretical consequence of the male bias in the categories that structure most political economic analysis is that features associated with women are treated as different from the norm. This difference then becomes the explanation for women's fate in labor markets. The labor market thus remains gender neutral and simply reacts to the different qualities that men and women bring to the labor market (e.g., commitment to the workforce; education; role in childbearing). Although women's greater role in reproduction and its effects on women's labor force participation are certainly important in understanding gender segregation and gender inequality in labor markets, attributing segregation to nonmarket factors does not grapple with the ways that gender is embedded in the market mechanism and thus structures the work opportunities of both men and women. Moreover, such a conceptualization does not explain the tenacity of such gender divisions in the face of dramatic declines in fertility, increases in women's education, and women's higher rates of labor force participation.

Marxists and neoclassical economists agree on little, but both, following the impeccable logic of their genderless analysis of labor markets, argue that gender divisions in labor markets should be evanescent. Marx (1977) believed that capital's drive to squeeze surplus value out of workers would lead ineluctably to the hiring of women, which would lead to the erosion of gender divisions in labor markets. For neoclassical political economists, the market mechanism should wear away gender divisions in labor markets over time. If some employers pay higher wages to men when women are equally capable of doing the work, other employers will drive them out of business by hiring cheaper female labor.[3] Both Marxist and liberal political economists expect gender to become less meaningful in labor markets over time. It is therefore puzzling that gender segregation remains a remarkably tenacious feature of labor markets.

Part of the "woman problem" in political economy is finding a theoretical language in which to address it. Marxist feminists have tried most fervently to gender political economy, and they have done so by expanding the analytic scope of Marx's critique of capitalism. The best-known approach in this vein of work is dual systems theory, which, deeply influenced by the development of patriarchy as a feminist concept in the early 1970s, wedded a theory of patriarchy to Marx's theory of capitalism (Eisenstein 1979; Ferguson and Folbre 1981; Hartmann 1979; Walby 1986). Capitalism remained a realm of class oppression; patriarchy represented a system of gender domination; and the interaction of capitalism and patriarchy determined women's position in capitalist society.[4] In most Marxist-feminist accounts, patriarchy has two benefits for capitalism. First, it assures that female labor will be cheap, and second, women's uncompensated domestic labor produces use values, such as cooked meals, that allow capitalists to pay men lower wages as well. But they parted company with Marx regarding the consequences of waged work for women. Since women were channeled into low-paying jobs, they remained dependent on male wage earners, so their incorporation into wage labor did not threaten patriarchy (Armstrong and Armstrong 1987; Beechey 1987; Brenner and Ramas 1984; Coulson, Magas, and Wainwright 1975; Dalla Costa 1973; Gardiner 1975, 1976; Morton 1971; Seccombe 1973, 1975; Vogel 1983).[5] Yet for all the talk about women, gender was brought in through the back door of patriarchy, so capitalism (and hence labor markets) remained a gender-blind system (Young 1981).

Most Marxist-feminist accounts fall into the trap of dualisms identified by Ava Baron (1991)—capitalism/patriarchy, public/private, production/reproduction, men's work/women's work—with class assumed to be integral to the first term of each pair and gender to the second. Such conceptualizations leave the gender-biased analytic apparatus of conventional approaches untouched. Of course, part of the reason for this analytical separation is that patriarchy undoubtedly preceded the development of capitalism. Yet treating gender as a residue of premarket (or nonmarket) relations is a dubious move. Gender is not merely "a hangover from precapitalist modes of production" (Connell 1987, 104). It was at the heart of labor markets from the beginning of capitalist development and remains a core feature of industrial organization today (Bradley 1989). As such, capitalism is historically gendered (Barrett 1988), and gender is embedded in capitalist labor markets (Mackintosh 1991). A capitalism unfettered by gender has thus never existed except in the minds of scholars. A gendered analysis of labor markets must bring gender into the heart of production and introduce gender as a category of analysis that affects all spheres of life.

The first step in developing a gendered political economy is to incorporate gender as a category of analysis. I adopt Joan Scott's definition of gender as "the social organization of sexual difference." It is not a synonym for women, so gender can be at work even when women are not present. Gender is a signifier of relationships of power, and gendered "meanings vary across cultures, social groups, and time" (Scott 1988a, 2). Gender positions women and men differently in society, structures their lived experiences in distinct ways, and refers not only to social positions and social relations but also to ideas (Rose 1992).

The second step is to integrate gender directly into the study of labor markets. Feminist labor historians have shown persuasively that gendered discourses of work shape the way that employers define their economic interests; in other words, employers' beliefs about gender partially constitute their ideas about rational economic practice (Downs 1995; Rose 1992). Employers have historically considered men and women to be qualitatively different types of labor and have therefore viewed productivity and labor control through a gendered lens. Consequently, they define jobs in gendered terms. On the basis of their assessments of the gendered character of work on the shop floor, employers use gender as a criterion for recruitment. Gendered hiring practices, in turn, produce the gender division of labor on the shop floor and perpetuate the deep occupational and sectoral segregation that exists all over the world. Once embedded in labor markets, gendered discourses of work shape gendered outcomes in labor markets independently of the nonmarket factors so often highlighted by scholars. Integrating gendered discourses of work into political economy brings gender into the heart of the market and allows for a truly gendered analysis of labor markets.

## Research Findings and the Plan of the Book

Chapter 1 begins the analysis by attacking the twin pillars of current theorizing of feminization, EOI and cheap labor. That narrative contains grains of truth, but through an analysis of cross-national patterns of feminization and the process of feminization in Indonesia, I call into question the level of causal weight attributed to these two factors. The primary force driving feminization is not market orientation (export orientation versus inwardly directed industrialization) but the balance of employment between labor-intensive and capital-intensive sectors. Since the primary phase of EOI promotes employment growth in labor-intensive sectors, it is strongly associated with feminization. As EOI deepens, however, employment growth shifts to more capital-intensive sectors, and masculinization usually ensues. Moreover, even when controlling for the type of industrialization, women's share of employment varies, and I argue that two additional factors need to be introduced to account for these differences: the supply characteristics of women workers, and mediating institutions. Perhaps the most contentious finding is that women's lower average wages are only one reason—and perhaps not the most important one—that employers in labor-intensive sectors hire women. Gendered discourses of work help to explain why employers hire women, even when men and women earn the same wages, and why many employers are reluctant to cut costs by hiring "cheap" female labor.

Since labor intensity is such an important determinant of the location of women's employment, Chapter 2 explores the reasons behind this relationship. Scholars have argued that women are absorbed in labor-intensive lines of work because they are unskilled, unstable, and cheaper to employ than men. In fact, women's instability as workers is more a consequence than a cause of labor practices in labor-intensive industries, and women's relegation to labor-intensive work has little to do with low skill levels, as training times for jobs varied little between the labor-intensive and capital-intensive firms I surveyed. Wages, however, are an important determinant of women's concentration in labor-intensive sectors. Hiring women conveys wage savings to employers, including labor-intensive employers, but surprisingly it is capital-intensive rather than labor-intensive sectors that could cut wage costs the most by hiring women. In addition to wages, high rates of turnover—which allow labor-intensive industries to seamlessly cycle women on maternity leave in and out of the workforce—and gendered discourses of work account for women's concentration in labor-intensive lines of work.

Chapters 3, 4, and 5 turn attention to an in-depth analysis of one case, Indonesia. Chapter 3 outlines the changes in supply and institutions that facilitated feminization in that country. Before and during the waves of feminization that swept through Indonesia, improvements in education, reductions in fertility, and increased labor force participation rates made women both more available and more appealing as workers. The authoritarian state demobilized political organizations, such as unions and radical Islam, which could potentially have obstructed feminization, and the state virtually stopped enforcing protective legislation. The state played a large role in these developments, but the mobilization of female labor was an unintended consequence of policies designed to accomplish other developmental goals. This series of changes assured that an appealing supply of women existed and that mediating institutions facilitated rather than impeded the absorption of female labor into factory work. The stage was thus set for a wave of feminization, but it took a change in industrialization policy to set it in motion.

Chapter 4 demonstrates how EOI generated increased demand for female workers by promoting massive employment growth in labor-intensive sectors. From the early 1980s until the financial crisis of 1997, labor-intensive sectors created the bulk of new jobs in Indonesia, although feminization occurred not only in these industries but also in almost every sector of Indonesian manufacturing. Feminization unfolded in three waves, each corresponding to a different stage of Indonesian industrialization. Although the shift in industrialization policy can explain the broad contours of feminization in Indonesia, the feminization of manufacturing did not simply grow out of already female-intensive sectors but involved sectoral feminization as well. In other words, labor-intensive sectors that had previously hired few women began to employ higher proportions of women than they had done in the past. The chapter shows how employers in a number of sectors increased their reliance on women workers by shifting selected jobs from men to women, and it highlights certain dynamics that cut across the three waves of feminization and explain its spread and variability—stickiness, spillover, and snowballing.

Chapter 5 illustrates the dynamics of feminization at the factory level. Two conditions increase the probability that a factory will undergo feminization: competitive markets, and the presence of male and female production workers on the shop floor. Sectors and firms in highly competitive markets face constant pressure to increase efficiency and quality, so the pressure to find ways to squeeze more productivity from their workers is intense. Feminization is one device that employers use to raise productivity. Since less competitive (usually more capital-intensive) sectors do not face the same level of competitive pressure, they do not innovate at the margins to the same degree as the more competitive sectors. The presence of women production workers also affects the likelihood of feminization. Gendered innovations in the labor process grow out of shop floor experiments, and the absence of women in many of the most capital-intensive sectors thus makes feminization less likely. Although these two variables help to explain variation between capital- and labor-intensive sectors, they cannot explain variations between labor-intensive sectors. The chapter thus also examines, through a series of intrasectoral comparisons of firms in the garment, plywood, and textile industries, how gendered discourses of work produce different gendered outcomes. It shows that feminization is never a foregone conclusion and that employers facing similar competitive situations adopt varying gendered practices. Feminization is thus a far more contingent process than it is portrayed to be in the literature.

Chapter 6 takes insights developed in the case study of Indonesia and applies them to a cross-regional comparison with nine other countries. Cross-national evidence supports the contention that shifts in industrialization are crucial components of generating feminization and shows that Latin American countries, which pursued a more capital-intensive route of industrialization, feminized less than countries in East and Southeast Asia. This chapter also demonstrates that women's share of sectoral employment is higher in countries where labor has been excluded from political power. Labor-excluding authoritarian developmental states in Asia and inclusionary populist politics that created relatively strong unions in Latin America resulted in disparate gendered legacies that had profound consequences for women's incorporation into factory work. Latin America has lower levels of female employment in manufacturing not only because it pursued different industrialization policies but also because it had stronger unions. Supply variables, with the exception of fertility, explained little of the cross-national variation in women's share of employment, but as expected, lower fertility rates facilitated feminization, which suggests that demand-side factors and labor market institutions are more important determinants of women's employment opportunities than cultural factors.

The Indonesian experience with feminization demonstrates that there are features in addition to women's lower wages which make them appealing as workers. But it also shows that though capital absorbs female labor with great alacrity, the continued segregation of women into low-wage sectors mitigates the impact of their integration into factory labor. The conclusion focuses on the impact of feminization on gender inequality in labor markets in Indonesia. In particular, by highlighting how and why women are drawn into the industrial workforce, it sheds light on how feminization brought limited, although not insignificant, benefits for women. The pattern and process through which women entered the manufacturing workforce was crucial. Feminization increased women's access to work in the formal sector, but most of the higher-paying sectors remained closed to them. Although women often earned wages equal to men's in the low-pay sectors, after more than a decade of feminization, men's average wages in manufacturing were still much higher than women's. These inequalities persist because markets reproduce and redraw rather than erase the gendered boundaries in production which perpetuate gender inequalities in the labor market. Diverting the market from this path requires disrupting the gendered processes within labor markets which reconfigure rather than undermine these gender inequalities.

# 1

# From Cheap Labor and Export-Oriented Industrialization to the Gendered Political Economy Approach

> Industrialization in the post-war period has
> been as much female led as export led.
>
> SUSAN P. JOEKES, 1987

Theorists unfailingly highlight two factors as crucial in generating the waves of feminization that swept through much of the developing world after World War II: changes in the global organization of production, and women's low wages. In the late 1960s and early 1970s, multinational corporations began to relocate labor-intensive assembly operations from developed countries to cheaper production sites overseas. At the same time, export-oriented industrialization (EOI) became the favored development policy in many developing countries. These twin occurrences generated higher demand for cheap and easily exploitable labor to fuel export drives (Frobel, Heinrichs, and Kreye 1980; Nash and Fernandez-Kelly 1983). Since exporters competed in global markets, they were extremely sensitive to labor costs, with immense gendered consequences. Exporters were especially keen to hire women, because their subordination to men meant that they could be paid low wages.[1] Those that eschewed cheap female labor in favor of more expensive male labor would therefore find themselves at a competitive disadvantage in the cutthroat global economy. EOI and patriarchy thus combined to make women the ideal workforce in countries that relied on exports to propel industrialization drives (Elson and Pearson 1981a; Fox 1993; Joekes 1987; Lim 1983, 1990; Safa 1986).

The purpose of this chapter is to unpack the arguments that underlie the conventional wisdom and to cast some doubt on their persuasiveness. Although they contain a grain of truth, a closer look at both the manner in which feminization unfolds and the cross-national patterns of feminization calls into question the level of causal weight attributed to them. I argue that it is not market orientation (export orientation versus inwardly directed industrialization) that matters but rather the balance of employment between labor-intensive and capital-intensive sectors. Moreover, I argue that two additional factors need to be introduced to analyses of feminization in order to account for cross-national variations in women's share of manufacturing employment: the supply characteristics of women workers, and mediating institutions. I suggest that low wages are only a partial explanation why employers in labor-intensive sectors hire women. Gendered discourses of work—ideas about men and women as distinct types of labor—are necessary to explain not only feminization but also why many employers are reluctant to cut costs by hiring "cheap" female labor.

## Industrialization Paths and Feminization

The feminist literature on women's work in export-processing zones has long emphasized the importance of export orientation and labor intensity in determining the propensity of particular sectors of manufacturing to employ women (Elson and Pearson 1981a; Joekes 1987; Lim 1983).[2] According to these authors, export and labor intensity compel factories to reduce labor costs as much as possible in order to compete. The pioneering works written in the early 1980s, before masculinization occurred in export-oriented countries such as South Korea and Taiwan, gave exporting and labor intensity equal weight. Yet labor intensity is the more important factor. Labor-intensive industries, regardless of whether they export, face competitive markets because entry costs are low.

Labor intensity and capital intensity are usually measured as value-added per capita. Sectors with high value-added per capita are capital intensive; those with low value-added per capita are labor intensive. The Industrial Statistics Database of the United Nations Industrial Development Organization (UNIDO), which includes sectoral female employment data from 1981 to 1995 as well as sectoral data on output, value-added, total employment, and wages, allows for an assessment of the importance of labor intensity in promoting women's employment.[3] I ran an ordinary

**Table 1.1.** Regression equation with log of percent female as dependent variable

| | |
|---|---|
| Capital intensity | −0.244*** |
| | (0.011) |
| (Constant) | 0.390** |
| | (0.179) |
| R-squared = 0.522 | |
| Adjusted R-squared = 0.519 | |
| N = 8,238 | |

*Source:* UNIDO Industrial Statistics Database.
*Note:* Unstandardized regression coefficients with standard error in parentheses; p values indicated by *, **, and *** for values less than 0.1, 0.05, 0.01.

least squares (OLS) regression analysis with the natural log of *Percent Female* as the dependent variable and the natural log of *Capital Intensity,* measured as value-added per worker, and forty-eight country dummy variables to control for a host of national factors that could affect the level of female employment. The model explains 52 percent of the variance in female employment, and the coefficient for capital intensity is statistically significant and has a substantive impact in the expected direction—a 1 percent increase in capital intensity leads to a 0.244 decrease in percent female (see Table 1.1). In other words, as capital intensity increases, women's share of employment decreases.

Shifts in employment between labor- and capital-intensive sectors will therefore have gendered consequences. The type of industrialization that a country pursues has dramatic effects on the balance of employment in labor- and capital-intensive sectors of manufacturing and thus has predictable effects on men's and women's shares of employment. Political economists have identified two main forms of industrialization: import-substitution industrialization (ISI) and EOI. ISI is based on production for the local market and involves high levels of protection for domestic producers; it also tends to promote the growth of capital-intensive sectors. Scholars distinguish between two phases of ISI, primary and secondary (Gereffi 1990; Haggard 1990). Although primary ISI entails the production of some labor-intensive goods such as textiles, it is usually more capital intensive than primary EOI. As primary ISI progresses to secondary ISI, industry becomes even more capital intensive, which strengthens the masculine tendency of this type of industrialization. ISI is likely to lead to the employment of men because it promotes capital-intensive industries—although primary ISI has led to feminization in some cases: in Indonesia during the 1970s, for example, impressive employment growth in an inward-oriented labor-intensive industry, textiles, generated some feminization.

EOI is a mirror image of ISI. Whereas ISI emphasizes production for the domestic market, EOI promotes manufactured exports. Its first stage, primary EOI, is highly labor intensive. Since job growth occurs overwhelmingly in labor-intensive sectors during the primary phase of EOI, demand for female labor rises. Like ISI, EOI becomes more capital intensive with the shift from the primary to the secondary stage, although employment in labor-intensive sectors remains large (Gereffi 1990). EOI is therefore more likely to result in feminization than ISI, but since the move to secondary EOI results in increased capital intensity, the reliance on female labor usually diminishes over time. Most existing studies of feminization concentrated on the primary rather than the secondary phase of EOI, which led them to associate EOI erroneously with feminization. It is the primary phase of EOI that is most strongly linked to an increased presence of women in manufacturing work.

In practice, countries often combine EOI and ISI, and when they do, it is necessary to look closely at the net impact on job creation of capital- versus labor-intensive sectors. When employment in labor-intensive sectors grows more quickly than that in capital-intensive sectors, feminization is likely to ensue. The crucial point, then, is not market orientation but how the type of industrialization affects the balance of sectoral employment.

## Waves of Feminization

Historically, primary EOI led to waves of feminization across the globe because it generated enormous job growth in labor-intensive industries. Although East Asia's dynamic "tiger" economies—Hong Kong, Singapore, South Korea, and Taiwan—and Mexico's *maquiladoras* are at the forefront of thinking about the export-led model of industrial development and its impact on women workers, the precursors of export-driven growth in the contemporary era were actually Puerto Rico and Ireland. Puerto Rico embarked on its export drive, Operation Bootstrap, in the 1950s (Rios 1990); Ireland began to promote exports in 1960, with the establishment of the first export-processing zone in the world at Shannon Airport (Pyle 1990). It soon became apparent that many multinational companies that invested in both countries preferred to hire women. About 60 percent of the newly created jobs in Puerto Rico went to women (Rios 1990). In Ireland, companies responding to the export-promotion scheme employed more women than the average for manufacturing as a whole—about 40 percent versus 31.8 percent (Pyle 1990).

Ironically, policymakers in both places formulated the new industrialization programs to reduce male unemployment, and each later took measures to rein in the tendency of export factories to employ women. Puerto Rico responded by promoting a more capital-intensive form of export-oriented industrialization (Rios 1990). The Irish government passed new incentives in 1969 that explicitly stated a minimum goal of 75 percent male employment in new investments (Pyle 1990). Ireland, more successful than Puerto Rico, managed to hold down female employment in sectors that were highly feminized internationally, allocating 74 percent of jobs in newly approved projects in the early 1970s to men. By the late 1970s, however, the commitment to this goal flagged, and in 1975 the government dropped the "predominantly male" provision of investment laws, and the state investment board stopped reporting jobs by sex. In 1978 the government gave up discouraging the employment of women and lobbied for the repeal of the protective legislation that prevented women from working at night.

Mexico was another early promoter of exports as a path to reducing male unemployment. The government initiated the Border Industrialization Program (BIP) in 1965 in order to offset male unemployment in northern Mexico in the aftermath of the bracero program, which had allowed Mexicans to enter the United States as agricultural workers. The BIP led to the establishment of the *maquiladoras*—factories on the Mexican side of the U.S.-Mexico border which produce for export, primarily to the United States (Fernandez-Kelly 1983). In spite of the government's desire to promote male employment, the *maquilas* were keen employers of women, especially during the first fifteen years of operation. In 1975, about 85 percent of all *maquila* workers in Ciudad Juarez were women (Fernandez-Kelly 1983), and in 1980 women composed 77 percent of the workforce in all *maquiladoras* (Geografia e Informatica Instituto Nacional de Estadistica 1983).

The political economy of the post–World War II era pushed many countries onto this labor- and female-intensive path. Few incentives existed for capital-intensive firms to relocate to poor countries solely because of lower labor costs, as wages were a smaller component of their total costs than in labor-intensive sectors. Capital-intensive investments were more appealing as import-substituting investments, where large capital outlays could be justified by privileged access to local markets. An export strategy of development thus required governments to accept that they would attract labor-intensive industries, which would unfailingly desire to hire many women.

Following on the heels of Ireland, Puerto Rico, and Mexico, feminization swept through many Caribbean nations and East Asian newly industrializing countries (NICs): South Korea, Taiwan, Hong Kong, and Singapore. Likewise, the "tiger cubs" in Southeast Asia (Malaysia, Thailand, the Philippines, and Indonesia), as well as Bangladesh, Sri Lanka, and Mauritius, followed a similar pattern as they expanded export promotion. In recent years a number of Central American countries, China, and Vietnam have also followed this path. Unlike the early exporters, these countries were fully conscious that the chosen development strategy would create many jobs for women and rarely interfered with the mobilization of female labor; in fact, government officials often facilitated and even encouraged factories to employ women by repealing protective legislation (Lim 1978), helping with the recruitment of female workers (Arrigo 1980; Ong 1987; Rosa 1989; Wolf 1992), advertising in investment brochures (Grossman 1978), pleading outright for the hiring of women in "lighter" jobs (Lim 1978), and even subsidizing child care (Phongpaichit 1988).

In all the East Asian NICs except Singapore, as well as in the *maquiladoras* in Mexico, the female share of employment peaked between 1975 and 1980 and subsequently declined. The masculinization in many of the countries that had begun export promotion policies in the 1960s and early 1970s is an interesting twist in the story, as manufacturing in these countries remained export intensive. In the East Asian NICs a large part of the explanation is that employment growth in labor-intensive sectors shrank, relative to capital-intensive sectors. The main cause was the relocation of labor-intensive industries to other countries, especially to Southeast Asia, but employment in relatively capital- and male-intensive sectors also expanded. In Mexico, masculinization in the *maquiladoras* accompanied feminization at the national level. The increasing prominence of male workers in the *maquiladoras* was a result of the masculinization of historically feminine industries (i.e., garments, electronics), the growth of relatively masculine sectors such as transport and furniture, and an increase in the share of technical workers relative to operators (Catanzarite and Strober 1993; Sklair 1993; Tiano 1994). In all these countries, masculinization occurred during the second phase of EOI and coincided with shifts in employment from labor-intensive to more capital-intensive sectors of manufacturing.

## Thickening the Plot: Mediating Institutions and Labor Supply

The type of industrialization affects gendered trends in employment in the manufacturing sector as a whole through its effects on the expansion and contraction of sectoral employment. Yet this is only part of the story. If it is only capital or labor intensity that matters, then there should be little cross-national variation in gendered shares of sectoral employment. Yet as can be seen in Table 1.2, marked cross-national sectoral variations exist. For example, although the textiles industry is labor intensive and relatively feminine in all the countries in the table, the *share* of female employment in the sector varies by country. The difference between the maximum and the minimum percent female for each sector is calculated in the column farthest to the right, and these differences range from 11 to 72 percent. Even when we control for export orientation, the differences are dramatic. Moreover, the disparity between Latin America and Asia is stunning. In Table 1.2, the maximum percent female for a sector is enclosed by a light border and the minimum with a dark border; the count of maximums and minimums is then calculated for each country at the bottom of its column. Almost all the minimums are in Latin America, while all the maximums are in Asia. An explanation focusing solely on labor intensity cannot explain these cross-national variations. Labor intensity is crucial for understanding changes over time within countries in women's share of manufacturing employment, and it can also predict in a probabilistic fashion which sectors are likely to be the most feminine in any given country, but cross-national variation in women's share of sectoral employment suggests that labor-intensity is only part of the story.

I believe it is necessary to supplement the argument based on labor intensity with other features of the domestic political economy, in particular

**Table 1.2.** Female share (%) of employment by country and sector

| Sector | Argentina 1985 | Brazil 1985 | Mexico 1985 | Indonesia 1994 | Malaysia 1985 | Philippines 1988 | Singapore 1985 | Thailand 1985 | ROK 1985 | Taiwan 1985 | Max. – Min. |
|---|---|---|---|---|---|---|---|---|---|---|---|
| Food | 23 | 27 | 22 | 46 | 33 | 27 | 38 | 31 | 43 | 47 | 25 |
| Beverages | 10 | 10 | 3 | 38 | 30 | 10 | 31 | 24 | 24 | 30 | 35 |
| Tobacco | 16 | 40 | 26 | 88 | 47 | 58 | 40 | 53 |  | 47 | 72 |
| Textiles | 35 | 39 | 25 | 56 | 64 | 47 | 65 | 78 | 65 | 65 | 53 |
| Garments | 74 | 67 | 77 | 79 | 89 | 80 | 89 | 97 | 75 | 79 | 30 |
| Footwear | 37 | 10 | 30 | 78 | 56 | 51 | 43 |  | 61 | 65 | 48 |
| Wood Processing | 6 | 19 | 6 | 39 | 24 | 11 | 40 | 27 | 24 | 40 | 34 |
| Paper | 14 | 7 | 12 | 23 | 39 | 22 | 42 | 45 | 24 | 30 | 33 |
| Industrial chemicals | 8 |  | 5 | 22 | 16 | 15 | 18 | 28 | 19 | 28 | 23 |
| Other chemicals | 29 | 44 | 33 | 58 | 42 | 29 | 38 | 52 | 36 | 44 | 29 |
| Iron and steel | 3 | 7 | 3 | 2 | 13 | 7 | 10 | 8 | 6 | 13 | 11 |
| Non-ferrous metals | 5 | 4 | 7 | 7 | 16 | 8 | 33 | 9 | 9 | 20 | 28 |
| Non-electrical machinery | 7 |  | 18 | 8 | 17 | 10 | 21 | 14 | 12 | 18 | 17 |
| Electronics | 22 | 34 | 50 | 60 | 74 | 64 | 72 | 41 | 51 | 59 | 52 |
| Transport | 6 | 6 | 8 | 11 | 20 | 8 | 10 | 17 | 9 | 18 | 14 |
| Professional & scientific | 22 | 36 | 50 | 57 | 71 | 68 | 69 | 60 | 46 | 55 | 49 |
| Total Minimums | 7 | 3 | 7 | 1 | 0 | 1 | 0 | 0 | 0 | 0 |  |
| Total Maximums | 0 | 0 | 0 | 4 | 4 | 0 | 3 | 4 | 0 | 3 |  |

*Sources:* See the Statistical Appendix.

with factors that shape the *supply* of appealing and available women for work in factories and the *mediating institutions* that affect employer access to this labor. The assumptions of most existing analyses of feminization—that women are available to work in factories, that women are attractive potential employees, and that employers can hire them—are wildly unrealistic. An ensemble of political factors both determines women's availability for employment and facilitates or obstructs their entry into the workforce, and these factors vary cross-nationally.

Among factors that shape the supply characteristics of female labor, government policy—through its effects on women's fertility, education levels, and labor force participation rates—affects the availability of women to work in factories and their attractiveness as potential employees. Lower fertility levels make women more appealing to employers, especially in countries where employers have to pay for maternity leave: if women begin having children later in life, employers that hire young women can be relatively assured that it will be years before they claim maternity leave or leave the workforce to concentrate on family duties. Basic education, especially literacy and numeracy, also affect employer demand for women's labor: if a country's educational system produces fewer women than men with the basic skills needed in the workplace, many employers will be reluctant to hire women. The organization of reproduction in the family and norms about women's participation in waged work outside the home not only affect the supply of women available for work but also the demand for their labor by employers (Stichter 1990).

Likewise mediating institutions affect the capacity of employers to hire women and thus have an important impact on patterns of female employment. Labor market institutions such as unions, the structure of collective bargaining, and protective legislation all mediate between the supply of female labor and capital's demand for it, limiting or facilitating employer access to female workers. Unions can prevent the replacement of male workers with female workers. Centralized bargaining that sets wages throughout an industry prevents employers from undercutting male wages by hiring women. Protective legislation, if enforced, can prevent women from working night shifts, which in turn limits the capacity of factories that use shift work to employ women. In some advanced industrialized countries, certain industries rely on vocational education to produce workers with the requisite skill sets (Hall and Soskice 2001). If women have difficulty gaining entry into vocational education systems, they will be excluded from the areas of employment that rely on the skills imparted through these training programs. In addition, conservative political parties and religious organizations can potentially lay roadblocks in the path of employers that seek to employ women. Thus, rather than assuming that employers can readily hire a supply of women workers, careful attention must be given to the mediating institutions that intervene between the supply of gendered workers and employer demand for gendered workers. As with supply factors, these mediating institutional features vary from country to country and across time within particular countries.

## Insights from Indonesia

A common problem in many studies of feminization is that they focus solely on labor-intensive and export-oriented industries that employ women. This biased sample assures that scholars will conclude that export-oriented and labor-intensive industries do employ women. Without examining the manufacturing sector as a whole, however, it is impossible to assess which factors carry the most causal weight. Moreover, few studies take a longer historical perspective; most examine developments that take place over just a few years.

A holistic and historical view of gendered patterns of industrialization in one country can offer insights that previous studies have missed. When Indonesia embarked on its industrialization drive in the early 1970s, men held the majority of jobs in medium and large firms, but by the mid-1990s men and women each composed about half of the production workforce. In 1971, only three of twenty-five sectors employed more women than men (tobacco, garments, and "other"). Over the next twenty-five years, women's share of the production workforce increased in nineteen of twenty-four sectors, and women became the majority in six additional sectors (textiles, footwear, other chemicals, plastic, electronics, and professional and scientific equipment). As feminization theorists have argued, an important aspect of this transformation was the rise of EOI. Whereas ISI concentrated investment in relatively capital-intensive sectors and generated little employment growth, EOI favored labor-intensive industries and created enormous job growth. In the early 1980s, Indonesia began to make tentative moves into EOI and by the late 1980s was fully engaged in an export promotion strategy. The labor-intensive sectors that were the major success stories of EOI generated much of the new employment for women. Feminization of the greatest magnitude occurred in sectors with high and medium-high levels of labor intensity, particularly in those that were major exporters.

Yet the transformation was both much deeper and more varied than the EOI narrative suggests. First, many but by no means all export sectors were female intensive. For example, wood industries were overwhelmingly export oriented and labor intensive, yet men remained the majority of that sector's workforce. Even more surprising, the most female-intensive industry in Indonesia was an inward-oriented and relatively capital-intensive sector, tobacco. Second, even among labor-intensive export industries, the degree of feminization that took place varied dramatically: although significant feminization occurred in both textiles and wood-processing industries, the change in women's share of employment was greater in wood products (38 percent) than in textiles (20 percent). Third, even when controlling for exporting and labor intensity, I found that women's actual share of employment varied widely: for instance, women were a higher proportion of the workforce in footwear than in wood products even though both industries were extremely labor and export intensive. Fourth, the scope of feminization extended far beyond export industries and affected almost every sector of manufacturing. And finally, the extent of feminization within sectors was uneven, some firms feminizing and others sticking with men. In sum, even when controlling for labor intensity and exporting, one finds that the degree of feminization and women's share of employment varied both between sectors and between firms within sectors, and that even sectors relatively unexposed to international competition were feminized.

The variability in gendered practices holds even when we control for wages and labor intensity. Figure 1.1 breaks down wages and capital intensity into four categories each—low, medium-low, medium-high, and high—and places capital intensity on one axis and wages on another.[4] Each sector is then placed in the box that corresponds to its level of capital intensity and wages. The figure shows that the most labor-intensive sectors employ the highest share of women—58 percent—and that the sectors that pay the lowest wages, regardless of the level of capital intensity, employ

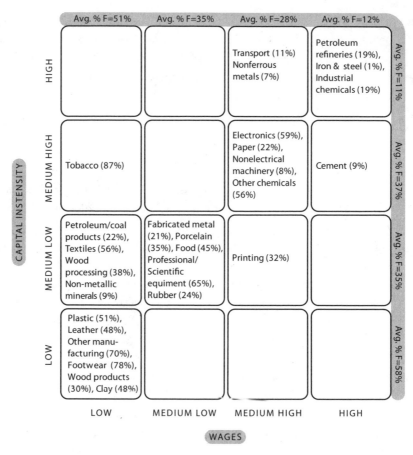

**Figure 1.1.** Women's employment by wages and capital intensity, Indonesia, 1996. *Source:* Biro Pusat Statistik, *Statistik Industri Besar dan Sedang 1996* (1997).

more women. The general relationship between labor intensity, wages, and female employment is confirmed, but many labor-intensive sectors employ a lot of men, and some capital-intensive sectors employ many women. The large differences in the level of female employment between the sectors inside each box indicate that sectors with similar wages and levels of capital intensity have substantial leeway in selecting a gendered work force. For example, in the low/low box, wood products employ only 30 percent women, whereas garments and footwear employ 78 percent; in the medium-high/medium-high box, nonelectrical machinery has only 8 percent women, whereas electronics has 59 percent. Significantly, the disparities in women's employment are lowest for the highly capital-intensive sectors, but all other boxes with at least two sectors show wide dispersions in the percentage of female workers employed.

Given the capacity of some relatively labor-intensive sectors to rely on male labor and the choice of some capital-intensive sectors to employ women, a structural account that explains sectoral proclivities (labor intensity versus capital intensity) must be complemented by a more interpretive and historical explication of the gendered development of sectoral and firm-level labor practices. The sharp disparities between sectors with similar levels of wages and capital intensity indicate that gender exerts an impact on employer choice, independent of wages.

## Cheap Labor?

Scholarship on feminization underestimates the power of gender in labor markets by framing it primarily as an issue of lower wages. Authors are correct to note that competitiveness in export sectors forces employers to reduce production costs. Hiring women, however, is not necessarily the obvious tactic for doing so. Many employers opt to hire women when faced with extremely competitive markets, but others continue to employ men and still manage to compete effectively. Wages, of course, are important, and my aim is not to dismiss the wage argument in its entirety but to complicate it.

The wage advantages that employers can secure by hiring women instead of men vary from country to country. Southeast Asia, for example, exhibits a different pattern of gender inequality in wages from East Asia (Bai and Cho 1995). Guy Standing (1996) compared wages in the Philippines and Malaysia and found that wage disparities between men and women for similar classifications of workers were small. In contrast, the wage inequalities between men and women in South Korea were found to be among the widest in the world (Amsden 1989; Standing 1999). Yet women constitute a larger share of the manufacturing workforce in Southeast Asia, where gender wage differences are smaller.

In Indonesia, although women's average wages are indeed lower than men's average wages, this figure is less useful, since it is partly a reflection of men's higher shares of employment in the higher-paying capital-intensive sectors. In the early 1990s the Indonesian government systematized a minimum wage policy, and minimum wages set by sector and by region became the standard for pay in many industrial sectors (Manning 1998). Consequently, gender differences in pay in low-wage industries diminished, and I found no wage discrimination between men and women at the factory level by 1997–98.[5] I collected gender-differentiated wage data at fourteen factories, and the ratio of the average female to the average male wage ranged from 0.96 to 1.06, with the average being 1.0.[6] There are significant gender inequalities in labor markets in Indonesia (see Chapter 2), but the relative equality of wages between men and women at the factory level is not a trivial point. It contradicts the assertions by some scholars that employing a woman as opposed to a man *automatically* results in wage savings.

Hiring women can in fact incur costs that make their labor more expensive than male labor, especially in contexts where the gender wage gap is relatively small. In Indonesia, women received more generous overtime bonuses for night shifts than men.[7] For employers that paid taxes for workers, women cost more, being taxed at a higher rate than married men. By law, women were entitled to two days of paid menstruation leave every month and three months of maternity leave, with full wages paid by the employer rather than by the state. Many employers evaded payment of maternity and menstruation leave, of course, but many did pay them. Those that did so often devised elaborate tactics for reducing the impact on production. Some employers offered incentive pay to women who worked during their two days of monthly menstruation leave, which often amounted to receiving four days' pay for two days' work. Employers hired young unmarried women, provided family planning services at factory clinics, and encouraged rapid turnover through a regime of forced overtime, which caused many young women to resign after marriage. Despite the costs associated with these benefits and practices, employer interest in hiring women remained keen. Understanding both why employers hire women when men's labor can be obtained at the same wage rate and why employers in capital-intensive industries often shun female labor requires the consideration of gendered discourses of work.

## Gendered Discourses of Work

A virtually omnipresent fact of industrial life is the categorization of jobs in a factory as "men's work" and "women's work." Men and women seldom do the same jobs on the shop floor, and the profound gender segregation is hard to miss when one enters a factory. A constant theme in the literature on women factory workers is that employers associate a number of positive features with female labor that are not reducible to lower wages. I use the concept of gendered discourses of work to capture these ideas that employers hold about men and women workers.

Many scholars who have studied the massive flow of women into factory work in developing countries since 1970 address the attributes that I refer to as gendered discourses of work, but they integrate them differently into their analyses.[8] The scholarship that gives gendered discourses of work a causal role in shaping shop-floor divisions of labor usually focuses on a small number of factories and rarely offers theoretical explanations for broader gendered trends in employment. Further, they seldom trace change over time in gender divisions of labor, even when they pay careful attention to other dynamics on the shop floor. The varying impact of gendered discourses of work on actual divisions of labor is therefore usually overlooked. Those offering theories of feminization, in contrast, rarely incorporate examinations of shop-floor job allocation into their analyses. Although they acknowledge the existence of managerial beliefs about the characteristics of women workers (e.g., docility, dexterity, tolerance for monotony), they place the main causal weight on low wages. Since the causal force of gendered discourses of work are seen as pushing in the same direction as wages, they are usually subsumed under the wage argument, and the independent causal impact of gendered discourses of work is lost.

Authors also vacillate between treating gendered discourses of work as managerial subterfuge or as traits that women actually possess (Elson and Pearson 1981a; Fernandez-Kelly 1983). For example, at one point Elson and Pearson (1981a, 92) argue: "It might seem to follow that the labor force of world market factories is predominantly female because the jobs to be done are regarded as 'women's work.' But to note that jobs are sex-stereotyped is not to explain why this is so. After all, capitalist firms are compelled by competitive forces to select their labor force and constitute their division of labor on the basis of profitability, not ideology." On the following page, however, the authors note that women's "nimble fingers" are the result of training, and they specifically mention that industrial sewing is similar to sewing in the home on domestic sewing machines. Elson and Pearson shift from calling these traits "ideological" to agreeing that women have them and to showing how they obtain them.

I argue that whether women possess these traits is irrelevant; the crucial point is that employers believe that they do. As elegantly stated by Salzinger (2003, 9), these images are important not because they reflect reality but because they produce it. In other contexts, feminist labor historians and sociologists have shown persuasively how gender shapes the way that employers put their economic interests into practice (Downs 1995; Humphrey 1987; Milkman 1987; Rose 1992). These scholars demonstrate that rational economic practice is partially constituted by gender and that employers view productivity and labor control through a gendered lens. Gendered discourses of work are therefore integral to understanding the gendered dynamics of hiring practices.

I adopt a synthetic conceptualization of gendered discourses of work, combining Foucault's (1990) notion of discourse, Connell's (1987) praxis-oriented perspective, and poststructuralist feminist approaches (Riley 1988; Scott 1988a). I take from Foucault the notion that discourse produces subjects. In this case, the gendered worker on the shop floor is created in part through the discourses produced by management about gendered workers. From a Foucauldian perspective the issue is not whether women are patient, disciplined, and diligent but that the subject of the woman worker as a patient, disciplined, and diligent worker is produced through discourse. Poststructuralist feminists have shown the utility of paying attention to how gendered subjects are constructed relationally through discourse: male and female workers are produced relationally through a series of binary oppositions—for example, careless/careful, lazy/diligent, undisciplined/disciplined, strong/weak, heavy/light. Connell's praxis-oriented approach calls attention to how these discourses, once produced, become embedded in institutions and gain materiality, becoming part of the structure of everyday life and shaping relations within it. The importance of binary oppositions and their embeddedness in everyday practice is most evident in the separation of men and women into different job categories in the factory. Combining these varied approaches to discourse acknowledges the contingency of these discourses (they do not represent "truth"), and integrates into the analysis their operation in everyday factory practice. Discourse both structures how and forms a lens through which subjects in the factory view the labor process; discourse is both created and re-created—and possibly changed—by practice on the shop floor.

In Indonesia, management generally presented the distinctions between men and women in dichotomous terms: women were more careful, diligent, disciplined, patient, easier to manage or control, and better suited for light and monotonous work; men, in contrast, worked quickly but often carelessly, did not follow orders as well as women, were naughty, and complained more, but they were better than women at heavy work.[9] Supervisors seldom mixed men and women in the same jobs because they believed that if men were put in women's jobs (or vice versa), productivity would fall. For certain jobs some managers were neutral, observing that either men or women would do. In these cases, the main obstacle to introducing women into men's jobs was wariness of male resistance to an influx of women.

Gendered discourses of work not only include factors that help managers decide on the best-gendered worker for a given job but also encompass broader features of interest to employers, such as labor control. Some managers regarded women as being less likely to go on strike, but most focused less on the propensity to strike and stressed that women were easier to control. They emphasized women's willingness to follow instructions without delay and without talking back, flexibility about doing work outside their job classifications, willingness to stay at work stations, and punctuality. The number of strikes rose precipitously in Indonesia in the late 1980s and early 1990s, and many of these strikes occurred in sectors in which women made up the majority of the production workforce (Kammen 1997), so it is unsurprising that many managers did not mention a lower propensity to strike as a reason to hire women. Managers' perceptions about gender-differentiated rates of absenteeism were also important.[10] For example, if management had problems with too many women taking maternity leave, then job classifications perceived as being relatively androgynous might be directed toward men.

So why do gendered discourses of work matter for explaining feminization? Feminization involves either a gendered redefinition of work—jobs that men previously claimed become redefined as women's work—or the assignment of new job categories to women rather than to men. But what leads employers to establish or change a particular gender division of labor? I argue that hiring women is one solution that employers deploy to enhance productivity and labor control. Since gender is a key organizing principle in the factory, managers believe that placing the wrong-gendered workers in a job will negatively affect productivity. Consequently, when productivity is suboptimal, employers often attribute it to having wrong-gendered workers in the job, and replacing male workers with female workers is one solution for rectifying the situation.

The structural imperative to remain competitive, however, does not result automatically in specific gendered changes in the labor process. A process of *translation* must occur whereby managers assess, given the resources at their disposal, how best to deal with the competitive situation that they face. Labor-intensive and export-oriented industries are more likely to feminize because they feel the forces of competition most acutely and are therefore more likely to tinker with the labor process in order to squeeze more productivity from their workers. Consequently, rates of feminization are higher in these industries than in more capital-intensive and protected industries. Gendered discourses of work broaden the scope of factors to be considered in assessing how employers weigh the relative costs and benefits of hiring men versus women. Wages are one, but not the only, consideration. Employers facing similar competitive constraints come to different gendered decisions about hiring, some opting to employ men and yet others, women.

The critique of the conventional wisdom regarding feminization has highlighted four key areas that a theory of feminization must incorporate: labor/capital intensity, labor supply, mediating institutions, and gendered discourses of work. These four components combined constitute the theoretical framework of this book, the gendered political economy approach.

## The Gendered Political Economy Approach

The gendered political economy approach comprises three nodal points —labor supply, mediating institutions, and capital/demand—each of which incorporates gender as a category of analysis. Gender is therefore at work not only in the family, the culture, and the state but in markets as well. It is also a comparative framework that highlights differences between countries which affect women's share of employment.

The nodal point capital/demand breaks down into two components: gendered sectors, and gendered discourses of work. Each of these components captures, in a different way, the gendered nature of production and how it affects capital's demand for women workers. The two components combine to form an approach that incorporates gender into the political economy rather than treating it as a residue from nonmarket spheres of activity. The first component, gendered sectors, simply reflects an important empirical regularity of gendered employment in manufacturing: labor-intensive sectors are far more likely to hire women than capital-intensive sectors; capital-intensive sectors are more likely to employ men. Once sectors become gendered male or female, the stamp of femininity or masculinity, though not indelible, has enormous staying power. Gendered sectors constitute the structural component and help to explain why some countries have employed more women than others over the course of industrialization. In other words, it explains broad regularities in women's absorption into factory work across national and historical contexts.

The second component of the capital/demand nodal point, gendered discourses of work, captures the effect on hiring decisions of employer perceptions about women workers. The most obvious evidence of the role of gender in organizing production is the pervasive but variant gender division of labor present on the shop floor. One consequence of this stubborn fact of industrial life is that feminization often entails a redrawing rather than an erasure of the line between men's and women's work. Employers do not randomly replace women with men; rather, they carefully choose specific job categories to feminize while leaving others untouched. Over time, gendered discourses of work can transform the way a sector is gendered. For example, electronics is a highly feminine industry in many countries, even though it is relatively capital intensive. Feminization in electronics has largely been a result of employers' defining many of the jobs within electronics assembly as suitable for women. Thus, although labor intensity has a gendered logic—labor-intensive sectors are more likely to hire women than capital-intensive sectors—gendered sectors to some extent reflect long-term processes through which gendered discourses of work are embedded in production processes. Gendered discourses of work are essential for explaining why employers facing similar competitive constraints make differently gendered hiring choices.

Gendered sectors and gendered discourses of work thus determine capital's demand for female labor. But just because capital wishes to hire women does not mean that it can, which brings us to the second nodal point, labor supply. This point focuses attention on the characteristics of gendered workers before they enter the labor market and on the availability of gendered workers. Do state policies and cultural practices facilitate or obstruct the mobilization of a female workforce? Assuming that features of the labor supply nodal point facilitate capital's access to female labor, one more hurdle, labor market institutions, must still be cleared before significant feminization can occur.

The third nodal point, mediating institutions, identifies institutions that intervene between the supply of gendered labor on the market and capital's demand for gendered labor. Mediating institutions that regulate employer access to labor need to be scrutinized carefully for their gendered impact—do they facilitate or hinder employer access to female labor? The labor supply and mediating institutions nodal points both highlight factors that explain cross-national variations in women's sectoral share of employment.

Figure 1.2 pulls together the three nodal points and illustrates how they interact to produce gendered outcomes in industrialization. Significant feminization occurs only when demand for female labor increases, when women's labor is available and appealing, and when mediating institutions facilitate the channeling of women to the factories. Feminization may also take place if demand for female labor remains constant when significant changes occur at the labor supply and mediating institutions nodal points, but the magnitude would be modest. Differences in the degree of feminization between countries can be attributed to variations at all three nodal

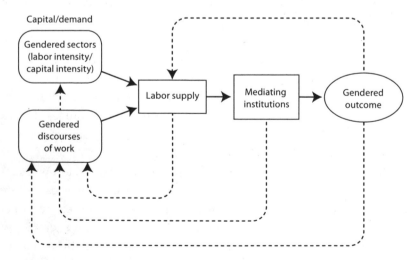

**Figure 1.2.** The gendered political economy approach.

points, whereas sectoral variations between countries (i.e., why the textiles sector employs fewer women in Mexico than in Thailand) are largely attributable to variations in labor supply and mediating institutions.

The dark arrows in Figure 1.2 portray the initial causal chain, but over time there are long-term interactions between the nodal points, and these interconnections are denoted by the dashed arrows. For example, if women become more appealing workers as a result of significant reductions in fertility, this result can have a feedback effect on employer demand for women workers. Changes in mediating institutions can produce similar feedback effects. The very process of feminization itself can have feedback effects on gendered discourses of work and on the labor-supply nodal point. If capital's demand for women workers is high, for example, parents are likely to invest more in their daughter's education; likewise, more employers hiring women can have spillover effects on other employers and hence create yet more demand for women workers. When positive feedback loops such as this are created, feminization can continue for many years, which is precisely what happened in Indonesia.

Before I embark on an analysis of the Indonesian case, it is necessary to probe more deeply into the reasons why women tend to be concentrated in labor-intensive sectors; otherwise, a core causal pattern identified in the book remains somewhat mysterious—although empirically validated, the underlying logic is unclear. Moreover, understanding the reasons behind women's concentration in low-paid, labor-intensive sectors is a crucial first step to devising ways of changing this fact. Uncovering the reasons for the link between labor intensity and women's employment is the task of the next chapter.

# 2

## Feminized Ghettos?

### The Structural Contours of Women's Employment

$P$ick any sector in any country, and chances are that if it is a relatively female- or male-intensive sector in that country, then it is also relatively female- or male-intensive in other countries. These similarities between countries are surprising—given the cross-national differences in gender relations, institutions, and industrialization paths—but the underlying reason is labor/capital intensity: women are overwhelmingly concentrated in labor-intensive sectors; men work in a wider range of sectors and claim the majority of jobs in capital-intensive sectors. It is essential to explore the underlying causes of women's concentration in labor-intensive sectors in order to illuminate not only why feminization occurs but also what the sources are of much of the gendered wage inequality that pervades labor markets.

Although the link between labor intensity and women's employment is widely accepted, the causes of it are a matter of dispute among scholars. Two views prevail, one that focuses on wages and another that highlights worker stability and skills. My analysis leads to different conclusions. Whereas most scholars emphasize the qualities of the workers, I stress how labor intensity affects the types of labor organization that a sector develops. Employers in capital-intensive sectors can afford to set up internal labor markets that reward tenure with significant increases in wages, which discourages turnover in the workforce. In contrast, employers in labor-intensive sectors cannot afford to set up internal labor markets. They provide few incentives for long tenure and hence have higher rates of turnover.

Varying rates of turnover have gendered consequences. High turnover allows employers to cycle women on maternity leave in and out of the workforce more easily, so hiring women is more appealing to those employers than to firms with low rates of turnover.

Although turnover rates do affect the gendered hiring preferences of employers, scholars tend to exaggerate gender differences in rates of turnover and to overlook how employer practices contribute to the differences that do exist. As measured by absenteeism and length of tenure, women are usually slightly more unstable workers than men. But the most interesting finding is that the differences between sectors are far more significant than the differences between men and women within sectors, which suggests that the crucial variable determining stability is not gender but sector-specific labor practices. Indeed, capital-intensive sectors that hire women do not set up internal labor markets with career ladders but adopt labor practices that induce turnover. A comparison of training times between capital-intensive and labor-intensive industries, moreover, reveals little difference in the training requirements for men's and women's jobs, which casts doubt on skills as an explanation for women's concentration in labor-intensive sectors.

The most persuasive existing explanation for women's concentration in labor-intensive sectors is that these sectors pay lower wages and are therefore more attracted to hiring less expensive female labor. Yet evidence from firm-level data in Indonesia shows that although some wage savings can be gained by hiring women, the degree of saving varies from sector to sector and is greatest in capital-intensive, not labor-intensive, sectors. I argue that gendered discourses of work are an essential additional factor to be considered. It is a combination of lower wages, employer practices that induce high turnover rates, and gendered discourses of work that explain women's concentration in labor-intensive industries.

## Worker Stability

Dual labor market theory is perhaps the best-known theory that highlights women's instability as workers as the primary explanation for their concentration in labor-intensive lines of work (Doeringer and Piore 1971; Gordon 1972; Sabel 1982). The theory posits that a combination of product market pressures and skill requirements generates two diverse market segments, the primary and secondary markets. Primary firms usually produce for the stable element of demand in product markets, secondary firms for the unstable component. In the primary market, skill specificity, on-the-job training, and custom lead firms to create internal labor markets that provide career ladders offering opportunities for workers to gain new skills and better wages. High wages, good working conditions, employment stability, career ladders, and a host of other positive features characterize jobs in the primary market. Employers create internal labor markets in order to reduce turnover (i.e., to increase stability), as training workers with the requisite firm-specific skills is costly. Firms in the secondary market, in contrast, do not train workers, either because they hire workers who already possess general skills—skills that are transferable to and from other workplaces—or because the work itself is unskilled. Since most of the work is relatively unskilled, the costs of recruitment, screening, and training are low, and turnover is not a concern. Consequently, jobs in the secondary market tend to have low wages and paltry fringe benefits, poor working conditions, high labor turnover, little chance of advancement, and arbitrary and capricious supervision.[1]

Stability characterizes not only the jobs in the primary sector but also the workers who fill them. Unstable workers with low job attachment are willing to take secondary jobs, as they are more tolerant of poor working conditions and are uninterested in advancement, whereas stable workers seek out the primary jobs. Dual labor market theorists argue that instability is an inherent characteristic of the worker as well as a product of employment in a particular labor market, creating a vicious cycle. The causal chain, however, begins with the negative characteristics of the worker, which are merely reinforced by employment in the secondary market. Women end up in the secondary market because they are unstable workers and hence not worth training. Dual labor market theory is vulnerable to criticism from two directions. The first has to do with stability, the other with skill (see below).

The stability of workers can be measured in a number of ways, absenteeism and turnover being the most prevalent. Scholars often assume that women have higher rates of absenteeism and turnover, but empirical studies show conflicting results. I deal with each of these measures in turn, relying on both the secondary literature and the data that I collected in Indonesia. The firm and sector are the appropriate levels for comparing

male and female rates, since firm-specific and sector-specific labor practices affect the level of absenteeism. Firms offer varying incentives to encourage stability, and sectors have different wage levels, different hours
(e.g., one shift with overtime, two twelve–hour shifts, three eight–hour
shifts, etc.), and varying intensities of work. Comparisons should also be
made between similar workers: that is, between production workers rather
than between, say, male management and female production workers.

Although it is generally assumed that women have higher rates of absenteeism than men, some studies have shown that men and women have
similar rates (Anker and Hein 1985; Hein 1986; Joekes 1987). In my sample,
firms rarely separated absences by gender in their records, and even when
they did, pregnancy leave was often excluded. Only three textile companies (one spinning, one weaving/spinning, and one weaving/spinning/
dyeing) collected data that separated men and women and included maternity leave in the absenteeism figures.[2] Women's absence rates were generally higher, but the differences were not very large, considering that
maternity and menstruation leave were included. The male rate of absenteeism varied between 5.21 and 12.67 percent, and women's rates ranged
from 6.54 to 9.7 percent.[3] Women's absenteeism was lower in two of eight
years, about 1 percent higher in two years, and in the remaining four the
difference was substantial, between 2 and 4 percent. It is significant that the
factory showing the largest differences in absenteeism was the newest factory, established in 1992. Tenure was relatively long at this factory, so many
women hired in 1992 and 1993 began to have children at the same time,
which pushed up the level of absences as these women took maternity
leave.

Since so few firms compare men's and women's levels of absenteeism
directly, a second-best alternative is to compare the rate of absenteeism
with the percentage of women employed in a factory. These findings are
tenuous because of problems of ecological inference; I assume that if
women's rates of absence are higher than men's, then factories that employ
more women should have higher levels of absenteeism. Table 2.1 lists levels of absenteeism by sector.[4] Some factories provided data for multiple
years, and all available data are reflected in the calculations in the table.
The automobile factories had much lower rates of absenteeism than other
sectors. At the firm level, the difference between the lowest and highest
rates was 4.8 percent (5.3 percent for a plywood factory minus 0.5 percent

**Table 2.1.** Absenteeism by sector

| Sector | Percent absent | Percent female |
|---|---|---|
| Textiles ($N = 24$) | | |
| Mean | 3.09 | 50.08 |
| Median | 2.93 | 52.5 |
| Standard deviation | 0.69 | 24.17 |
| Automobiles ($N = 16$) | | |
| Mean | 1.83 | 0 |
| Median | 1.63 | 0 |
| Standard deviation | 1.08 | 0 |
| Plywood ($N = 5$) | | |
| Mean | 4.29 | 55.6 |
| Median | 4.25 | 44 |
| Standard deviation | 0.88 | 15.88 |
| Garments ($N = 4$) | | |
| Mean | 3.38 | 91.5 |
| Median | 3.43 | 92 |
| Standard deviation | 1.03 | 5.2 |

for one of the automobile producers), with about 63 percent of the cases falling in the range of 2 to 4 percent.

The relationship between the level of female employment and absenteeism can also be tested statistically. I ran two models, the first simply with *Percent Absent* as the dependent variable and *Percent Female* as the independent variable; the second model was the same but added a dummy variable to control for sector-specific features of the automobile industry: namely, much higher wages and stricter regulations about attendance. Since sector-specific features affect levels of absenteeism for both men and women, it is necessary to examine how controlling for dramatically different sectoral labor practices affects absenteeism. Because the other sectors are relatively similar in terms of pay and benefits, the automobile sector is the most likely to have a large sector-specific effect on absenteeism. In the first model, Percent Female explains 34 percent of the variance in absenteeism, and the coefficient for Percent Female is positive and statistically significant but not very large. A 1 percent increase in Percent Female leads to a 0.02 increase in absenteeism (see Table 2.2). If a firm employed 100 percent women as opposed to 100 percent men, the absenteeism rate would be 2 percent higher. The coefficient for Percent Female in the second model is not statistically significant, so the results are at most suggestive. When

**Table 2.2.** Regression equation with percent absent as dependent variable

| Model 1 | Coefficient | Standard error of b |
|---|---|---|
| Percent female | 0.020*** | 0.004 |
| (Constant) | 0.021*** | 0.002 |
| R-squared = 0.340 | | |
| Adjusted R-squared = 0.326 | | |
| $N = 48$ | | |

| Model 2 | | |
|---|---|---|
| Percent female | 0.010 | 0.006 |
| Automobiles | −0.009** | 0.005 |
| (Constant) | 0.028*** | 0.004 |
| R-squared = 0.340 | | |
| Adjusted R-squared = 0.369 | | |
| $N = 48$ | | |

Note: Unstandardized coefficients; $p$ values indicated by *, **, and *** for values less than 0.1, 0.05, and 0.01.

controlling for automobiles, the impact of Percent Female on absenteeism practically vanishes, with a 1 percent increase in Percent Female leading to a 0.01 increase in absenteeism. Employing 100 percent women instead of 100 percent men would raise absenteeism only slightly—by 1 percent.

Although the direction of the effect is what dual labor market theorists would lead us to expect, the impact is not as large as they suggest. If garment factories can get 3.4 percent absenteeism (see Table 2.1) with an overwhelmingly female workforce (92 percent) that is paid low wages and given few incentives to stick around, while automobile factories get 1.8 percent by employing all men and paying high wages, it is not obvious that a 1.6 percent difference in absenteeism would lead them to employ only men. Rather, these small differences in absenteeism would be only one factor weighed among many. Lowering absenteeism is costly, and hiring men, setting up career ladders, and paying higher wages may not be the most cost-effective path to follow. The wage premium buys less than 2 percent in increased attendance per year, since women would reduce their absences in an automobile factory for the same reasons that men do. The most startling aspect of these data is that the impact of employing women on levels of absenteeism is so small. The main reason that the difference is not larger is that Indonesian women rarely claim menstruation leave and tend to have fewer unexcused and illness-related absences than men. The small difference is especially surprising, given that maternity leave is included.

When the better working conditions and pay in automobiles are controlled for, the 1 percent difference in absenteeism would result in only about three more days of absences per year for each woman employed.

Dual labor market theory emphasizes turnover even more strongly than absenteeism, since it has an important impact on the cost structure of imparting firm-specific skills to workers. Scholars who have examined gendered turnover rates have come to some interesting conclusions. As in absenteeism, firm characteristics play an important role in determining levels of turnover (England 1992; Manning 1979). Controlling for higher wages and differences in management practices shows that women are not necessarily less stable workers; in fact, women may actually be more stable than men in monotonous work or in a single occupation, especially if it is a low-wage job (Humphrey 1987; Tjandraningsih 1991). Humphrey (1987) has observed that women in Brazilian manufacturing tend to work under conditions of much stricter supervision than men do. He found that when men are submitted to these conditions at low wages, they quit at higher rates than women. For men to submit to this monotony and discipline, they must either be paid higher wages or see the job as a step in a career ladder (Fernandez-Kelly 1983b; Humphrey 1987). Of course, the reason women are more willing to endure these working conditions is that other choices in the labor market are often equally unpleasant.

Research demonstrates that gender is an inconsistent predictor of turnover rates. A number of studies show that when age and skill are controlled for, the difference in turnover between men and women virtually disappears (Anker and Hein 1985; Humphrey 1987). Bai and Cho (1995) found that female manufacturing workers' rate of turnover, measured in terms of the rate at which a worker changed jobs, was lower than men's in Seoul, Kuala Lumpur, Bangkok, and Manila. Hein (1986) discovered little difference between women's and men's turnover rates in Mauritius, and the differences were higher between factories than between men and women, which points to the vital influence of firm-specific practices on worker stability. Anker and Hein (1986) found similar turnover rates for men and women in Cyprus, Ghana, India, Mauritius, and Sri Lanka. Although women quit work as a result of family-related issues, men were more likely to leave for another job. Cohn (2000) has reviewed the literature on turnover and finds that studies are inconclusive: about one-third find women's rates to be higher, one-third find them to be about the same, and one-third find them to be lower.

Before turning to the empirical evidence from Indonesia, I should note that employers do not necessarily regard high turnover as a negative feature. In fact, certain employers take active measures to encourage workers to resign after a few years on the job. The main reason that turnover can be advantageous to employers is that it keeps wages low, which is especially important in jobs where productivity peaks can be reached in a relatively short period of time. Cohn (1985, 2000) has introduced the concept of synthetic turnover to capture the idea of management policies that increase turnover rates. Women are frequently the targets of such policies; simply inferring that women are unstable workers, then, overlooks the impact of employer practice on a worker's decision to quit. Cohn argues that in firms with hierarchical structures and tenure-based salary scales, workers become more expensive without necessarily becoming more productive, creating an incentive for firms to find ways to shed workers. Marriage bars were a common device used historically by employers—and still used in many countries that do not have enforceable equal rights legislation—to cycle women out of the workforce. Of course, if women simply quit when they married, it would be unnecessary to enact marriage bars, so their existence provides strong evidence that women would often prefer to continue working after marriage.

A weakness of Cohn's theory, however, is that it fails to capture the dynamics of induced turnover in sectors such as garments in Indonesia during the export boom. The absence of tenure-based salary scales can also increase turnover, especially if the likelihood of finding another job is high. Garment firms in Indonesia, for example, rarely offered well-defined job ladders; wage increases were also rare, and most workers depended on annual increases in the minimum wage to secure higher pay. Consequently, workers had little incentive to stay at one firm as long as other factories continued to hire; they left jobs for slightly better wages or working conditions, out of boredom with the routine, because of a poor relationship with a supervisor or disagreement with a particular policy of the firm. One frustrated textile employer complained to me that when a factory across the street began to feminize its workforce, all his best female workers left simply because uniforms were not required at his competitor's workplace.

In other words, when women's labor is in demand, women may leave more frequently because they have little to lose by switching employers.[5] High turnover rates in low-wage firms, then, may mean not that workers are unstable but that the structure of incentives gives workers little reason to stay.

In addition, fostering synthetic turnover is not simply a matter of preventing wage increases from rising faster than increases in productivity. There are at least two additional benefits. First, physically demanding jobs that require strength or stamina give employers incentives to shed older workers and replace them with younger and more energetic employees. The workers most likely to experience productivity declines after reaching peak productivity are those who work in sectors that rely on extensive overtime or long shifts. It is not coincidental that women's tenure in textiles is longer than in garments and plywood. Textile plants usually run three eight–hour shifts, so overtime is limited. Plywood firms, in contrast, generally have two twelve-hour shifts, and garment factories are usually one-shift operations that rely on high levels of overtime. Long shifts and high overtime hours encourage turnover in all workers but take an especially high toll on women, once they marry and assume greater family responsibilities.

Second, encouraging turnover is a way to avoid paying maternity leave as well as to get around the supposed higher rates of absenteeism that are often wrongly associated with women's having family responsibilities.[6] I found no employers enacting marriage bars, but they voiced a strong preference for hiring young, single women—most obviously because employers could be relatively certain that young women would not take maternity leave in the short term. In contrast, the chances of a married woman in her reproductive years becoming pregnant in the short term were high.[7] Inducing turnover was a way to get women to quit before they claimed maternity leave.

Maternity leave also helps to explain why labor-intensive sectors are more likely to hire women than capital-intensive sectors. Even if women return to work after having a child, the combined impact of their absence and the adjustment of work assignments during their final months of the pregnancy poses difficulties for the management of capitalist enterprises. It is not that maternity leave makes women unstable workers—women often return from maternity leave, and they retain all the firm-specific skills that they have acquired—but rather that the challenge for employers is how to cover the lost labor during the leave. Managers face three choices. The first is to make do without the worker until she returns to the factory, but this choice could negatively affect output. The second is to hire a few more workers than are necessary for production jobs. The excess workers serve as floaters that cover for absent workers. This is an unappealing option, however, because it raises labor costs.

The third choice is to hire a replacement. But this course of action is risky, as employers could end up with excess workers if the woman on maternity leave returns to work. Women would be more likely to return to work after maternity leave in firms that offer career ladders and high wages. Since turnover in these firms is low, it is unlikely that other workers would have resigned in the meantime. It is ironically women's potential *stability* that presents the biggest problem for these employers. Capital-intensive firms fall in this category because they can afford labor practices that provide significant rewards for long tenures. In contrast, labor-intensive firms cannot afford to erect career ladders for the majority of their workforce, but they can handle women's maternity leave more easily than capital-intensive firms because they have higher turnover rates. By the time a worker returns from maternity leave, there is a good chance that another worker will have resigned, which allows employers to hire replacements and cycle women on maternity leave in and out of the workforce relatively seamlessly.

Although capital-intensive firms could opt for forms of labor organization that induce turnover, it is overwhelmingly the labor-intensive firms that adopt such practices, a fact that provides additional insights into the reasons women end up in these sectors. They do so not because they are unstable workers but because capital-intensive firms that reward tenure prefer not to deal with the costs and logistical problems associated with maternity leave. And since they are paying relatively high wages, they can easily secure a male workforce. The argument presented here also suggests that capital-intensive sectors employing large numbers of women will adopt practices that induce turnover. Electronics, for example, is a relatively capital-intensive industry, but it is also female-intensive in many countries; unsurprisingly, labor practices in electronics are more similar to those in garments than to those in automobile manufacturing. Gender, then, affects how firms structure labor practices, which in turn affects the stability of women workers.

With these caveats in mind, how did male and female turnover ratios compare in my sample of firms? Since the empirical data that I collected in Indonesia rarely allow for accurate calculations of turnover, I have instead relied on tenure and resignation rates: if women generally have higher turnover than men, then they should have shorter tenures and higher quit rates. A comparison of median tenures shows that within sectors men's tenure was longer, but the difference was less than one year for textiles and negligible for garments (see Table 2.3). The largest difference was in plywood, where average median tenure was 6.6 years for men and 3.4 years for women. It is impossible to compare men's and women's rates for automobiles, since no women were employed in the firms from which I obtained tenure data, but it is notable that the median tenure for women in textiles, 7.36 years, was comparable to the 8.0 years for men in the automobile factories. The differences in median tenures between some sectors were substantial, suggesting that practices within sectors were extremely important in determining the length of tenure for both men and women. One could simply conclude that women's years of tenure were lower, but the difference was large in only one sector, plywood, where it was at least partially attributable to gender differences in promotion possibilities (discussed in more depth below) and to the twelve-hour shifts that further complicated balancing motherhood and work.

**Table 2.3.** Median tenure rates

| Sector | Men | Women |
| --- | --- | --- |
| Textiles ($N = 11$) | | |
| Mean | 8.18 | 7.36 |
| Median | 8 | 7 |
| Standard deviation | 2.04 | 2.94 |
| Automobiles ($N = 4$) | | |
| Mean | 8 | n/a |
| Median | 6 | n/a |
| Standard deviation | 4.69 | n/a |
| Plywood ($N = 10$) | | |
| Mean | 6.6 | 3.40 |
| Median | 6 | 3 |
| Standard deviation | 2.41 | 1.26 |
| Garments ($N = 7$) | | |
| Mean | 2.43 | 2.29 |
| Median | 2 | 2 |
| Standard deviation | 1.72 | 1.11 |

**Table 2.4.** Resignation rates (%)

| Sector | Men | Women |
| --- | --- | --- |
| Textiles ($N = 27$) | | |
| Mean | 9.03 | 9.96 |
| Median | 6 | 6.4 |
| Standard deviation | 9.09 | 12.21 |
| Plywood ($N = 7$) | | |
| Mean | 11.04 | 21.24 |
| Median | 8.2 | 20.9 |
| Standard deviation | 6.11 | 8.46 |
| Garments ($N = 19$) | | |
| Mean | 20.87 | 23.89 |
| Median | 12.6 | 27 |
| Standard deviation | 22.55 | 12.52 |

The data provide weak support, then, for the assertion that women are more unstable than men; in fact, a stronger argument could be made that given the right organization of production, women have long tenures.

For resignation rates, the same pattern is repeated. Textile firms, once again, fostered stability among employees. Men and women had roughly the same resignation rates: 9.03 percent for men and 9.96 percent for women (see Table 2.4). The garment sector was once again the most unstable, with both men and women showing high resignations rates: 20.9 percent of male employees and 23.9 percent of female workers. Plywood showed a large difference between men and women, with only 11 percent for men but 21.2 percent for women. (I could not obtain resignation rates for the automobile factories, but some automobile plants provided turnover figures, and in general the rates were low: in one assembly factory the average rate between 1990 and 1997 was only 1.87 percent. Another assembly plant, however, reported a much higher rate, 15.3 percent.) The pattern evident in the tenure data resurfaced in the analysis of the resignation rates, with sectoral variations being wider than gender differences except in plywood.

Although the average median resignation rate was higher for women than for men in all three sectors, the difference between men and women was small in garments and textiles, and differences between sectors were greater than gender differences within sectors, which once again points to the importance of sector-specific labor practices in determining worker stability. To understand why gender differences in worker stability were larger in plywood than in the other sectors, it is necessary to take a closer look at another factor of great importance in dual labor market theory— skill.

## Skill

A number of authors have observed that dual labor market theory conflates capital intensity with a high level of firm-specific skills and labor intensity with unskilled work (Armstrong 1982; Cagatay and Berik 1991). But some jobs in highly capital-intensive industries may require little training. As stated bluntly by a supervisor in the machining section of a capital-intensive firm in Great Britain, "I could train a pair of chimpanzees to do this job" (Armstrong 1982, 30). Conversely, some labor-intensive jobs require as much training as some jobs in capital-intensive industries. Theorists from all perspectives agree, however, that women are confined overwhelmingly to jobs that are formally classified as unskilled or semiskilled and that these jobs tend to be in labor-intensive firms. This fact is then discussed in various ways. Authors, both feminist and nonfeminist, may simply assume that the work women do is indeed, on average, less skilled than men's work. Other feminists, however, have pointed out that women's jobs often require just as much skill as men's jobs but that women's jobs are devalued because women perform them (Armstrong 1982; Kim 1994). Still others have observed that women are excluded from work categorized as skilled (Acero 1995; Banerjee 1991; Downs 1995; Hirata 1989; Pena 1997; Rose 1992) and that women are not rewarded with high pay even when their work *is* classified as skilled.[8]

Some feminist scholars have taken the argument further and questioned the concept of skill as an objective economic category (Baron 1991; Beechey 1987; Phillips and Taylor 1980; Rose 1992). These scholars usually acknowledge that training is costly for employers and that some jobs are more difficult to master than others, but they assert that deciding which jobs qualify as "skilled" versus "semiskilled" versus "unskilled" is far from an objective process. Designating skill definitions is a social process, and since the assignment of a skill category creates hierarchies, it is also political. Women are at a disadvantage in the translation from job to skill category, and theorists define two dynamics that lead to the devaluing of women's work. First, employers assume that certain abilities associated with being female, such as dexterity or a high tolerance for monotonous work, are innate qualities that all women possess (Brenner 1998; Collins 2002; Downs 1995; Elias 2004; Elson and Pearson 1981a; Humphrey 1987; Kim 1994; Rose 1992; Wolfe 1993). Women's skills are thereby naturalized and deemed unworthy of monetary reward. The second is that male workers regarded as "skilled" labor will defend this designation in the face of deskilling (Baron 1991; Cockburn 1983; Coyle 1982; Rose 1992). Skill categories, then, cannot be taken at face value and should be treated with a healthy dose of skepticism.

The feminist literature only partially describes the gender and skill dynamics that I found in Indonesia. Supervisors and factory managers ascribed specific features to each gender and viewed men and women as distinct kinds of labor, but their definitions did not necessarily lead to a devaluation of women's abilities, and average male and female wages at most factories that I visited were roughly equal.[9] The discourse was one of complementarity, with management emphasizing that each gender was better at certain kinds of work and that it was best to go along with these "natural" capacities. If anything, in many of the factories it was the male workers that management demeaned, calling them "muscle men" (*tukang otot*), undisciplined, and mouthy.[10] Yet despite the positive appraisal of women as production workers, women rarely made it into maintenance jobs, and supervisory trajectories were extremely circumscribed except in garments —where there *were* many women in supervisory positions. Management did not place women in maintenance, which paid slightly higher than direct production work, because they believed that dirty and heavy work intimidated women. Only one company's spinning unit had introduced women systematically into maintenance, but there the tasks were subdivided into "light" maintenance, which involved routines such as cleaning the machines, and "heavy" maintenance, which entailed opening up and repairing large machines.

For supervisory jobs, there was a reluctance to let women manage men, not necessarily because upper management thought that women were poor managers but because they feared that men would disobey orders given by female supervisors. Since women usually composed 85 to 97 percent of the operators in medium- and large-scale garment factories, and since men had a significant presence only in the cutting and packing sections, women's promotion possibilities were better in garments than in textiles and plywood, where there were few female supervisors and it was rare for women to be promoted to a position higher than team leader. Even in majority-female sections, a significant male presence in most production sections in textiles and plywood narrowed the promotion possibilities for women. In the major automobile plants, women were not hired at all in production, even for the most menial tasks.

A comparison of the automotive plants with the more labor-intensive sectors provides a way to explore the utility of dual labor market theory for explaining women's lack of access to high-paying work in capital-intensive sectors. The automobile industry is a quintessential primary-sector employer, offering high wages in exchange for stability. It is capital intensive and has career ladders on which production workers can expect significant pay increases over time. Garments, textiles, and plywood, in contrast, are labor-intensive sectors with relatively low wages and—one would expect, given the theory—comparatively low levels of skills.

The best way to compare the sectors is not to take supposedly objective classifications of skill levels and note that one kind of factory has fewer "skilled" workers; the feminist intervention in this area has shown that one should be suspicious of skill classifications. The key issue for dual labor market theory should in fact be training, as this is the cost borne directly by the company. I interviewed supervisors to determine the training times for a range of positions, making it explicit that they should distinguish between competence (the worker can perform the operation) and speed (competence plus quantity). As Coyle (1982) has observed, with labor processes increasingly fragmented, speed becomes a highly valued skill. Basic competence can often be acquired rather quickly, but the worker may not work fast enough to be considered productive. Once the worker acquires the rudimentary knowledge required to perform the task, she must also learn to do the job more quickly, and reaching a productivity peak may take a year for some jobs.

An important preliminary note is that the end of three months is a central cutoff point for employers in Indonesia, since the first three months are legally considered a trial period. Employers can fire a worker for any reason during this period, but firing workers afterward requires permission from the labor dispute-resolution committee and payment of severance based on the length of service. A strong incentive therefore exists for employers to set up training so that worker productivity can be assessed within the initial three months.

Within sectors, female jobs usually required as much as or more training than male jobs. In garments, the most routinely valued job was the sewing operator position. New operators were put on the simplest tasks, and as they became more secure in the simple operations, they often learned more complicated tasks such as attaching collars. A sewer with no experience could learn to do the simplest operation efficiently in three months, but to become a "skilled" operator capable of performing a number of sewing operations efficiently took at least a year. In weaving factories, the jobs that required the most training were sizing, weaving, and inspection; women always predominated in inspecting and were often weaving operators. Inspecting operators could learn the basics of their jobs in a few months, but to be able to distinguish grades could take up to a year. Weavers could also learn the basics in about three months, but it took longer to be able to handle a large number of looms. In spinning, ring spinning was routinely named as the job that required the longest amount of time to learn well, about one month for the basics but up to a year to be able to handle a large number of spindles. Ring spinning was also the most female-intensive section of production in most spinning factories. In garments and textiles there were no well-defined career ladders for the vast majority of jobs, and the job structure was extraordinarily flat. All the workers were simply "operators," and although incentive structures might vary between sections, they did not reward men more than women.

In plywood there was slightly more hierarchy. Once again, the majority of jobs could be learned in less than three months, and most managers claimed that by the end of the three months even the most difficult tasks in this group of jobs could be done well by most workers. The two exceptions were grading and machine operation. Most firms had two levels of grading: the lower-level workers needed around six months to perform adequately and a year to be skilled enough to get promoted to "operator," the second level. (In plywood factories, "operator" refers to production workers with higher status and pay.) In grading, the operator oversaw a group of graders with less experience, and this was the only operator job that women performed regularly. The machine operator positions were a male domain. Young male workers learned the job by serving as assistants to the operators, and once an operator quit, retired, or was promoted, his assis-

tant moved into the operator job. Supervisors placed reliable male workers in the assistant position, and it was usually about three months to one
year, depending on the machine, before the worker could do all aspects of
the job independently. That operators received higher wages may be one
reason that male tenures were much longer than female tenures in plywood. Although operator jobs were less than 10 percent of all jobs in the
factory, they provided a promotion route for a portion of the male workforce. In addition, men had access to more supervisory positions than
women, and lower-level supervisors were often promoted from the production workforce.

Dual labor market theory would posit that automotive jobs require more
training than the jobs in the labor-intensive sectors, but in fact the automotive factories were, across the board, similar to the other sectors. To
simplify exposition, however, I will discuss only the assembly plants. Assembly plants had systematic training programs, with a set period of one
month for learning the company rules, the overall production system, and
safety; another month as a "helper"; and the third month working independently but under close supervision. By the beginning of the fourth
month the worker was expected to do the job smoothly and to keep up with
the line. Jobs such as $CO_2$ welding and spray repair took a little longer to
master, but about 60 percent of the jobs could be learned well in three
months and the remaining 40 percent in six months. As one manager explained to me, the jobs had to be simple because the lines moved quickly.
Each operator was expected eventually to learn at least three different jobs,
and after six months to a year he was rotated to his second job. There were
three grades for operators, from class three to five, with foremen being able
to achieve up to class six and supervisors up to class eight. Wage increases
in addition to routine cost-of-living raises were tied to moving up the job
ladder and to job performance. Over time, workers could expect to increase
their basic wages significantly, as can be seen by contrasting the lowest
and highest operator wages in one firm: Rp. (rupiahs) 340,000 versus Rp.
900,000. Such dramatic increases were impossible for production workers
in textiles, garments, or plywood unless they made it into management.

Longer training time, then, is not the reason that women do not work in
automobile assembly plants. Even the time it takes for a worker to complete three job rotations in an automobile assembly factory, about a year
and a half, is well within median tenure ranges for female workers in tex-

tiles and plywood. For many jobs in garments, textiles, and plywood, women require similar amounts of time to become proficient. The difference is that capital-intensive firms can afford to erect job ladders and provide high wages to workers with long tenures, whereas labor-intensive sectors cannot. The tendency of those studying labor relations to focus on highly male-intensive sectors and relatively privileged (male) workers has produced a skewed and oversimplified view of the characteristics and location of women's work. The comparison of automakers with the labor-intensive sectors shows that the training required by the automobile firms is comparable to that for the labor-intensive firms, which casts some doubt on the claims by dual labor market theorists about the importance of firm-specific skills in relegating women to labor-intensive sectors.

Before discussing the impact of wages on women's concentration in labor-intensive sectors of manufacturing, I think it worthwhile to comment on the implications of these findings for a new literature that offers a skill-based argument quite similar to dual labor market theory: the varieties-of-capitalism approach (Hall and Soskice 2001). Scholars in the varieties-of-capitalism tradition have directed attention to the impact of different types of skill regimes on gender segregation in labor markets (Estévez-Abe 2005; Estévez-Abe, Iversen, and Soskice 2001). Although this literature focuses on occupational segregation throughout the economy and analyzes highly institutionalized labor markets in Western Europe, North America, the Antipodes, and Japan, the logic of the approach should extend to gender segregation in manufacturing. Drawing on the work of Polachek (1981), scholars in this tradition argue that since women fall behind their male cohort in the acquisition of firm-specific skills and in promotions during leaves related to childbearing, it is irrational for women to invest in firm-specific skills if they plan to have children. Women therefore invest in "general skills," skills that are easily transportable to other workplaces. Employers that rely on firm-specific skills will in turn be reluctant to hire women, since it is impractical and costly to train replacements for women who are on maternity-related leave. Employers that rely on firm-specific skills thus engage in statistical discrimination against women. Consequently, women are concentrated in employment that relies on general rather than firm-specific skills.[11]

The argument has a chicken-and-egg character: is it women's rational behavior that underlies segregation, or statistical discrimination by employers? The prong of the argument that rests on women's behavior has both empirical and logical weaknesses. Empirically, England (2005) found that wage depreciation related to extended absences was not higher in traditionally male jobs, which means that it would in fact be rational for women to invest in firm-specific skills. Logically, given that male-dominated jobs have higher wages than female-dominated occupations, investing in firm-specific skills would be perfectly rational for women, even if they fell behind their male cohort, as long as the income in that occupation was higher than in alternative employment. Furthermore, the argument that women would fall behind men in terms of skill assumes that the pace of skill acquisition is constant and ongoing. But many jobs are characterized by fairly steep learning curves in the initial phases, with more modest slopes afterward. The argument also assumes that men's work experience during the leave period would impart significant and qualitatively new skills to workers rather than new applications of existing skills. Women may indeed fall behind their male cohort in promotions, but this holds true for all jobs, not just those requiring firm-specific skills. The only rational reason for women not to invest in firm-specific skills is that employers refuse to hire them. Since acquiring firm-specific skills is by definition dependent on being hired in the first place, the argument really boils down to one of statistical discrimination.

My empirical material also highlights weaknesses in the varieties-of-capitalism approach to assessing skills. Scholars read skills from tenure rates and national systems of vocational education but do not actually analyze the investment in training at the firm level in male-intensive and female-intensive occupations. As my analysis shows, albeit in a small sample of industries, some sectors that employ men and that fit the usual criteria for firm-specific skills (high tenure rates, internal labor markets) differ little from more female-intensive sectors in the amount of training and experience required to become competent on the job. Similarly, the variations in median tenure rates found in manufacturing in Indonesia did not correspond with variations in training, which suggests that tenure could be a poor proxy for firm-specific skills, at least in developing countries.

Moreover, thus far the "skill-regime approach" has not effectively engaged with alternative explanations for much of the variation in segregation that they seek to address. For example, it is equally possible that patterns of segregation could be explained by the social exclusion of women from historically male systems of vocational education which channel workers to employers in certain sectors of manufacturing, and equally possible that powerful unions and centralized collective bargaining—which characterize the countries that these scholars classify as rich in firm-specific skills—are reducing incentives for hiring women through the equalization of wage rates throughout the industry (McCall and Orloff 2005). In other words, although the logic underlying the argument is impeccable—industries relying on firm-specific skills will be reluctant to hire women because it is more difficult for them to hire replacement workers— it remains to be seen whether the jobs performed by men and women differ dramatically in the amount of training time required to produce proficient workers. Moreover, the logic underlying their classification of countries into different skill regimes flies in the face of arguments made about systems of skill acquisition in the countries that they study. As Thelen (2004) has argued, in countries where established vocational and firm-based training imparts high levels of skill, the heart of the matter has been the free-rider problem, which is a problem precisely because many of the skills imparted are transferable and transportable: that is, they are not truly firm-specific skills. Employers would be more likely to invest in training if poaching could be prevented. In countries with strong employer associations and centralized bargaining, such guarantees could be provided collectively, but in countries without these institutions, firms established internal labor markets that provided significant seniority-related benefits.

Finally, the varieties-of-capitalism explanation, even if ultimately supported with stronger empirical evidence, cannot deal with an important part of the puzzle of gender segregation: the overwhelming similarity between countries in the kinds of jobs that women perform (Charles 2005; McCall and Orloff 2005). At most, they can potentially account for certain highly capital-intensive sectors such as metalworking being more male-intensive in some economies (Germany, for example) than in others (the United States, for instance) (Charles 2005).

## Wages

Whereas worker stability and skills are of limited utility in explaining observed gender divisions of labor in Indonesia, wages are an important component in explaining patterns of segregation. Although Chapter 1 poked some holes in the cheap-labor argument, the goal was not to dismiss it entirely but to incorporate it into a more complex story about the forces behind feminization. Evidence drawn from wage data can help one assess the extent to which low wages influence labor-intensive sectors to hire women.

The fact that men and women in Indonesia often earned similar wages within factories does not address the issue of whether employers that hire mostly women have lower wage bills than those that rely primarily on male labor. If sectors that employ primarily women pay wages below those warranted by the level of capital intensity, then this is strong evidence that sectors relying on female labor reduce labor costs by doing so. It is vital to bring capital intensity into the picture, since capital-intensive sectors can afford to pay higher wages; the observation that steelworkers are paid more than garment workers is hardly shocking. By ranking sectors according to average capital intensity and average wages, it is possible to appraise whether female-intensive sectors are paying wages wildly out of line with their level of capital intensity.

In Indonesia, average sectoral wages corresponded roughly to the level of capital intensity (see Table 2.5). More capital-intensive firms paid higher wages, with the notable exceptions of beverages and tobacco. When sectors were ranked by average capital intensity, the ranking of the average wage for the sector was within three positions of its capital intensity ranking in twenty of thirty sectors. In ten additional sectors, the difference was four places or more. Of these ten sectors, three paid wages lower and seven paid wages higher than their capital-intensity ranking.

When these data were broken down in gendered terms, women were seen to constitute a majority of the workforce in nine sectors and men in twenty-one sectors. Female-intensive sectors had wages in line with their capital-intensity ranking in five sectors (56 percent), above the ranking in three (33 percent), and below the ranking in one (11 percent). In the twenty-one sectors that employed primarily men, in contrast, fifteen paid wages in line with their level of capital intensity (71 percent), four paid wages above (19 percent), and two below (10 percent). This distribution shows that women are not more disadvantaged than men in terms of working in sectors that paid wages incommensurate with the level of capital intensity. Overall, women were paid at a level in line with the structural features of the sector. The real issue is the overwhelming relegation of women to the

Table 2.5. Capital intensity ranking versus wage ranking

| Sector | Capital intensity ranking | Wage ranking | Difference in ranking | Percent female |
|---|---|---|---|---|
| Petroleum refineries/gas | 1 | 1 | 0 | 19 |
| Iron and steel | 2 | 3 | −1 | 1 |
| Industrial chemicals | 3 | 2 | 1 | 19 |
| Transportation | 4 | 7 | −3 | 11 |
| Nonferrous metals | 5 | 8 | −3 | 7 |
| Beverages | 6 | 16 | −10 | 39 |
| Electronics | 7 | 10 | −3 | 59 |
| Cement | 8 | 4 | 4 | 9 |
| Tobacco | 9 | 29 | −20 | 87 |
| Paper | 10 | 6 | 4 | 22 |
| Glass | 11 | 12 | −1 | 16 |
| Nonelectrical machinery | 12 | 9 | 3 | 8 |
| Other chemicals | 13 | 5 | 8 | 56 |
| Printing | 14 | 11 | 3 | 31 |
| Fabricated metal products | 15 | 13 | 2 | 21 |
| Porcelain | 16 | 11 | 5 | 35 |
| Coal/petroleum products | 17 | 24 | −7 | 22 |
| Food | 18 | 17 | 1 | 45 |
| Professional/scientific equipment | 19 | 14 | 5 | 65 |
| Rubber | 20 | 18 | 2 | 24 |
| Textiles | 21 | 21 | 0 | 56 |
| Wood processing | 22 | 20 | 2 | 38 |
| Other nonmetallic minerals | 23 | 19 | 4 | 9 |
| Plastic | 24 | 22 | 2 | 51 |
| Leather | 25 | 26 | −1 | 48 |
| Other manufacturing | 26 | 28 | −2 | 70 |
| Footwear | 27 | 23 | 4 | 78 |
| Garments | 28 | 25 | 3 | 78 |
| Wood furniture, etc. | 29 | 27 | 2 | 30 |
| Clay | 30 | 30 | 0 | 48 |

Source: Biro Pusat Statistik, *Statistik Industri Besar dan Sedang 1996*, data file.

more labor-intensive sectors. Two-thirds of the sectors in which women constitute a majority were relatively labor intensive.

Another way to test for the impact on the wage bill of hiring women is to run an OLS (ordinary least squares) regression on firm-level data from the BPS survey of medium and large establishments, with the natural log of *Wages per Capita* as the dependent variable, and *Percent Female*,[12] the natural log of *Capital Intensity*, and twenty-eight sector dummies as the independent variables (see Table 2.6).[13] The model explains 66 percent of the variance in wages, and when sector is controlled for, the higher the level of female employment, the lower the average wage. A 1 percent increase in

**Table 2.6.** Regression equation with log of wages per capita as dependent variable

|                     | Coefficient | S.e. of b |
|---------------------|-------------|-----------|
| Capital intensity   | 0.508***    | 0.003     |
| Percent female      | −0.002***   | 0.000     |
| Constant            | 3.42***     | 0.039     |
| R-squared = 0.663   |             |           |
| Adjusted R-squared = 0.662 |      |           |
| N = 22,963          |             |           |

*Source:* Biro Pusat Statistik, *Statistik Industri Besar dan Sedang 1996,* data file.
*Note:* Unstandardized coefficients; *p* values indicated by *, **, and *** for values less than 0.1, 0.05, and 0.01.

female employment results in a 0.2 decrease in average wages. By increasing the employment of women by 50 percent, a factory gains a sizable 10 percent wage reduction.

A closer examination of the sectoral data, however, shows that the wage savings vary by sector and diminish as the level of labor intensity increases. I divided sectors into quintiles according to the share of female employment (0–20, 21–40, 41–60, 61–80, 81–100) and compared the lowest quintile with the highest. The difference was highest in capital-intensive sectors and lowest in labor-intensive sectors, so labor-intensive sectors gained less of a reduction in average wages by substituting women for men than did capital-intensive ones. Thus, although the contention of feminization theorists that employing women results in wage savings is supported, it is important to add the caveat that the potential gains for labor-intensive sectors are small in comparison with the capital-intensive sectors. Even though it is certainly fair to argue that capital-intensive sectors are less attracted by the lure of lower wages than labor-intensive employers (Joekes 1982, 1987), it is still puzzling that only three relatively capital-intensive sectors in Indonesia employ over 30 percent women: beverages (39 percent), electronics (59 percent), and tobacco (87 percent).

Since tobacco is the starkest example of a female-intensive sector paying wages wildly out of line with its level of capital intensity, this exception is worth examining more closely. It is the most feminine sector in Indonesia; it is also relatively capital intensive. In most countries, tobacco is in the top three capital-intensive sectors, but tobacco is lower in capital intensity in

Indonesia because the law required a certain percentage of *kretek* (clove cigarettes), the most popular tobacco product in the country, to be rolled by hand. Since the 1960s, women have predominated in the hand rolling of *kretek;* many firms placed women on the automatic machines as well. Each machine can roll as much in one minute as an experienced hand roller can complete in an entire day, so the hand-rolling requirement has served to protect women's jobs.

The tobacco industry pays among the lowest wages in Indonesian manufacturing, and it is likely that the strong preference for hiring women influenced the adoption of a low-wage regime. Most women in the rolling sections have low educational levels, are married, and tend to be older than women in other industries. The willingness to retain older workers and to accept women's reproductive responsibilities has also resulted in long work tenures, with one study showing that about 20 percent of female *kretek* workers in two East Java villages had remained in their first factory job for over ten years (Saptari 1995). By accepting women workers that few other employers will take, the *kretek* industry has been able to pay extremely low wages.[14] They could afford to pay higher wages but they do not, since they are willing to hire women that other employers shun. Tobacco employers select a subset of women and structure their wage system around the weak bargaining position of this population, which allows them to pay lower wages than other sectors at similar levels of capital intensity. Gender therefore has an independent effect on how employers structure wages, and it is puzzling that tobacco manufacturers in other countries, as well as other capital-intensive employers in Indonesia, have not followed their example. Gendered discourses of work offer one possible explanation.

## Gendered Discourses of Work

Another factor that helps to explain women's concentration in labor-intensive sectors is gendered discourses of work. Many labor-intensive industries are characterized by assembly-line work that is relatively light, clean, and safe—features that employers almost universally identify as being especially conducive to the employment of women. Employers, draw differing interpretations, of course, about the match between the jobs in their factories and gendered workers, so gendered discourses of work are an imperfect predictor at the firm level. They are however, a fairly reliable predictor at the sectoral level. The conclusion that work in any one sector is relatively light, safe, and clean is far easier to reach in garments than for steel. Since heavy machinery is more likely to characterize capital-intensive than labor-intensive firms, these gendered notions more frequently lead to links between women workers and labor-intensive sectors than in capital-intensive industries.

Moreover, gendered discourses of work provide insight into why women are sought out by some relatively capital-intensive industries and shunned by others. In electronics, for example, production lines similar to those in labor-intensive industries are used. Likewise, tobacco companies in Indonesia have actively sought out women both to roll the cigarettes and to operate the machines that have largely supplanted hand rollers. The automobile industry is a bit of a paradox, since it is perhaps the only male-intensive assembly-line industry. Yet employers there have resisted hiring women, even though they could cut wages considerably by doing so. One reason is the perception of managers that work on the line is heavy, dangerous, and unsuitable for women (see Chapter 6).

## Conclusion

This chapter has probed the multitude of reasons behind the relationship between labor intensity and women's employment. Labor-intensive sectors are more likely to hire women as a result of women's lower average wages, the higher levels of turnover in such industries, and gendered discourses of work. Arguments based on women's instability, in contrast, were found to have limited explanatory weight. In fact, women's instability was found to be more an effect of sector-specific labor practices than a cause of women's concentration in labor-intensive industries, thus turning the argument of many scholars on its head: gendered outcomes in the labor market are a function not simply of women's role in the family but of intentional efforts by employers to induce high turnover among all workers and especially among women. In sectors that adopt labor practices that encourage long tenure and that allow women to balance family duties with work responsibilities, gender differences in worker stability nearly vanish. Labor-intensive industries hire women not only because their average wages are lower but also because these industries have higher turnover than capital-intensive industries and can therefore more easily rotate women on maternity leave in and out of the workforce. The few capital-intensive industries in Indonesia that hire women alter their labor practices in ways that mimic those of labor-intensive industries. This analysis leads to pessimistic conclusions about the potential for women's upward mobility in the industrial workforce and suggests that capital-intensive industries offering career ladders and promotion tracks are unlikely to open their doors to women.

# 3

# Appealing Women and
# Permissive Institutions

Although an expansion of employment in labor-intensive relative to capital-intensive sectors will generate demand for women workers, whether a supply of appealing potential workers is available and whether mediating institutions will permit employers to access this labor pool are far from certain results. Rather than assuming that employers can hire women, this chapter documents the multitude of changes in labor supply and mediating institutions that made women both more attractive and more accessible workers in Indonesia; it thus highlights the factors that created a supportive environment for feminization. A less conducive environment would have slowed, but not stopped, feminization.

In Indonesia, developments at the labor supply nodal point in the 1970s and early 1980s made women an increasingly desirable and available workforce. First, Suharto's New Order regime expanded primary education as part of its development program, creating a large pool of young female workers with junior and senior high school education. Second, family planning policy resulted in a dramatic reduction in fertility. Third, increased landlessness and economic crisis in the early 1980s drove women into the workforce, leading to higher female labor force participation rates.

In addition to these changes at the labor supply nodal point, a number of important developments at the mediating institutions nodal point diminished potential obstacles to the mobilization of women workers. Most important, the authoritarian state emasculated unions, thus removing the main obstacle to significant feminization. The demobilization of labor was part of a larger state project to eliminate potential political opposition. As part of the same effort, the state dismantled existing political parties and limited the activities of religious organizations as well. Islamic social and political organizations were therefore not in a position to oppose the expansion of women's involvement in manufacturing work.[1] Finally, the state relaxed its interpretation of protective legislation, so few legal restrictions remained on female labor.

These changes at the supply and institutional nodal points facilitated feminization by expanding the pool of potential women factory workers and by allowing the flow of these women into the factories. When industrialization policy shifted to EOI (export-oriented industrialization) in the 1980s, a mobilized female workforce was ready. And since the authoritarian state had repressed most social forces that could have potentially opposed the greater integration of women into factory work, a wave of feminization ensued. An overlooked side effect of authoritarian rule is that it can facilitate feminization by demobilizing potential sources of opposition. After laying out the developments at the three nodal points longitudinally, I discuss in more depth each of the supply and institutional factors that facilitated feminization.

## Sequencing

For a sense of the dynamics of feminization, the nodal points can be thought of as choke points that open and close, with an opening—represented by a change at the supply or institutional nodal points—increasing the flow of potential workers to factories. An overview of these changes can be seen in Figure 3.1.

The demobilization of the organizations that could have impeded feminization—unions, political parties, and political Islam—were the earliest developments that facilitated feminization by removing obstacles that might have obstructed it once capital's demand for female labor increased in the 1980s. The next set of significant developments occurred at the labor supply nodal point: small but steady gains in basic education for women, and moderate reductions in fertility over the course of the 1970s. The enforcement of protective legislation, moreover, weakened in the late 1970s. These changes expanded the supply of, and employers' access to, women workers and set the stage for the first wave of feminization in the late 1970s.

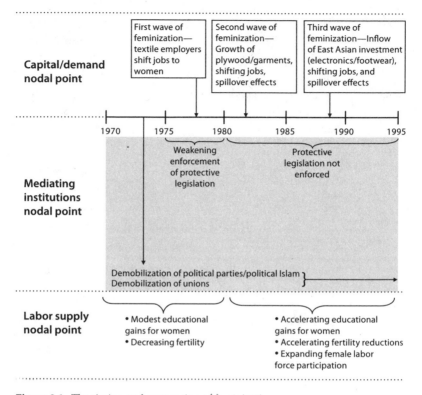

**Figure 3.1.** The timing and sequencing of feminization.

In that first wave, employers in textiles responded to the changes in women's fertility and education by shifting selected jobs to women. When women's educational levels rose and fertility declined moderately, and as the state granted more exceptions to the ban on night work for women, factories began to hire more women. Since employment in labor-intensive sectors had not expanded significantly, however, the degree of this early feminization was modest.

The second wave of feminization began in the transition years between import-substitution industrialization (ISI) and full-blown export promotion—1979 to 1986. The demobilization of unions and political parties remained in effect throughout the entire period, and the state intensified the repression of labor in the early 1980s. In addition, the trends in fertility decline and educational improvement evident in the 1970s accelerated, and the enforcement of protective legislation ceased. The main new development was an increase in women's labor force participation rates, which rose largely as a result of changes in agriculture and of economic crisis and created a larger pool of women workers available for mobilization into the factories. When the first major exporting industries began to develop in the early 1980s—primarily plywood and garments—demand for female labor expanded. As these sectors grew over the course of the decade, they benefited from the steadily expanding female labor force participation rates, decreasing fertility, and increases in basic education which continued into the 1990s.

The third wave of feminization, driven by foreign investors from East Asia and led by footwear and electronics, further increased demand for female labor, and the previous developments at the labor supply and mediating institutions nodal points facilitated their access to an attractive pool of potential female workers.

Although the state played an important role in many of these changes, with the exception of the relaxation of protective legislation, feminization was largely an unintended consequence of policies designed to accomplish other developmental, political, and societal goals. The state's indifference to women was evident in its discourse on their role in the economy. Rather than encouraging them to enter the workforce, the state expounded on women's "special" role in development as mothers and wives (Caraway 1998; Manderson 1980; Rahayu 1996; Sen 1998; Sullivan 1991, 1994; Suryakusuma 1987; Wieringa 1993). In the 1980s, some emphasis was placed on women's role as a human resource in the economic sphere, but this change in government discourse came *after* rising female labor force participation rates and the increased emphasis by international organizations on women and development policy. By 1988 the national economic policy statement called for an upgrading in women's skills and education to enable them to take advantage of work opportunities (Sen 1998), but once again this change followed rather than led increases in women's labor force participation rates.

Changes in mediating institutions and labor supply preceded each wave of feminization and were facilitating factors rather than causes of feminization. They facilitated feminization by assuring that capital's demand for female labor could be filled. The "temporal ordering" (Pierson 2004) of developments was crucial; if these facilitating factors had come into play *after* rather than *before* an increase in capital's demand for female labor, the degree of feminization would have been less impressive.

## Education

As a result of the expansion of primary and secondary schooling, educational levels for both men and women rose substantially during the Suharto regime (1967–1998) (Oey-Gardiner 1993). Employers in large factories rarely hired production workers over the age of twenty-four and tended to employ workers with a junior or senior high education, so the educational level of the fifteen-to-nineteen and twenty-to-twenty-four age groups provides an estimate of the supply of educated labor available to work in factories.

In 1971, few men and even fewer women had completed junior and senior high school in the areas that were, and that became, Indonesia's industrial centers (North Sumatra, Jakarta, West Java, Central Java, East Java, and East Kalimantan). Nationwide, only 9 percent of women and 13 percent of men between the ages of fifteen and nineteen had a junior high school education; 6 percent of women and 12 percent of men between the ages of twenty and twenty-four had completed junior high school (Biro Pusat Statistik 1975). By 1980, substantial increases in junior high school education levels for both men and women had occurred, and even larger increases followed in the 1980s and 1990s, especially for the fifteen-to-nineteen age group (Biro Pusat Statistik 1983, 1992). Between 1980 and 1990, large jumps in the percentage of senior high school graduates in the twenty-to-twenty-four age group took place, with women keeping pace with men in most industrial centers. By 1990, when the export drive began to take off, between 24 and 44 percent of women aged fifteen to nineteen were junior high school graduates, and between 17 and 41 percent of women aged twenty to twenty-four had completed senior high school.

Educational levels of both men and women, then, improved significantly between 1971 and 1990, and although on average men still had higher levels of educational attainment, women gained as well. In most cases, the disparity in educational achievement for men and women aged fifteen to nineteen shrank, and by 1990, of the provinces with a significant industrial base, only Jakarta showed significant differences in educational attainment between men and women at the junior high level (see Table 3.1). Two important conclusions can be drawn from these data. First, the percentage of women in both the fifteen-to-nineteen and twenty-to-twenty-four age groups with junior and senior high education increased dramatically, creating a substantial pool of women with the levels of education sought by employers. Second, educational disparities between men and women were low in the former age group, and although higher in the latter group, they had shrunk to about 5 percent for junior high school and about 10 percent for senior high.

Although there were more educated men available to work than women, the number of women with junior or senior high education increased substantially and was more than sufficient to fulfill the potential demand. The difference between the percentage of the population that was economically active and the percentage of the population in the age groups that had junior and senior high education in 1990 was higher for women than for men (see Table 3.1). In most cases, the percentage of men who were economically active was higher than the percentage of individuals with these educational qualifications, whereas there was a surplus of educated women in North Sumatra, Jakarta, East Kalimantan, and in the fifteen-to-nineteen age group in West Java. The figures indicate an ample supply of women with the basic educational credentials desired by employers, and the personnel managers in the factories that I visited confirmed it. They rarely complained about the difficulty of recruiting workers (male or female) who had a junior or senior high school education (even before the financial crisis that swept through Indonesia beginning in 1997), noting that they usually had more qualified applicants than vacancies.

## Family Planning

Economic development was one of the cornerstones of the Suharto regime's political program, not just as an end in itself but as a way to avoid political instability. The regime set out to distinguish itself from Sukarno's "Old Order," which had failed to foster economic stability, much less growth. Suharto even christened himself *Bapak Pembangunan*, the Father of Development. In the 1970s, international development experts identified population growth as a factor that inhibited economic development in the Third World, and the New Order regime shared these concerns (Robinson

**Table 3.1.** Education and economic activity by province, 1990

|  | Males, 15–19 | Males, 20–24 | Females, 15–19 | Females, 20–24 |
|---|---|---|---|---|
| North Sumatra |  |  |  |  |
| % Elementary | 40 | 22 | 39 | 27 |
| % Junior high | 44 | 23 | 42 | 19 |
| % Senior high | 5 | 39 | 6 | 33 |
| % Econ. active | 39 | 79 | 32 | 49 |
| Jakarta |  |  |  |  |
| % Elementary | 32 | 18 | 36 | 25 |
| % Junior high | 52 | 20 | 44 | 17 |
| % Senior high | 10 | 54 | 9 | 41 |
| % Econ. active | 29 | 73 | 35 | 47 |
| West Java |  |  |  |  |
| % Elementary | 52 | 36 | 52 | 41 |
| % Junior high | 29 | 16 | 26 | 11 |
| % Senior high | 5 | 30 | 5 | 19 |
| % Econ. active | 48 | 80 | 30 | 34 |
| Central Java |  |  |  |  |
| % Elementary | 52 | 39 | 53 | 42 |
| % Junior high | 32 | 17 | 28 | 11 |
| % Senior high | 4 | 26 | 5 | 19 |
| % Econ. active | 52 | 83 | 41 | 50 |
| East Java |  |  |  |  |
| % Elementary | 47 | 32 | 48 | 37 |
| % Junior high | 35 | 18 | 31 | 13 |
| % Senior high | 5 | 31 | 6 | 21 |
| % Econ. active | 49 | 81 | 34 | 44 |
| East Kalimantan |  |  |  |  |
| % Elementary | 41 | 23 | 40 | 27 |
| % Junior high | 39 | 22 | 37 | 18 |
| % Senior high | 5 | 40 | 6 | 29 |
| % Econ. active | 45 | 84 | 28 | 40 |

*Source:* Biro Pusat Statistik, *Sensus Penduduk* (various years).

1989). The solution to the "problem" of population growth was to enact family planning policies, and the government established the *Badan Koordinasi Keluarga Berencana Nasional* (BKKBN), or National Family Planning Coordinating Board, in 1970. The family planning policy's main goal was to reduce population growth, but unintended consequences included higher female labor force participation rates and the creation of more attractive potential women workers.

The BKKBN expanded aggressively during the 1970s and 1980s, and through the involvement of local governments and women's organizations linked to the state, family planning services became available to women throughout Indonesia. Indeed, the state pressured women to participate in the program through the involvement of the *Pembinaan Kesejahteraan Keluarga* (PKK), or Family Welfare Movement, a state-linked organization that involved women at the village and neighborhood levels in delivering and promoting family planning services (Sullivan 1991). Local officials, working with the PKK and village luminaries, persuaded large numbers of women to sign up for family planning.[2] The military also sometimes "encouraged" women villagers to participate in the program, and the major women's confederation, KOWANI (Kongres Wanita Indonesia [the Indonesian Women's Congress]), supported family planning as well (Vreede-de Stuers 1976). The main Islamic organizations in Indonesia also endorsed family planning, and women's groups linked to these organizations, as well as female preachers, helped to connect state-sponsored family planning to individual women (Baried 1986; Marcoes 1992). Factories also dispensed family planning services to female workers, and in the 1993 industrial handbook the government included family planning as part of its industrial relations philosophy (Ford 1999).

By all accounts, the program achieved great success.[3] In the late 1960s the fertility rate was 5.6 births per woman, but it declined to 4.7 in 1976, to 3.2 in 1987, and 2.9 by 1992. Broken down by age, the fertility rate declined by 44 percent for women aged fifteen to nineteen and by 36 percent for those twenty to twenty-four between 1976 and 1991 (Bureau of the Census 1992). By 1994, the median age at first birth for women then aged twenty-five to forty-nine had increased to 20.3 years (Studies in Family Planning 1996). Given the dramatic declines in fertility, the median age at first birth for younger subgroups was probably higher.

Women began to marry, and therefore to have children, at a later age.[4] The Marriage Act of 1974, which raised the legal age of first marriage to sixteen, was partially responsible.[5] In 1971 the mean age of marriage was 19.3 years, but by 1985 the average age of first marriage had increased to twenty-one years (Gertler and Molyneaux 1994). By 1994, 82 percent of women fifteen to nineteen and 37.5 percent of those twenty to twenty-four had never married (Studies in Family Planning 1996).

Declines in fertility and increases in the average age at which women married and had their first child were significant for a number of reasons. First, if women had children later in life, even just two years later, factories could count on keeping young women employed for longer uninterrupted periods, which reduced the costs associated with maternity leave and turnover. Chances were that an eighteen-year old woman would work at least three years before taking maternity leave. Second, given that many married women continued to work even after having children, the reduction in the fertility rate meant that women claimed maternity leave less frequently. These two factors made women more attractive to employers than they had been in the past.

## Changes in Agriculture and Economic Crisis

A number of changes in the agricultural sector in the 1970s freed a proportionately larger number of women than men to work in manufacturing. Specifically, alterations in the gender division of labor in rice farming reduced women's opportunities to obtain agricultural work, and increased landlessness raised the level of proletarianization of both men and women.

A variety of changes in rice farming affected women negatively. A shift in harvesting techniques from the *ani-ani,* a small knife traditionally used by women, to the sickle, a larger implement employed by men, reduced women's work opportunities in rural areas. The introduction of hulling machines, which replaced the labor-intensive process of hand pounding performed by women, had a similar effect (Oey-Gardiner 1985; Stoler 1977). Large landowners also rationalized the transplanting and weeding of rice, labor-intensive tasks usually undertaken by women (Husken 1989). Agricultural work had been an important source of seasonal income for rural households, so the loss of women's access to it freed some for year-round jobs in other activities. These factors may have contributed to a higher rate of proletarianization for women than men over the course of the 1980s, with the wage-labor force for women expanding at a rate of 7.36 percent on Java, and just 5.79 percent for men. Using census data, Pincus (1996) shows that manufacturing accounted for 47.4 percent of this increase for women and only 34.3 percent for men. Oey-Gardiner (1993) also finds that in urban areas, new female entrants into the labor force exceeded males between 1980 and 1990, whereas in rural areas men and women entered the workforce in roughly equal increments.

The increased concentration of land ownership and rising levels of landlessness, especially on Java, expanded the availability of both men and women for wage labor.[6] On Java, one study found that 73 percent of families owned farmland in 1963 but only 57 percent by 1983 (Husken and White 1989). Another study produced similar results, with only half of families owning rice land and 40 percent having no cultivation rights (White and Wiradi 1989). Many Indonesians who had sustained themselves entirely in agriculture were compelled to engage in irregular waged work (both agricultural and nonagricultural), long-term waged work, self-employment, or a combination of self-employment and irregular waged work in order to earn a living. The statistical evidence bears this out. A 7 percent decline in the economically active population (both men and women) employed in agriculture took place between 1971 and 1980 (Oey-Gardiner 1985),[7] supporting the contention that an increasing percentage of the working-age population turned elsewhere for work opportunities. Factory jobs were an attractive option, since they provided wages year round, offered higher status than agricultural labor, and had the added benefit of being indoors.[8]

The economic crisis that hit Indonesia in the early 1980s also led to increases in women's labor force participation rates. The early 1980s were a transition period in which Indonesia moved from an inward-oriented to an export-oriented development policy. Women's labor force participation had remained relatively constant in the 1970s, the rate increasing only from 32.1 percent in 1971 to 32.4 percent in 1980. In the 1980s, however, women flooded into the labor market, and their participation rates increased to 37.6 percent in 1985 and to 44.8 percent in 1987 (Oey-Gardiner 1991). In urban areas, the increase was especially pronounced among young women, and between 1982 and 1988, even rural areas experienced surges in the participation rates of younger women (Benjamin 1996). The greatest gains occurred among young and less educated women, especially those in their twenties, and among primary- and lower-secondary-educated women in urban areas. Significant differences remained in the labor force participation rates of married versus single women, so the decline in birthrates for women was an especially important development that contributed to higher rates of workforce involvement (Manning 1998). Increases in participation rates *preceded* the big burst of investment in manufacturing in the late 1980s.

## Protective Legislation

Although a number of provisions in Indonesia's labor laws pertain specifically to women, only one directly limited the capacity of employers to hire women for factory work—the prohibition of night work for women.[9] Since many factories run twenty-four hours a day and utilize a rotating shift system, the ban on night work potentially hampers the capacity of employers to hire women workers. If employers cannot use women at night, they must abandon rotating shifts or employ men in women's jobs on the night shift or forgo the use of female labor for shift work. A ban on night work can thus restrict women's employment.

The Dutch colonial government first implemented this prohibition in 1925, and from the law's inception it contained an escape clause permitting a workplace with "special business requirements" to gain an exemption. This exemption was meant to protect industries that found female labor to be indispensable (Elliot 1997; Locher-Scholten 1987). In the 1951 Indonesian law, the exemption continued for sectors where "the employment of women during night time cannot be avoided for reasons of public interest and welfare," with the condition that the work, "according to its nature, place and condition, is suitable to women" (Sison 1989, 94). The assumption that certain kinds of jobs are better done by women, then, was built into the law from its inception. The conditions for exemption are sufficiently vague that the state can interpret them broadly. If a waiver is granted, employers are expected to provide transport facilities for women workers on the night shift so that they do not have to return home at night alone.[10]

During the 1970s, some employers found the night work prohibition to be an obstacle to hiring women. Manning's (1979) survey of firms in the weaving and cigarette industries revealed that 25 percent of the highly mechanized employers cited the law as a reason for not hiring additional women.[11] Some managers with long experience in the textile industry also spoke during interviews about the difficulty of employing women at night in the 1970s, and Mather (1985) reported that religious leaders in Tangerang, a major industrial area in Jakarta's western suburbs, encouraged managers to employ men on the night shift in the late 1970s.[12] In recent years, however, employers in the sampled firms reported no problems with placing women on the night shift. Since many of these factories began production in the 1980s, enforcement of protective legislation, which began to ease in the late 1970s, had ceased almost completely by the 1980s.

Another way to gauge the extent to which protective legislation is an obstacle to the hiring of women is to compare firms that run two and three shifts with those that operate just one shift. If the percentage of women employed in two- or three-shift factories is higher or about the same as in one-shift factories, then the prohibition has not had a significant negative effect on female employment. Overall, 56 percent of all employees working in factories that run one shift are women, whereas the figures for those with two and three shifts are 44 and 47 percent respectively. One-third of female workers are in factories that run three shifts, which is high, considering that two of the largest employers of women, tobacco and garments, are primarily one-shift operations. Since the overall rate in manufacturing might simply reflect the fact that male-intensive sectors happen to be more likely to run three shifts—because of capital intensity and other technological factors—it is also necessary to examine women's share of employment in three-shift operations within sectors.

Table 3.2 compiles data for the sectors that employ the bulk of the manufacturing workforce. In several industries that have played an important

Table 3.2. Employment by gender, sector, and shifts

| Sector | Percent female by number of shifts | | |
| | 1 | 2 | 3 |
| --- | --- | --- | --- |
| Food | 57 | 37 | 29 |
| Beverages | 54 | 40 | 33 |
| Tobacco | 87 | 64 | 83 |
| Textiles | 64 | 53 | 52 |
| Garments | 79 | 80 | 59 |
| Footwear | 75 | 81 | 79 |
| Wood processing | 29 | 40 | 45 |
| Furniture, etc. (wood-based) | 32 | 30 | 37 |
| Other chemicals | 59 | 57 | 46 |
| Rubber | 22 | 25 | 22 |
| Plastic | 47 | 50 | 51 |
| Fabricated metal products | 19 | 26 | 24 |
| Electronics | 53 | 60 | 65 |
| Transport equipment | 10 | 7 | 12 |
| Other (incl. toys) | 74 | 50 | 79 |

Source: Biro Pusat Statistik, *Statistik Industri Besar dan Sedang 1996*, data file.

role in the export boom—footwear, wood processing, wood furniture, plastic, and electronics—women's share of employment in three-shift factories is higher than in one-shift factories. Of the six sectors listed that show decreases in the number of women employed as the number of shifts increase, two are of little importance: for tobacco, there is only a 4 percent difference between those that run one and three shifts; in garments, only 5 percent of the labor force works in three-shift factories. The food sector, which reveals a decrease in the percentage of female workers with an increase in the number of shifts, is perhaps the most internally differentiated sector. I therefore also checked the data for five-digit ISIC (International Standard Industrial Classification) breakdown for the eleven food subsectors that employ at least 10,000 workers. Women's share of employment in three-shift factories was higher than in one-shift factories in four of these eleven subsectors, lower in five, and about the same in two. Although in some cases, such as textiles, there does appear to be a slight negative impact on female employment when employers run three shifts, there are more cases where women's employment is higher in three-shift factories. The weight of statistical and experiential evidence suggests that night work legislation was not a damper on the use of female labor in the 1980s. In other words, the state has interpreted the law liberally since at least the early 1980s, and employers have consequently faced little trouble in placing women on the night shift.

## Weak Unions

Labor unions in Indonesia were extremely weak during the period under consideration (1970–1998). After Suharto's New Order regime came to power in 1967, the government set about demobilizing political organizations, including unions. Under Sukarno, unions had been active, sometimes militant, and had links to political parties (Hawkins 1971; Tedjasukmana 1958). Suharto cut these ties and banned the most powerful union, SOBSI (Sentral Organisasi Buruh Seluruh Indonesia [All-Indonesian Central Labor Organization]), which was close to the Communist Party. Under the leadership of Ali Murtopo, the intelligence apparatus cobbled together the remnants of various non-Communist labor-related groups into a peak federation, the *Federasi Buruh Seluruh Indonesia* (FBSI), or All-Indonesia Labor Federation, in 1973. FBSI was the sole legal union in Indonesia for twenty-five years. Created to control labor and keep unions out of politics, it was a feeble advocate for workers (Hadiz 1997; Schaarschmidt-Kohl 1988).

Throughout the 1970s, strike activity had been low, but after a currency devaluation in November 1978, a wave of strikes swept through industrial areas as the cost of many commodities rose precipitously (Kammen 1997). Minister of Manpower Sudomo concluded that the FBSI was not demobilizing labor nearly enough, a fault he attributed to its loose federal structure. In 1985, he restructured the union, adopting a more centralized form of organization, and renamed it the *Serikat Pekerja Seluruh Indonesia* (SPSI), or All-Indonesia Workers' Union (Hadiz 1997; Indonesian Documentation and Information Centre 1981–86). In 1991, SPSI relaxed this centralized structure and formally instituted mechanisms that made the central executive accountable to lower levels of the organization (Hadiz 1997).

Despite a membership of slightly under one million by mid-1991, however, the union remained a weak vessel (Manning 1993). Although its role varied by region and even by factory, depending on the orientation of local leaders, SPSI was not a national player. Its leaders at the local level, as well as officials from the Department of Manpower, were notorious for corruption and collusion with factory owners.[13] It is a measure of the lack of importance the government assigned to SPSI that from the earliest days the union had difficulty funding its operations. The check-off system for deducting dues directly from workers' paychecks was operated largely by the Department of Manpower, and even so, these funds were not enough to cover expenses, so the union was dependent on the state and foreign labor organizations to subsidize its work (Hadiz 1997). Collective bargaining agreements were primarily at the enterprise level and rarely included provisions substantially better than those already guaranteed by law.

On a day-to-day level, military involvement in labor control was pervasive and especially severe in the 1980s (Hadiz 1997; Indonesian Documentation and Information Centre 1981–86; Kammen 1997; YLBHI 1990, 1991, 1992, 1993, 1997). State intelligence agencies systematically monitored labor and acted to prevent and repress labor activity. Coordination between the Manpower Department and security agencies intensified when Sudomo was transferred to head the department in the 1980s. Sudomo had previously served as the head of Kopkamtib, a military body with virtual martial-law powers that coordinated the army's operational, intelligence, and sociopolitical machinery. He developed a series of institutions to detect and prevent industrial disputes, effectively creating formal channels through which labor union leaders and business cooperated with intelligence operatives in the area of labor relations—a menacing twist on tripartite corporatist arrangements (Tanter 1990). In addition to intervening in strikes, military men also found jobs as personnel directors in factories, which added a sinister element to everyday relations between management and workers.[14] Retired military personnel even obtained positions in the union itself (Lambert 1997). Workers who participated in strikes could expect military intimidation, and for those identified as leaders, interrogation by the military or the police and firings were common.[15] In some cases, leaders were raped and/or murdered.[16] Efforts by NGO (nongovernmental organization) activists to set up independent unions in the 1990s foundered under a combination of repression, difficult registration requirements, and internal conflicts.[17]

In sum, as part of its efforts to "depoliticize" society, the Indonesian state demobilized labor by creating a tame union firmly under state control. Enmeshed in clientelistic webs, the union colluded with management, the military, and government agencies. When workers became militant, the military intervened. Given the weakness of the national union, male unionists were hardly in a position to stop employers from feminizing factory labor, either through outright opposition or through negotiating encompassing collective bargains.

## Islam

Restrictions on women's activities in the public sphere can make it difficult for employers to hire women. Conservative interpretations of religious texts about women's proper role in society are one factor that can severely curtail women's labor force participation rates, and these rates are low in many countries where Islam is the predominant religion. This generalization is not a blanket statement about Islam, however, as even among primarily Muslim countries there are wide variations in women's involvement in waged work.[18] Nevertheless, since it is the religion of about 85 percent of Indonesians, a few words on Islam are necessary.

Historically, Islam in Indonesia has placed relatively few restrictions on women's activities, especially on Java. Women have long engaged in a variety of economic endeavors that require them to leave their homes and to mix with men. Stoler (1977) notes that on precolonial Java, both men and women engaged in handicraft and agricultural production, and indigenous forms of exploitation extracted both male and female labor. The Dutch later worked within the framework of the preexisting gender division of labor, which required both male and female workers for rice cultivation. They also mobilized both male and female labor for export agriculture, and as a consequence women were not confined solely to the subsistence sector.[19] On Java, women have dominated petty trade at least since the beginning of the nineteenth century (Boomgaard 1981), and they constituted a large share of employees in plantation and manufacturing workforces (Elliot 1997; Locher-Scholten 1987). At the very least, Islam in Indonesia has not prevented women from engaging in work outside of the home.

The increasing popularity since the 1980s of the *jilbab*, a head covering that conceals the hair and neck, is not an indication of higher restrictions on women, as university campuses and workplaces are full of women in *jilbab*. Islamic courts that administer family law in Indonesia are among the most liberal in the Muslim world, and women have even become Islamic judges (Lev 1996). Women retain their rights to property they owned before marriage; within marriage women continue to own and dispose of property like single women; and divorced women take their property with them. Women can also initiate legal action (Manderson 1980). Finally, prominent male Muslim intellectuals, such as former President Abdurrahman Wahid, have contested conservative interpretations of religious texts about women's role in society and politics (Istiadah 1995). Woodcroft-Lee (1983) analyzed the content of two Islam-oriented popular journals in 1979–80 and found that they had favorable views of women pursuing academic or professional careers after marriage and of women entering into community welfare work, religious education, and even politics.

Even if Islam had been a more conservative force in Indonesia, Suharto's New Order state would have assiduously managed its political role. Suspicion of political Islam has a long lineage in Indonesia, from the Dutch colonial regime to the first president, Sukarno, who strenuously opposed Islam as the basis of the state. He developed Pancasila as the state ideology, and one of its five principles is simply belief in God rather than in the god of any particular religion. Fighting religion-based insurgencies in West Java, South Sulawesi, and Aceh absorbed much of the military's energy in the 1950s, which undoubtedly inculcated an aversion to the politicization of religion in many military officers. Nevertheless, during the early Sukarno years there were two large Islamic parties, Masyumi and Nahdatul Ulama (NU), as well as a host of smaller ones.[20] But Sukarno later banned Masyumi after members of the party became involved in a regional insurrection in the late 1950s (Kahin and Kahin 1995). The internal divisions within the Muslim community made the task of "managing" Islam easier for the state.[21] As Ruth McVey (1983, 200) astutely observed, "Nothing united Indonesia like Islam, neither does anything divide it so deeply."

This tense relationship between the state and Islam continued in the Suharto years. After mobilizing the youth wing of NU to murder Communists in the aftermath of the failed coup attempt in 1965, Suharto set about demobilizing and neutralizing Islamic political parties. The need to neutralize political Islam became especially apparent in the 1971 elections, when in spite of the onslaught of propaganda from Golkar, the government party, NU performed well (Wertheim 1986). As with labor, Suharto gave the task of emasculating the political parties to Ali Murtopo. Through pressure, bribery, manipulation, and co-optation, he succeeded in January 1973 in cramming all the Islamic-oriented political organizations into a single *Partai Persatuan Pembangunan* (PPP), the United Development Party.[22] The forced marriage of different streams of the Islamic community was a recipe for infighting among political enemies and all but assured that the PPP would never become a force to reckon with. When it did perform relatively well in the 1982 elections, Suharto brought the depoliticization of Islam to full fruition by requiring all social organizations to accept the state ideology, Pancasila, as their official basis (Wertheim 1986).[23]

The "floating mass" policy of the government, moreover, prevented parties from organizing at the village level. The religious activities of the two largest organizations, NU and Muhammadiyah, continued, but their open politics ceased. The local government—all members of the ruling party— and the military, with a structure parallel to the state that gave it a presence at the village level, kept a close eye on their activities, forcing Islamic organizations to concentrate on the cultural realm and to avoid overtly politicized Islam. The state encouraged the cultural emphasis by building mosques, sponsoring proselytization, and expanding Islamic education (Hefner 1993). Suharto deftly gave with one hand as he took with the other, and when this did not work he used outright repression (as exemplified by the Tanjung Priok massacre in 1984).

Nevertheless, the activities supported by the state ironically helped foster a revitalization of Islam during the 1980s. Suharto adroitly co-opted this renewed surge of activity by dumping his Catholic and Protestant allies in the military and embracing the new generation of Muslim intellectuals in a new state-backed organization, the Ikatan Cendikiawan Muslim Indonesia (ICMI), or Indonesian Muslim Intellectual's Association (Hefner 1993). The president even went on pilgrimage to Mecca in 1991, signaling that being a devout Muslim was back in style (Raillon 1993). This maneuver by Suharto took Islam away from the PPP as a political identifier. Since it had become acceptable both to be a good Muslim and to be in the ruling party, Suharto had neutralized, at least temporarily, the threat that Islamic revitalization might lead to a more politicized movement demanding an Islamic state.

Muslim organizations effectively mobilized on occasion, most notably to oppose aspects of the 1974 marriage law which were seen to be in violation of Islam, and the provisions that offended them most were diluted. Organized religion, however, has done little to counter other government initiatives related to women, such as family planning and sending Indonesian women overseas as domestic workers. One author even reported that local religious authorities facilitated the recruitment of young women workers in the factories in Tangerang, West Java, just outside the capital (Mather 1985).

Islam in Indonesia, then, has not adopted an especially restrictive view of women's role in society and has placed few restrictions on women's public activities. Even had Islam been a more conservative force, the state would have carefully circumscribed religiously based political action. Suharto thus successfully co-opted, neutralized, sidelined, or repressed the main Islamic organizations in the country.

## Conclusion

Among the range of developments at the labor supply and mediating institutions nodal points that facilitated feminization, the improvement in women's basic education and the lowering of fertility rates created a pool of potential women workers attractive to employers. At the same time, women poured into the workforce in the early 1980s in response to economic crisis and shrinking access to agricultural jobs. The government first relaxed and then ceased enforcement of the main piece of protective legislation that limited the extent to which factories could hire women workers, and unions were a feeble shell that could not obstruct employers bent on feminizing. The state demobilized the political parties and prevented grassroots political activities that could have provided political bases for opposing women's increased presence in factory work. And the state checked the possibility of more radical Islamic restrictions on women by effectively "managing" sources of political mobilization.

The analysis in this chapter, rather than simply assuming that a supply of women will emerge to satisfy rising demand and that this supply of women can be hired by employers, shows the means through which women became both more appealing and more available to potential employers. In the course of doing so, it highlights processes that are likely to be at play in other cases of feminization and suggests that where similar processes are absent, the degree of feminization will be more subdued.

# 4

# Spillover, Stickiness, and Waves

## The Dynamics of Feminization

$B$y 1980, the facilitating pieces were in place; all that was needed to generate an impressive wave of feminization in Indonesia was a substantial increase in demand for women workers. Modest feminization occurred in textiles in the late 1970s, largely in response to changes in the supply of women and the easing of the enforcement of protective legislation. It was not until Indonesia's industrialization policies began to promote labor-intensive export sectors in the early 1980s that a second and more significant wave of feminization spread through the economy, followed by a third wave in the late 1980s, when foreign investors from the newly industrializing East Asian countries expanded their investments in labor-intensive manufacturing in Indonesia.

Although the shift in industrialization policy explains the broad contours of feminization in Indonesia, it is also notable that many of the labor-intensive sectors that increasingly hired women in the 1980s and 1990s had employed few women in 1971. In other words, feminization was not simply an outcome of the growth of already female-intensive sectors but a product of sectoral feminization as well. This chapter therefore looks more closely at how employers in a number of sectors increased their reliance on women workers by shifting selected jobs from men to women; traces how the gendered hiring preferences of many employers were transformed, giving women access to a wider variety of jobs in manufacturing; high-lights dynamics that cut across the three waves of feminization—sticki-

ness, spillover, and snowballing; and demonstrates how regional variations in the propensity to employ women affected the degree of feminization that took place.

## Industrialization in Indonesia

In the 1960s, Indonesia was one of the least industrialized countries in
the world for its size (Hill 1990a), and manufacturing employment in
medium-sized and large firms totaled only about 840,000 workers in 1971
(see Table 4.1). The Suharto regime sought to quicken the pace of economic
growth, and over the course of thirty years it pursued a variety of industrial policies. Industrialization in Indonesia during the New Order can be
divided into three major stages: import-substitution industrialization (ISI),
1968–78;[1] the transition period, 1979–86; and (EOI), 1987–97.[2]

The first stage, ISI, promoted manufacturing industries that produced
primarily for the local market, and Indonesia relied mainly on oil revenue
for its foreign exchange. Under ISI, capital-intensive sectors expanded
most rapidly. Employment generation was unimpressive, with employment
in medium- and large-scale manufacturing increasing by only 130,000

**Table 4.1.** Employment by level of labor intensity (production workers), 1971–1995

| Level of labor intensity | 1971 | 1980 | 1985 | 1990 | 1995 |
|---|---|---|---|---|---|
| Low[a] | | | | | |
| Employment | 8,392 | 52,754 | 76,956 | 119,209 | 181,342 |
| Share of total employment | 0.01 | 0.05 | 0.06 | 0.05 | 0.05 |
| Medium-low[b] | | | | | |
| Employment | 198,062 | 297,900 | 334,761 | 391,869 | 707,690 |
| Share of total employment | 0.24 | 0.31 | 0.25 | 0.18 | 0.20 |
| Medium-high[c] | | | | | |
| Employment | 594,847 | 554,836 | 785,296 | 1,182,943 | 1,580,212 |
| Share of total employment | 0.71 | 0.57 | 0.58 | 0.55 | 0.46 |
| High[d] | | | | | |
| Employment | 38,987 | 63,697 | 158,444 | 474,192 | 1,000,332 |
| Share of total employment | 0.05 | 0.07 | 0.12 | 0.22 | 0.29 |
| Total employment | 840,288 | 969,187 | 1,355,457 | 2,168,213 | 3,469,576 |

*Sources:* Biro Pusat Statistik, *Statistik Industri Besar dan Sedang* (various years), and *Sensus Ekonomi 1985* (1988).
[a]Transport equipment, nonferrous metals, iron and steel, industrial chemicals.
[b]Tobacco, glass, beverages, electronics, paper, nonelectrical machinery, other chemical industries, cement.
[c]Textiles, wood processing, other nonmetallic minerals, fabricated metal products, porcelain,
food, professional and scientific equipment, rubber, printing.
[d]Plastic, leather, other manufacturing, footwear, clothing, wood products, clay.

workers between 1971 and 1980 (see Table 4.1). Between 1971 and 1980 the share of employment in sectors with low labor intensity increased from 1 percent to 5 percent and from 24 to 31 percent in those with medium-low labor intensity. In contrast, relatively labor-intensive sectors' share of employment declined or barely increased; the employment share of sectors with medium-high labor intensity fell by 14 percent; and those with high labor intensity rose by just 2 percent. The textiles industry was the only labor-intensive sector to show large increases in employment, adding about 100,000 jobs. Other relatively labor-intensive sectors that had previously employed many workers, such as rubber and food, lost about 225,000 jobs. ISI began to wind down when a drop in oil prices led to a foreign exchange crisis in the late 1970s. As a result, the government acted to foster the growth of other sources of foreign exchange by encouraging a number of labor-intensive sectors to produce more for the export market.

During the transition period from 1979 to 1986, Indonesia took tentative steps toward EOI. An export certificate program, one of the first measures implemented to promote exports, operated much like a subsidy for exporters.Garments, textiles, and wood/rattan furniture were the main beneficiaries, and over time the number of eligible products expanded. The export certificate program and the devaluation of the rupiah in November 1978 created the first export-oriented garment producers and encouraged some textile producers to begin to export.[3] The government also sought to promote new investment in processing industries such as sawmills, plywood, and furniture by restricting the export of whole logs in 1980 and banning it in 1985. The policy succeeded, and between 1978 and 1985 the number of plywood producers skyrocketed from nineteen to 101 (Barr 1998, 9). Employment figures reflect the success of this set of policies: between 1980 and 1985, employment in textiles, garments, and wood processing increased by about 13 percent, 300 percent, and 100 percent, respectively (see Table 4.1).[4] Other relatively labor-intensive sectors such as food, plastic, and rubber also underwent notable workforce expansions. Employment grew in relatively capital-intensive sectors, too, but not as quickly as in labor-intensive sectors, so their overall share of employment declined.

The transition period gave birth to a group of export industries and created tens of thousands of new jobs in labor-intensive industries. When full-blown EOI commenced, this trend accelerated and spread to almost every sector. Employment exploded in the export industries that had been fostered during the transition period, and new export industries emerged, but inward-oriented sectors also posted impressive growth. The liberalization of imports in May 1986 and a 31 percent devaluation of the rupiah in September 1986 were the first major steps that set Indonesia on the EOI path. More extensive liberalization of both trade and investment regulations took place over the next two years.[5] These policies made Indonesia increasingly attractive to foreign investors, especially investors from East Asia, and led not only to more remarkable export performance by industries that had already begun to prove their exporting mettle—garments, textiles, plywood, and rubber—but also to the rise of footwear and electronics as major new exporters. Employment in labor-intensive sectors boomed, doubling between 1985 and 1990 from just over 700,000 workers to more than 1.4 million and adding about 700,000 more jobs between 1990 and 1995. Although outpaced by labor-intensive sectors, capital-intensive sectors posted impressive gains in employment as well.

Between 1971 and 1995, then, a dramatic transformation of the structure of Indonesian manufacturing occurred. Employment more than quadrupled, the greatest expansion taking place after 1985. Sectors with the highest labor intensity grew most rapidly, increasing their share of employment from just 5 percent in 1971 to 29 percent in 1995. How did these profound structural changes in manufacturing affect women's employment?

## The Gendered Effects of Industrialization

Assessing the precise point when feminization began in Indonesia is impossible because of a gap in the statistical record. Between 1971 and 1993 the industrial survey did not break down employment by gender, which means that other sources of information must be mined for evidence that the shifts in gendered patterns of employment corresponded to changes in industrialization policy. The changes in gendered employment that can be established with statistics from the industrial survey provide before and after snapshots; thereafter I try to fill in the black box between 1971 and 1993.

When Indonesia embarked on its industrialization drive in the early 1970s, men held 63 percent of production jobs in medium and large firms (see Table 4.2). In 1971 only three of twenty-five sectors (tobacco, garments,

**Table 4.2.** Changes in women's share of industrial employment

| Sectors by labor intensity | 1971 | | 1996 | | Change in employment | Change in Percent female |
|---|---|---|---|---|---|---|
| | Production workers | Percent female | Production workers | Percent female | | |
| **Low** | | | | | | |
| Transportation | 4,742 | 2 | 102,039 | 11 | 97,297 | 9 |
| Nonferrous metal products | 0 | 0 | 13,645 | 7 | 13,645 | n/a |
| Iron and steel | 0 | 0 | 25,565 | 1 | 25,565 | n/a |
| Industrial chemicals | 3,650 | 42 | 45,362 | 19 | 41,712 | −23 |
| Average change | | | | | 44,555 | −7 |
| **Medium low** | | | | | | |
| Tobacco/cigarettes | 151,372 | 77 | 199,053 | 87 | 47,681 | 10 |
| Beverages | 4,161 | 26 | 17,655 | 39 | 13,494 | 13 |
| Paper | 6,730 | 25 | 70,810 | 22 | 64,080 | −3 |
| Other Chemicals | 22,029 | 48 | 82,287 | 56 | 60,258 | 8 |
| Non-metallic mineral products | 17,593 | 24 | 153,031 | 26 | 135,438 | 2 |
| Nonelectric machinery | 2,473 | 0 | 34,156 | 8 | 31,683 | 8 |
| Electronic equipment* | 4,048 | 45 | 138,991 | 59 | 134,943 | 14 |
| Average change | | | | | 69,654 | 7 |
| **Medium high** | | | | | | |
| Food | 275,309 | 28 | 394,747 | 45 | 119,438 | 17 |
| Textiles* | 145,190 | 36 | 542,296 | 56 | 397,106 | 20 |
| Wood processing* | 15,574 | 0 | 344,031 | 38 | 328,457 | 38 |
| Printing and publishing | 13,487 | 19 | 53,711 | 31 | 40,224 | 12 |
| Rubber* | 134,931 | 25 | 90,329 | 24 | −44,602 | 1 |
| Fabricated metal products | 16,259 | 9 | 135,833 | 21 | 119,574 | 12 |
| Professional/sci. equip.* | 47 | 0 | 13,860 | 65 | 13,813 | 29 |
| Average change | | | | | 139,144 | 23 |
| **High** | | | | | | |
| Garments* | 1,553 | 55 | 353,895 | 78 | 352,342 | 23 |
| Leather | 1,999 | 8 | 22,963 | 48 | 20,964 | 40 |
| Footwear* | 1,927 | 7 | 280,016 | 78 | 278,089 | 71 |
| Wood products* | 3,987 | 4 | 139,544 | 30 | 135,557 | 26 |
| Plastic | 5,394 | 44 | 145,957 | 51 | 140,563 | 7 |
| Other manufacturing (incl. toys) | 8,329 | 63 | 64,804 | 70 | 56,475 | 7 |
| Average change | | | | | 163,998 | 29 |

*Sources:* Biro Pusat Statistik, *Statistik Industri Besar dan Sedang 1971* (1973), and *Statistik Industri Besar dan Sedang 1996* (1998).
*Sector is export intensive.

and other manufacturing) employed more women than men. In contrast, in the mid-1990s men and women each composed about half of the production workforce. By 1996, women's share of the production workforce had increased in nineteen of twenty-four sectors, although the degree of feminization varied dramatically from sector to sector. Women maintained and widened their majority status in tobacco, garments, and other manufacturing; became the majority in six additional sectors (textiles, footwear, other chemicals, plastic, electronics, and professional and scientific equipment), and increased their share of employment (while remaining the minority) in ten sectors (food, beverages, leather, wood products, furniture, printing, nonmetallic mineral products, fabricated metal products, nonelectrical machinery, and transportation).[6] Despite these gains, men still outnumbered women in sixteen of twenty-four sectors, and three sectors masculinized (paper, industrial chemicals, and rubber).

As expected, shifts in industrialization policy that generated explosive growth in employment in labor-intensive sectors accounted for the macro-level changes in women's employment in manufacturing in Indonesia between 1971 and the 1990s. The labor-intensive sectors that were the success stories of EOI and that generated most of the new employment for women underwent striking gendered transformations, as many had been male intensive before the 1980s. The figures on the right side of Table 4.2 indicate the change in women's share of employment between 1971 and 1996. Some of the sectors in which women's share expanded dramatically were growth sectors in the export drive that began in the 1980s (export industries are indicated with an asterisk), but established industries such as food processing and tobacco grew and feminized as well, and even male-intensive, high-growth industries such as transportation and fabricated metal products feminized slightly.

Feminization of the greatest magnitude occurred in sectors with high and medium-high levels of labor intensity. The share of female employment in the highly capital-intensive sectors decreased (i.e., masculinization occurred) by 7 percent and increased moderately (7 percent) in the moderately capital-intensive sectors. The medium-high and high labor-intensive sectors showed strong feminization, with an average change of 23 and 29 percent respectively. Feminization was especially impressive in some labor-intensive sectors partially because they had employed mostly men in 1971. Of the seventeen relatively labor-intensive sectors, twelve employed 30 percent or fewer women in 1971. Relatively labor-intensive sectors that employed very few women (less than 10 percent) showed by far the highest average increases in women's presence. Feminization was also strong in sectors that had already employed significant numbers of women in their workforces in 1971, such as textiles and garments. The increases are not simply a function of low baselines, as some relatively capital-intensive sectors with similarly low baselines in 1971 did not feminize nearly as much.

The data in Table 4.2 support the contention that pressures for feminization were strongest in the most labor-intensive sectors, but it also raises further questions. Why did labor-intensive sectors that had previously employed mostly men begin to rely on more women in their workforces? In other words, why did their gender preferences shift so dramatically? Demonstrating the mechanics through which these sectors developed and were transformed not only pinpoints when feminization began in Indonesia but also reveals how sectoral feminization occurred.

## Waves and Paths

I focus on the three main labor-intensive sectors where I conducted research—textiles (spinning and weaving), garments, and plywood—plus footwear, where a rich secondary literature allows the drawing of some tentative conclusions. In addition, the heavy foreign presence in electronics permits some inferences about what happened there. Collectively, these sectors accounted for over half of all female employment in manufacturing in Indonesia in the mid-1990s.

Feminization unfolded in a series of waves. Textiles, in particular spinning and weaving, pioneered the first wave of feminization during the ISI years. Plywood and garments led the second wave, which coincided with the transition phase of industrialization. Footwear and electronics, along with the sectors from the second wave, propelled the third wave. Foreign investors did not play a significant role in the first two waves of feminization—which is surprising, given the overwhelming emphasis on the role of multinational corporations in the feminization literature—but they were a key component of the third wave. A central finding here is that feminization involved a redefinition of work. Jobs that had been associated primarily with men came to be performed by women. The story of feminization in Indonesia is therefore not simply that women's employment expanded in sectors that already employed women; rather, over the course of Indonesia's industrialization, many labor-intensive sectors and some relatively capital-intensive sectors that had overwhelmingly employed men increased their reliance on women workers. Without this sectoral feminization, the degree of feminization in Indonesian manufacturing as a whole would have been much smaller.

The process of feminization also created a set of dynamics that shaped the way it unfolded. The mobilization of women workers in the earlier stages of industrialization had spillover and snowballing effects within sectors and spillover effects on other sectors. The process of feminization also often proceeded unevenly within sectors, as many factories in feminizing sectors stuck with men even as competitors increased the ratio of women to men in their workforces. In the case of textiles, a shift in investment from regions with relatively low levels of female employment to regions employing higher percentages of women in the industry pushed feminization forward more rapidly.

### The First Wave: The Pioneers

In the first wave of feminization, beginning during the ISI period and continuing into the early transition period, textiles—especially spinning and weaving—were the trailblazing feminizers. The transformation of gendered employment practices in textiles had only a slight impact on women's overall share of employment in manufacturing, but the changes that occurred in the 1970s were important because they set the stage for the more dramatic transformations of the 1980s and 1990s. These textile employers were the pioneers who proved that women could be employed profitably in new lines of work.

At the beginning of ISI, spinning and weaving employed primarily men. In 1971 women composed 37 percent of production workers in weaving and a much smaller share in spinning—about 11 percent. Over the next twenty-five years, both activities feminized, and by 1996 women controlled 52 percent and 59 percent of the production jobs in weaving and spinning respectively. Not all factories feminized however; some firms in both spinning and weaving continued to employ mostly men while others were coming to rely more on women. When and how did these gendered transformations take place?

Managers in both spinning and weaving factories estimate that the shift to female workers in textiles occurred in the middle to late 1970s. During this period, employers in many factories began to experiment with using women in some sections of production. In Bandung (West Java), the major textile-producing area at the time, one factory manager noted that switching from male to female workers was a trend in the area when he feminized his weaving operation in 1973. Another manager who worked in Purwakarta (West Java) and traveled to spinning firms in other regions of the island observed that in the 1960s and early 1970s most spinning factories relied primarily on male workers but that by the late 1970s they had begun to use more women. The exact timing varied, but feminization in textiles did begin in Java during the middle to late 1970s.

Since spinning and weaving have distinct labor processes, the contours of feminization differed slightly. Large-scale weaving factories in Indonesia use both shuttle looms and automatic jet looms (AJL). The main impact of the difference in loom technology, aside from productivity, is that shuttle looms require an additional section of production with machines that wind the thread, the *palet* section. In factories with shuttle looms, most production workers are on the looms and in the *palet* section, while in those with AJLs, most workers are on the looms. In 1971, shuttle looms predominated in the weaving subsector, and men usually ran them, with the possible exception of Central Java, where the ratio of men to women was probably closer to 50–50. In both East and West Java, men were commonly found on the looms.[7] In my sample of ten weaving factories, six were established before 1975, and two-thirds reported using men on the looms when they commenced production; only one factory had employed women on the looms.[8]

Hardjono (1990) and Willner (1961) both found that employers tended to hire women in the *palet* section.[9] Women predominated in the *palet* section in the 1990s as well, but the number of workers in this section had declined because the winding machines were more efficient and required fewer workers. Moreover, since many employers had shifted from shuttle looms to AJLs, shuttle looms were a smaller proportion of total looms than in 1971, and in firms with AJLs there were no *palet* machines. Women therefore expanded their share of employment in weaving in spite of the rationalization or obliteration of the *palet* section that for many years had generated most of the female jobs in weaving.

Women maintained and increased their presence in weaving by colonizing the looms, which were more likely to be run by women than by men by the 1990s. In 1998 and 1999, seven of the ten factories in my sample employed primarily women on the looms; two used mostly men, but only one relied exclusively on men. The statistical data also show that by the 1990s the ISI-era firms had workforces that were 49 percent female, well over the 37 percent employed in 1971, which indicates a major shift. Firms established later—during the transition period or EOI—tended to employ more women from the beginning and had higher shares of female employment as well. Men nevertheless retained a substantial share of the jobs in weaving firms, as even feminizing employers were reluctant to place women in certain areas of production, such as sizing, and some firms did not feminize at all. Factories branched onto one of two paths—a feminizing or a nonfeminizing path.

A similar process occurred in spinning, although the change in women's share of work there was larger, partly because spinning was a much smaller sector in 1971 (only about 14,000 production workers) relative to later years. Spinning production began in earnest in 1974, and interview evidence indicates that most of these firms initially employed primarily men, although when they began production, women did constitute more than the 11 percent of the workforce indicated in the 1971 statistics. Of the four spinning factories in my sample which began production during the ISI period, women were in the minority in all except one. As with weaving, some firms feminized while others did not, and once again, feminization involved the regendering of work in the factory and began to occur well before exports commenced.

The production process in spinning involves two major segments, front spinning (blowing, carding, drawing, combing, and roving) and back spinning (ring spinning, winding, and sometimes twisting). In all the factories, even the male-dominated firms, women were concentrated in back spinning. The factories that employed relatively more women used a higher percentage of women in back spinning but placed women in front spinning as well. The specific areas in front spinning where women outnumbered men varied from firm to firm, but in those employing over 50 percent women, women were commonly found in drawing, combing, and roving. In back spinning, the firms with female majorities employed exclusively women as operators, and if men were used at all, it was for doffing (stripping off slivers of cotton from the carding cylinders or removing bobbins or spindles) and carrying materials between sections. In spinning, then, the shift to women involved expanding their role in back spinning and introducing them into front spinning.

Although foreign investors accounted for a small share of employment in textiles in Indonesia in the 1990s (18 percent in spinning and 7 percent in weaving—see Table 4.3), Japan was a major force in the textile industry, especially in spinning, in the ISI period.[10] Japanese spinning factories were far more male-intensive than local producers, with an astonishingly low level of 20 percent female production workers in their Indonesian operations. This finding surprised me; since women predominate in weaving, spinning, and knitting in Japan, I had assumed that Japanese factory managers would prefer to hire women in Indonesia as well.[11] One Japanese factory manager explained that in the 1970s there had been concerns about using women on the night shift, and he complained that in those years women had very high absenteeism. Japanese investors were probably especially careful as a result of anti-Japanese protests in 1974, when spinning production began to take off. The modest wage differentials between men and women in textiles may have also made the Japanese factory managers less insistent about employing women; in Japan there are significant wage savings associated with employing women (Brinton 1993). Recently, however this Japanese manager decided to try using more women in certain sections of weaving and spinning, so after many years of stagnation in the gender division of labor in that factory, it is feminizing as well. In addition, since the majority of Japanese textile firms were established in the ISI period, they are more likely to be affected by the stickiness phenomena (outlined below).

The first wave of feminization thus involved a group of textile employers that began to shift selected jobs from men to women even before In-

**Table 4.3.** Percentage of production workers employed in foreign-owned firms

| Sector | Percent of total production workers | Countries of main foreign investment |
|---|---|---|
| Spinning | 18 | Hong Kong, Japan, India |
| Weaving | 7 | Japan, Hong Kong |
| Garments | 23 | South Korea, Taiwan, Hong Kong, Japan |
| Footwear | 44 | South Korea, Taiwan, Hong Kong |
| Plywood | 9 | South Korea, Japan, Singapore |
| Consumer electronics | 51 | Japan, Hong Kong |
| Electronic components | 69 | Singapore, Taiwan, Japan, S. Korea, U.S.A., Malaysia |

*Source:* Biro Pusat Statistik, *Statistik Industri Besar dan Sedang 1996,* data file.

donesia initiated export-promotion policies. Although feminization during the first wave had a modest effect on women's overall share of manufacturing employment, it set an important precedent by demonstrating that women could be productive and reliable workers in modern industry.

### The Second-Wave: Emergent Exporters

The second wave of feminization occurred during the transition period, 1979–1986, and coincided with the first major growth spurt of exports. The feminization that continued in spinning and weaving was primarily an outgrowth of previous trends in the industry. Unlike the first wave, this second wave can be attributed to the emergence of new growth sectors, especially garments and plywood. The gendered transformations that occurred in the second wave were significant enough to affect women's overall share of employment in manufacturing. Although this cannot be shown definitively with national-level statistics, the case studies of garments and plywood, which accounted for one-third of the new employment generated between 1980 and 1985, lend credence to the claim that feminization began to take off during the transition period.

Additional available information supports the claim that the transition period was the turning point for significant feminization. A macrolevel indicator that provides some clues to when feminization began to gain speed is the list of job openings reported by factories to the Department of Manpower. In Indonesia, employers could legally specify whether they preferred to hire a man or a woman in their job postings. Table 4.4 lists the number of job openings reported to the Department of Manpower between 1983 and 1996.[12] Initially, demand for men outpaced the demand for women, but the gap began to narrow after 1983, and by 1986, job openings for women exceeded those for men. In subsequent years, demand for female workers exceeded that for male workers with the exception of 1989. It is notable that demand for women surpassed demand for men in 1986, which coincides with the first major liberalization package to promote export manufacturing, but it is also significant that the trend had already begun in 1985, when women's share of job openings reached 44 percent, a 15 percent rise in just two years. These data support the contention that feminization began to gather steam during the transition period as a result of employment growth in a number of labor-intensive industries.

**Table 4.4.** Job openings in manufacturing reported to the Department of Manpower, 1983–1996

| Year | Men | Women | Men − Women | Percent female |
|---|---|---|---|---|
| 1983 | 22,239 | 8,918 | 13,321 | 29 |
| 1985 | 10,760 | 8,360 | 2,400 | 44 |
| 1986 | 14,451 | 18,115 | −3,664 | 56 |
| 1987 | 14,229 | 14,597 | −368 | 51 |
| 1988[a] | 13,642 | 17,954 | −4,312 | 57 |
| 1989 | 22,823 | 20,794 | 2,029 | 48 |
| 1990 | 37,735 | 45,860 | −8,125 | 55 |
| 1991[b] | 13,996 | 15,990 | −1,994 | 53 |
| 1993[c] | 26,016 | 35,754 | −9,738 | 58 |
| 1995 | 67,073 | 71,493 | −4,420 | 52 |
| 1996 | 86,301 | 98,241 | −11,940 | 53 |

Source: Departemen Tenaga Kerja, Subdit Informasi Pasar Kerja, Dit Penyaluran Tenaga Kerja.
[a]March–December only
[b]January, March, July only
[c]January–March, October

Another indication of women's greater presence in the manufacturing workforce is that women workers began to appear as topics worthy of discussion in newspapers in the early 1980s. Major newspapers published articles about the need to protect women working at night[13] and about the opening of new job opportunities for women in industry, both in Indonesia and abroad.[14] In the early 1980s a Central Javanese newspaper carried a number of stories about the recruitment of female workers for factories in the Jakarta suburbs (Tangerang), South Kalimantan, and Maluku.[15] These stories show that factories were willing to incur significant expense in order to obtain female labor when it was unavailable locally and suggest that employers were increasingly seeking out women.

The increased demand for women workers is amply demonstrated by the experiences of the garment and plywood industries. In 1980, garment factories employed only about 15,000 people, and the majority of production was still in small workshops. Men had held almost half the jobs in 1971, and when the industry began to grow in the early 1980s, garments had an androgynous character. Although some new firms employed mostly women from the beginning, many continued to hire some men, since few women had sewing skills. In small-scale production, each sewer assembled the entire garment himself, so sewers were akin to skilled craftsmen, but in larger factories employers subdivided the work with each sewer performing just a few or even just one task. The growth in the large-scale sector in the 1980s therefore led to a fragmentation of the production process, which facilitated the shift to women workers. As Collins (2003) has noted, when employers in large factories do not depend on trained work-*men*, there is the possibility of hiring untrained or moderately trained women. Over time, managers in large factories that initially employed many men as sewers switched to a female workforce on the sewing lines. Factories shed male workers and/or shifted them to other jobs, shifts that went relatively smoothly because many factories were expanding. As they added sewing lines, employers also increased the workforce in cutting and finishing, so managers transferred male sewers to those sections, replacing them and male sewers who resigned with women. Large firms that began production after the transition phase inevitably put women on the sewing machines from day one.[16] At the beginning of the transition phase, then, firms started from different points of origin—some with mostly male employees, others with mostly women—but the great majority of large factories ended up with an overwhelmingly female labor force.

The association of women with sewing in the large factories is an interesting development, because many men still sew in Indonesia today. They are concentrated in the workshops and medium-scale factories that are enmeshed in subcontracting relationships with the larger firms. The medium-scale factories in particular offer less secure work at lower wages, and male sewers who cannot find employment in the workshops often end up there, since most large factories will not hire them.[17] Sewing has become "women's work" in the large-scale factory sector, and it is difficult for men to land sewing jobs there.

In 1971, plywood producers employed almost no women, but employment in plywood was negligible then. Based on my sample, my estimate is that at the beginning of the 1980s the share of female employment in plywood was around 40 percent. In 1996, 47 percent of production workers in plywood were women, so some feminization occurred. Most of the firms that started predominantly with women in the 1980s continued to rely on a majority-female workforce in the 1990s, while those that were male intensive remained so. New firms drew on advice from foreign advisers and partners or figured out the gender division of labor over time. Two of the nine firms in my survey reported significant increases in their use of female workers, one from about 50 percent to 77 percent, and the other from 35 to

44 percent. The former feminized in the mid-1980s when it reopened after a forced closing of several years (a perfect opportunity to replace the men); the latter started to feminize in 1997 when a new manager began to place women in a number of jobs historically performed by men.

All the plywood factories used women for the detailed manual work; men moved veneer between sections, and most machine operators were men. The main difference between firms was in the gender division of labor for feeding veneer into the machines and stacking it as it exited. Workers did this in teams of two to five people. Some were all women teams, others were all men, still others mixed men and women together, and within firms the gender composition of the teams varied from machine to machine. In plywood, the low end for the utilization of women was around 30 percent, as the light manual jobs that were almost always performed by women constituted approximately this share of jobs.[18] This percentage rose depending on the employer's preference to have men or women do the feeding and stacking jobs and willingness to try out women as machine operators. Because managers in most firms did not shift more of these stacking, feeding, and machine operator jobs to women, greater feminization did not occur.

As with textiles, local capital dominated in garments and plywood. The foreign presence in plywood was negligible at 9 percent, and the main investor was South Korea (see Table 4.3). This low level of direct foreign involvement was the result of restrictions on foreign investment in wood processing. In garments, the foreign role was more substantial at 23 percent, and the foreign garment firms employed a higher percentage of women in their workforce than the local firms. South Korea was the largest foreign investor in garments, accounting for about 10 percent of production workers, followed by Hong Kong and Taiwan (4 percent each) and then Japan (3 percent). Local firms averaged 75 percent women, while the figure was over 85 percent for the Asian foreign firms. Feminization would probably have been even stronger if East Asian investors had played a larger role in garments.

In sum, the second wave of feminization was more significant than the first wave, and the main reason for this difference was the change in Indonesia's industrial structure during the transition phase, which generated thousands of new jobs in labor-intensive sectors. Feminization would have been weaker, however, if garments and plywood had not undergone sectoral feminization. In garments, some employers started with a relatively even ratio of women to men but increased their utilization of women within a few years. In plywood there was a dual character, some employers starting with mostly women and others with mostly men. As with the first wave, feminization involved a redefinition of work in which jobs previously performed by men began to be done by women.

### The Third Wave: The East Asia Connection

In contrast to the earlier waves of feminization, foreign capital from East Asia played an important role in the third wave. Rising production costs in the East Asian NICs (newly industrializing countries) led investors from these countries, as well as from Japan, to turn to Southeast Asia in the 1980s and early 1990s. Although some invested in Indonesia during the ISI and transition phases of industrialization, investment surged in the late 1980s (Wells and Warren 1979; Wie 1991). By 1990 the NICs accounted for 30 percent of approved investments in terms of value and 58 percent of approved projects; more important, this investment flowed into labor-intensive and export-oriented manufacturing, with 84 percent of approvals in export-oriented projects (Wie 1991). Investment from Western countries was negligible in these sectors.

Footwear and electronics were the main beneficiaries of this new investment, but garments also attracted much interest from overseas. Investment in electronics and footwear took off in the 1990s after Indonesia was solidly on the EOI track. The foreign investors who led the way relied on a high level of female labor from the beginning. In footwear, South Korea was by far the most important foreign investor, accounting for 26 percent of all production workers. Taiwan placed second with about 9 percent, and Hong Kong third with 5 percent. These firms employed a substantially higher percentage of women than their local counterparts. Koreans, for instance, employed about 83 percent women whereas the local average was 74 percent (76 percent for large firms only).

In consumer electronics, Japan (47 percent) and Hong Kong (4 percent) predominated, employing 51 percent of production workers. The foreign percentage in electronic components was even higher at 69 percent, with Singapore (29 percent), Taiwan (9 percent), and Japan (8 percent) being the largest foreign investors. Both at home and abroad, Asian investors preferred to hire women in electronics, especially in their overseas operations.[19] Some foreign investors in consumer electronics employed fewer women than Indonesian firms. Japanese firms averaged 67 percent women, whereas Hong Kong averaged 84 percent, as compared with 70 percent for domestic capital. The difference between foreign and local investors was significant across the board in electronic components, however, with local firms averaging 68 percent, as opposed to 87 percent for Singapore, 82 percent for Taiwan, and 79 percent for Japan.

Electronics and footwear, then, constituted the new feminizing sectors of the third wave, and East Asian NICs accounted for a large share of this new investment. Indonesian investors in these sectors also employed primarily women, but the stronger preference by NIC investors for women workers in footwear and electronic components made the degree of feminization even greater.[20] These investors brought with them a conception of the ideal division of labor between men and women, and since they were unobstructed by local factors, they deployed that division of labor in Indonesia. In addition to the development of these new sectors, the growth of employment accelerated in sectors that had undergone feminization during the first and second waves. More than 600,000 new jobs were created in textiles, plywood, and garments between 1985 and 1995—almost one-third of all new jobs—which contributed to the overall trend of feminization during the third wave, which was the most impressive: by 1996 women claimed half of all manufacturing jobs.

## Stickiness, Spillover, and Snowballing

I have thus far treated the three waves in isolation from one another, but doing so obscures the links between them and underemphasizes the persistence of many male-dominated factories. Despite the overall trend of feminization, some firms in feminizing sectors resisted shifting jobs to women. To gain a better sense of the contours of feminization, it is necessary to explore three dynamics that cut across the three waves—stickiness, spillover, and snowballing—and to consider how regional differences affected the pace of feminization.

Once feminization began, it unleashed forces that pushed the process forward as new sectors emerged and old sectors grew. But many firms bucked the feminization trend, a resistance that would be surprising to most theorists of feminization. It is not so shocking, however, if the process at the firm level is taken into account. Since the gender division of labor is rooted in deeply held beliefs about the relative productivities of men and women in specific jobs, the example of other firms that have successfully feminized is not necessarily enough to convince managers that hiring more women is a sensible move. Gender divisions of labor therefore often have an inertial character (Milkman 1987). Even if management decides to feminize, shifting work from men to women in jobs that involve a large number of workers takes time because employers, usually unwilling to fire the entire male workforce, must wait for men to resign. Moreover, managers are often reluctant to place women in men's jobs while other men are still doing that work, as men seldom welcome women into their realms of activity on the shop floor. Feminization was therefore easier in firms that expanded, since employers could transfer men from jobs that they wanted to feminize to positions still deemed to be "men's work" in the new unit of production. New factories, of course, could hire women from the beginning.

The "stickiness" of the gender division of labor corresponds to some of the features of "path dependence" highlighted by Pierson (2004) and to the tenacity of employment systems described by Fligstein (2001). When firms settle on a particular gender division of labor, shifting to a significantly different gendered path can be extremely difficult. Given that gender divisions of labor tend to be sticky, older firms would be expected to have lower shares of women workers than newer firms.

A breakdown of factories within sectors according to when they were established confirms that those which began production during the ISI and transition periods were more male intensive in the 1990s than the firms established during EOI, even though in most cases they employed on average a higher percentage of women than they had in the past. Figure 4.1 represents employment by sector according to when production began. Although older firms did feminize—that is, women made up a larger proportion of employees in 1996 than in the 1970s—they still used fewer women than the factories established during later phases of industrialization. This pattern held even for the inward-oriented sectors, such as food, that underwent explosive growth in the 1980s and 1990s. The newer firms were relatively free of the sticky legacy of the gender division of labor; if they desired, they could (and many did) start with a majority-female work-

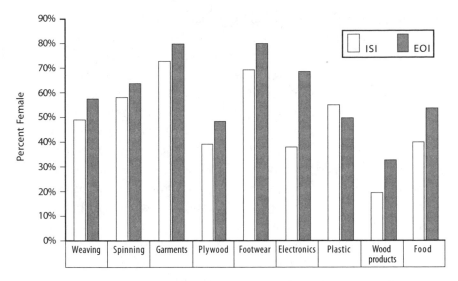

**Figure 4.1.** Women's share of sectoral employment by phase of investment. *Source:* Biro Pusat Statistik, *Statistik Industri Besar dan Sedang 1996*, data file.

force. As a result of stickiness in older firms, employment growth—through both the expansion of existing firms and the opening of new firms—facilitates significant feminization.[21]

Whereas stickiness slows feminization, "spillover" and "snowballing" effects drive the feminization process forward. Spillover captures the dynamic through which practices in one firm or in one sector influence those in another. Feminizing firms from the earlier phases of industrialization laid the groundwork for upsetting the association of work in specific sectors with male labor, and investors that entered the sectors in later years were more likely to use women from the beginning, once early feminizers had already shown that it was possible and profitable to employ women in, for example, spinning, weaving, garments, and plywood. The most common reason employers give for hiring women is that the jobs are "women's work"—but the 1971 statistics and the evidence of my case study show that in many instances, men had formerly done much of this work. These new employers could consider the work to be "women's work" only because of the earlier feminizers.

Spillover works in a number of ways, first by simply following common industry practices. As Fligstein (2001) argues, employment practices in existing industries influence employers in new industries. For example, a new local investor who enters an industrial terrain will observe the practices of other firms in the area to get a sense of how she wants to set up her business. Moreover, she will hire experienced managers who know about labor practices in the industry. If many existing firms already employ a lot of women, the chances are high that this practice will be replicated. Second, managers copy new practices that are perceived to be successful. Such "mimetic processes" (DiMaggio and Powell 1991) can spread firm-level practices through an economy. A number of managers in textiles confessed to me that their experiments with using women in additional areas of production were based on the knowledge that a competitor had successfully employed women in those jobs. Third, spillover can work through the transfer of management from one factory to another, both within a larger group and between companies. For example, at one of the plywood factories in the sample, a manager transferred from another factory in the group surveyed the gender division of labor soon after his arrival and determined that women could do some of the jobs that men were performing. He immediately began to feminize these job categories. Fourth, since factories are concentrated in industrial zones, the vision of thousands of women entering the factory gates undoubtedly led managers in other industries to consider the possibility of employing women workers as well. The existence of feminization in some sectors makes employers in other sectors more likely to consider shifting selected jobs to women. The data in Figure 4.1 also support this assertion about spillover effects; even though ISI firms did feminize, the EOI factories employed more women. Spillover effects can move in either direction, of course—feminization or masculinization—but in a previously male-dominated or relatively new industry, the emergence of many successful feminized firms injects a new dynamic into decisions about the gendering of workforces and makes the choice to employ women more likely.

The third dynamic, snowballing, takes place when employment grows rapidly in firms that already employ large proportions of women. Employment growth in the 1990s was most rapid in female-intensive sectors, and although some of this growth came from newly established factories, much of it was a result of the expansion of existing firms. Garment factories in Indonesia, for example, often started as relatively small enterprises that had just one or two assembly lines. As they grew, they added additional sewing lines and expanded the cutting and finishing sections. Since they had often begun with at least 80 percent women in their workforces, the growth of these firms had a snowballing effect on women's share of employment in manufacturing. Employment growth therefore not only provides an opportunity to feminize but also allows for the replication of existing practices on a larger scale.

## Regional Dynamics

In addition to the trio of dynamics that accompanied feminization in Indonesia, regional effects also shaped its course. In spinning and weaving, an important regional dynamic contributed to the degree of feminization. Feminization would have occurred in textiles even in the absence of this dynamic but to a lesser degree. This regional dynamic was rooted in regional variations in women's share of employment in textiles. Central Javanese firms tended to use a higher proportion of women than the other main areas of textile production, West Java (Bandung primarily) and Jabotabek.[22] In Central Java, women composed 60 and 62 percent of the spinning and weaving workforces in 1996. In West Javanese spinning factories, women were 62 percent of the workforce in weaving, but only 46 percent in spinning. In Jabotabek, the area that used the lowest proportion of women, 55 percent of workers in spinning and 45 percent in weaving were women in 1996.

Over time, the more female-intensive regions gained a larger share of new employment in textiles, thus contributing to the strength of the feminization trend. In weaving, Central Java and Jabotabek maintained their relative shares of employment in firms established during the ISI and transition phases (about 30 and 20 percent respectively), but in the EOI phase Central Java's share of employment in new investments increased to almost 50 percent, while Jabotabek's went down to about 10 percent. Although the ISI and transition phase companies in Jabotabek had the largest share of employees in spinning, with the advent of EOI, Jabotabek's share of new investment in spinning declined precipitously, whereas Central Java slightly increased its proportion, and West Java expanded its share to over half. The generation of more employment in the more female-intensive regions in the later phases of industrialization contributed to the degree of feminization, making it greater than if the new employment had occurred in the Jabotabek area.

The gendered political economy approach suggests two explanations for these regional disparities in Indonesia. First, there were differences in the supply characteristics of women workers between regions. Central Java had by far the highest levels of labor force participation rates for young women: in 1990, 41 percent of women aged fifteen to nineteen were in the labor force, while only 30 and 35 percent were active in West Java and Jakarta respectively. For women between the ages of twenty and twenty-four, Central Java remained on top with 50 percent of women economically active, in contrast to just 34 percent in West Java and 47 percent in Jakarta (Biro Pusat Statistik 1992).[23] In addition, a key factor to keep in mind for Jakarta is the large number of service-related jobs available to young women; these have more status and are less taxing than factory jobs and require minimal education. Educational levels for women are higher in Jabotabek and West Java, but the supply of educated young women in Central Java is sufficient to meet demand. In both age groups, the supply of women with elementary school education and above in Central Java far exceeds the number of women who are economically active. And in 1985, West Javanese women had higher fertility rates than the national average, which meant that West Java was pulling up the island's fertility rate, as fertility rates were lower on Java and Bali than the national average (Sanderson and Tan 1995). Mather (1985) also observed that the average childbearing age in West Java began about two years earlier than in Central Java in the 1970s.

Second, women have historically played a greater role in textiles in Central Java, creating gendered discourses of work that linked a broad array of jobs to feminine attributes. The paucity of textile studies that incorporate a gender perspective makes it impossible to determine the evolution of gendered discourses of work in each region, but the 1930 census conducted by the Dutch (Dutch East Indies 1933–36) indicates that 94 percent of Central Java's 216,000 textile workers were women. In West Java, women were only 80 percent of the 38,000 textile workers. In both cases the ratio of women to men is high, but Central Java was higher, as it is to this day. It is also notable that the total employment in textiles was much higher in Central than West Java, suggesting that the industry has deeper roots there. Textiles began to grow dramatically in West Java in the 1930s, and the production facilities in the region adopted more sophisticated looms from the beginning (Hardjono 1990). In Jabotabek the textile industry did not begin to generate significant employment until the 1970s.

## Conclusion

The shift to EOI and the ensuing promotion of labor-intensive sectors provided the impetus for strong feminization by expanding the share of employment in labor-intensive sectors in Indonesia. Feminization affected virtually every sector, but the labor-intensive sectors that had employed mostly men in 1971 feminized most sharply. I argue that feminization in Indonesia occurred in three successive waves, each corresponding to a separate phase of industrialization. Moreover, I suggest that feminization exhibited a set of dynamics that pushed the process forward—"spillover" and "snowballing"—but that the legacy of the past was evident in the "stickiness" of the gender division of labor in many firms. Finally, regional variations in levels of female employment in textiles were also important in determining the degree of feminization as investment shifted from areas with relatively low propensities to employ women to those with higher ratios of women to men in their workforces.

Through the analysis of the Indonesian experience, the dynamics whereby feminization is enacted became visible. Rather than merely relying on the causal logic of impersonal structural forces, the analysis showed how these structural forces were translated into practice by tracing how the gendered preferences of employers in particular sectors changed over time and how, given a conducive local environment, foreign investors imported gender divisions of labor that strengthened the feminization trend. Nevertheless, firms in the same sector and sectors with similar levels of capital or labor intensity adopted widely divergent gendered practices. Why did some textile firms rely on men while others depended on women? Why did some textile factories feminize while others did not? Why did sectors that paid similar wages and had similar levels of capital and labor intensity vary in their gendered labor choices? To better understand these issues, it is necessary to move to a lower level of analysis, the factory, and to take gendered discourses of work into account.

# 5

## From Profit to Practice

Gendered Innovations in the Labor Process

Feminization, according to most authors, is the path of survival for firms in competitive labor-intensive and export-oriented industries. Employers assure continued profits by exploiting cheap female labor. But, as David Harvey (1999, 116) observes, "There are, evidently, more ways to make a profit than there are to skin a cat." This chapter outlines a variety of gendered innovations in the labor process through which factories seek to raise productivity and profitability. Feminization is only one solution among many that managers adopt in their pursuit of profit.

Two comparisons constitute the heart of the analysis. The first, between highly masculine oligopolistic automotive companies and one of their subcontractors, examines their distinct gendered practices. The comparison demonstrates that two conditions increase the probability that a factory will adopt feminization as a gendered innovation in the labor process: competitive markets, and the presence of female production workers on the shop floor. Firms in highly competitive markets face constant pressure to increase efficiency and quality, so they must seek ways to squeeze more productivity from their workers. Since gendered discourses of work shape the way managers link profit to practice, feminization is one means of raising productivity. Less competitive—usually more capital-intensive—sectors do not face the same level of competitive pressure and hence do not innovate at the margins to the same degree as the more competitive sectors. Consequently, they are less likely to enact changes in the labor process which could lead to feminization. The second factor, the presence of women production workers, increases the likelihood of feminization as well. Gendered innovations in the labor process often emerge from shop-floor experiments, so the very absence of women in many capital-intensive sectors makes feminization less likely. These two factors help to explain why, on average, automobiles have feminized less than garments, plywood, and textiles, and they explain some intrasectoral variation in automobiles as well.

Although these two variables explain variation in the automotive industry and between capital- and labor-intensive sectors, they cannot account for variations between and within labor-intensive sectors, since all are in competitive industries and employ more than a token number of women. The second comparison illuminates how gendered discourses of work produce different gendered outcomes through a series of intrasectoral comparisons of firms in the garment, plywood, and textile industries. Adopting an interpretive approach, I show how gendered innovations in the labor process unfold. Whereas gendered discourses of work vary little between factories, gendered outcomes do. Variations in the linking process between the gendered workers and the particular job explain differences in gendered labor practices. The argument is therefore not that idea A causes outcome A, while idea B causes outcome B. Rather, it is an interpretive argument that offers insight into why firms facing similar competitive situations adopt varied gendered divisions of labor. Before elaborating the case studies, we must first explore how gendered discourses of work are related to broader gendered discourses in Indonesian society and demonstrate how deeply they permeate everyday practice on the shop floor.

## Linking Gendered Discourses of Work to Societal Gendered Discourses

Given the vast ethnic and cultural diversity in Indonesia, there is a host of societal discourses and practices about gender, and describing all of them would be beyond the scope of this book.[1] Instead, I focus on gendered discourses that are national in scope and consider how they provide a foundation for or point of linkage to the gendered discourses of work found in the factory.

First, a few words on *Indonesian* gendered discourses: that is, national as opposed to local (e.g., Javanese, Sudanese, Madurese, Balinese) conceptions of gender. Of course, local gender variations remain, but with the formation of a national state that molds gender relations through law, public policy, and public pronouncements, an Indonesian discourse on gender has emerged. Suryakusuma (1987, 6) vividly portrays this process, arguing that the "all-pervasive state . . . provides the structure for the development of a specific gender ideology which provides the official definition of how Indonesian women should be." Blackwood (1995) has also shown that gender representations emanating from state policies and programs, in conjunction with modernist Islamic discourse in national publications, both create new gendered identities in Indonesia and partially eclipse local gendered practices. Javanese influence is especially strong given Java's predominance in government and its cultural and political hegemony over other regions (Djajadiningrat-Nieuwenhuis 1987). Naturally, this discourse is challenged by elements of Indonesian society in the realms of local and national politics, but the outlines of a hegemonic discourse clearly emerged during the New Order period.[2]

The New Order regime adopted a discourse of separate but equal gender roles and emphasized the nurturing and selfless qualities of motherhood over other aspects of women's identities. The state's representation of Kartini, a famous Javanese princess during colonial times, epitomizes this vision of women's proper place in society. The Suharto regime played down her active and independent qualities and produced the image of a nurturing and self-sacrificing Kartini that perfectly matched the New Order discourse on women (Tiwon 1996).[3] Kartini is perhaps the quintessence of the perfect woman as portrayed in the national ideology of "Ibuism," which sanctions any selfless action taken by a mother in looking after her family, a group, a class, a company, or the state (Djajadiningrat-Nieuwenhuis 1987; Suryakusuma 1987).[4] As Sunindyo (1998) points out, it is not that women were never defined as mothers or housewives before the New Order but that the regime put the force of the state behind this particular definition.

Discourses on women's proper role, moreover, were spread through a variety of state-linked organizations. The Family Welfare Movement (PKK) penetrated villages and neighborhoods and administered government programs for women. It operated in gendered parallel to the state—the wife of the minister of internal affairs headed the organization at the national level, and at the village level the wife of the village headman was in charge. The structure of Dharma Wanita, the organization for the wives of civil servants and female civil servants, also mirrored the position of the husband: for example, the wife of a minister would be the head of Dharma Wanita for that ministry (Sullivan 1994; Suryakusuma 1987; Wieringa 1993).[5]

A core element undergirding national discourse on women is the term *kodrat wanita*, which is translated in a variety of ways: biological or female destiny (Sunindyo 1998); the intrinsic nature, true essence, or essential nature of woman (Tiwon 1996); and women's nature (Wieringa 1993). Wieringa connects the concept of *kodrat* to Hindu-Javanese roots; it is often associated with the idea that women are soft and weak (*lemah lembut*). *Kodrat* comes up repeatedly in discussions about the proper roles for women, whether from the period of the nationalist revolution or the New Order. For example, *Sarinah*, Sukarno's (1984) tract on women's role in the Indonesian national revolution, advanced a relatively progressive vision of the appropriate activities for women and argued that societal practices, rather than *kodrat*, caused women's subordination to men. He nevertheless clung to the notion of *kodrat* and criticized Western feminists for asserting that men and women were the same.[6] The emergence of the discourse that women are equal to but different from men is therefore not solely a creation of the New Order regime, although Sukarno never emphasized women's roles as mothers and wives to the same degree as the New Order. Rather, he strongly advocated women's participation in the national revolution and believed that it would not succeed without them. According to him, women's special connection to the social needs of society—a function of their *kodrat*—provided the justification for their participation in a variety of political mobilizations (Wieringa 1995).

Even Gerwani, the Communist-affiliated women's group that pushed for women's rights during the Sukarno years, did not fundamentally challenge the notion of *kodrat*, although members did dispute its association with shyness and meekness in public life (Wieringa 1995). Under the Suharto regime, however, *kodrat* was generally used to associate femininity with domesticity, even for women in the military (Sunindyo 1998). Armed forces publications frequently pronounced that women with positions in the military were not free from their *kodrat*, which naturally justified assigning them only particular kinds of tasks.

Female *kodrat* is a contested notion, and those that refer to it may disagree about its actual content, but its usage always assumes an opposition between female and male *kodrat*. *Kodrat* makes men and women different in spite of all their similarities as human beings and can be thought of as a shifting category filled with discourses about men's and women's essential natures. Essential difference is embedded in the concept; the implication of this essential difference is contested and has changed over time, but its existence is rarely challenged. *Kodrat* forms a bedrock dichotomy between male and female nature, which gets translated into—and is used to justify—gendered practices in society, including in the factory. The subterranean foundation of gendered discourses of work in Indonesia is *kodrat*.

Gendered discourses of work are not simply a feature of contemporary factory labor; they were present across historical periods and in nonfactory contexts. Studies of the Dutch period document specific gender divisions of labor—girded by essentialist notions of male and female labor—in sugar processing and on plantations, in subsistence agriculture in Java (Stoler 1985; Locher-Scholten, 1987, n.d.). European employers described Indonesian women as "cheap, accurate, responsible and willing" (Locher-Scholten n.d., 8) and as more patient and thorough than male workers, making them indispensable in the colonial era's sugar factories (Elliot 1997). On the tea estates, there is a long history of managers regarding women as more patient and accurate than men, and thus more suited to sorting work; similarly, their "cool" hands and delicate fingers were common justifications for using women as tea pickers (Grijns 1987).

Gendered discourses of work in the factory are inextricably connected to larger discourses about gender in society, but they are not mere replications. In concrete ways they shape real relations in the factory. The interesting question about gendered discourses of work is not whether they are "true" in the empirical sense but whether they influence the terms on which women gain access to work.

## Gendered Practices in the Factory

Upon walking into a factory in Indonesia, the visitor is immediately struck by the gender division of labor. Men and women rarely do the same jobs, even when they work in the same area of production, and some sections of production are the exclusive preserve of one gender. Gendered discourses of work are evident in the recruitment and placement of workers. The place to begin the journey through the gendered factory is with recruitment practices.

Although the specific process by which vacancies were filled varied from firm to firm, supervisors usually filled openings in their sections in one of two ways. In most factories, they initiated requests to hire additional or replacement labor, and part of the requisition process involved specifying the qualifications of the desired workers. Along with age and education, gender was a key "qualification" for available jobs, so gender was specified in job advertisements. The supervisor determined whether the open jobs required male or female labor, and requested the appropriate workers. For women, marital status was also important, and employers overwhelmingly preferred single women, since they could extract a few years of work from them before they married and started to have children.

In other factories, explicit or implicit company policy dictated particular gendered hiring practices. In these cases, supervisors did not need to specify gender on a hiring request, as the personnel department already knew, depending on which jobs were open, the number of men or women to be recruited. Workers were thus not considered equivalent just because they had the same age, education, and marital status; gender was an explicit point of differentiation in the workforce. Potential recruits of the same gender, however, tended to be regarded as interchangeable units, given similar education and age.

Recruitment was broken down along gendered lines because the division of labor in production was also gendered. Hiring a man for a woman's job would be disruptive, not only because supervisors considered the worker inappropriate for the job but also because most men resented being stuck in a task performed predominantly by women.[7] Some managers produced production plans that listed the number of required workers in their sections, breaking down each job or subsection and listing discretely how many men and women they required. Through their embeddedness in the everyday life of the factory, gendered discourses of work become common sense that are rarely questioned. For this reason, I often received tautological answers when asking why women or men did a particular job: "Because it's women's work," or "It's work that's compatible (*cocok*) with women," and so on. The respondents often acted as if I had asked a question with an obvious answer, and sometimes I had to ask a number of follow-up questions to get them to tell me what specifically about the work made it *cocok* for women or men. Recruitment practices, shaped by gendered discourses of work, are critical for sustaining gender divisions of labor (Elias 2004).

Gendered discourses of work, crucial in understanding how and why feminization occurs, are linked but not reducible to broader discourses about gender in Indonesia. They provide a vital lens through which managers not only interpret but also construct the organization of production.

## Masculine Oligopoly versus Mixed Gender Subcontractors

The automotive sector is relatively capital intensive, and the large firms occupy an oligopolistic position in the industry. Smaller firms that subcontract for the larger firms, however, face a more competitive market. In the subcontractor that I visited, Bekasi Motor, many of the operations that workers performed were similar to those at the large firms.[8] In fact, Bekasi Motor obtained much of its equipment from the large firm with which it contracted, equipment that the big company no longer had room for in its cramped Jakarta plant.

None of the large automobile concerns in Jakarta had ever employed women, and they had no plans to hire women in the future. In contrast, Bekasi Motor, which did stamping and machining work for one of the largest automobile producers in Indonesia, employed quite a few women. As a subcontractor, Bekasi Motor had a much tighter bottom line than the large companies. It could not exploit the oligopolistic position enjoyed by the big players, and its marginal position compelled the factory to pay relatively low wages. It started its workers at the regional minimum wage of Rp. 198,500; after at least five years they could hope to increase that to Rp. 250,000, but there would be no further increases. (Most of the garment, textile, and plywood factories that I visited, when incentives and premiums were taken into account, paid their workers as much and some paid more, in spite of the higher educational level of workers at Bekasi Motor.)

The workers at the large automobile firms are among the best paid in Indonesian manufacturing, however. The oligopolistic position enjoyed by the top firms allowed them to set up career ladders and to pay higher wages. The payoff was a more disciplined and stable workforce. The director of personnel at Bekasi Motor estimated that its absenteeism was about 8 percent for men, in contrast to an average of less than 2 percent in the big firms. Although Bekasi Motor did not collect data on turnover, the director of personnel said that workers resigned frequently—whereas workers in the big firms seldom resigned, and the average median tenure was eight years.

That Bekasi Motor faced a competitive environment completely different from that of the top-tier firms was evident in its labor practices and wage structure as well as in the multitude of gendered changes that it made in the labor process. At Bekasi Motor, women were a minority of the workforce, about 12 percent in stamping and 13 percent in machining before the financial crisis hit in 1997, and 10 percent and 31 percent respectively after the economic crunch.[9] Men were put on the large press machines and the machining jobs that were either dangerous or involved lifting heavy materials, whereas women operated the small presses and machining jobs considered to be light. Since Bekasi Motor faced competitive markets, it made many changes in the production process; and since women were present in the workforce, these adaptations sometimes resulted in gendered innovations in the labor process.

In previous years, Bekasi Motor had employed even more women. The general manager estimated that between 1990 and 1994 about 70 percent of production workers were women. Yet over time, upper management decided to reduce the firm's reliance on women, primarily because of menstruation leave and women's poorer productivity, which according to the general manager was 10 percent lower than men's on the same small press work. The manager of the press section disagreed with upper management, however, insisting that women's productivity on the small presses was higher and that he still preferred to use women. Top managers nevertheless eased women out of selected jobs where their performance was not deemed to be significantly better than men's in order to lower the burden of menstruation and maternity leave. Even at the low wages paid at the firm, Bekasi Motor had little difficulty finding men to do these jobs. At least two strikes occurred in the early 1990s,[10] and after the financial crisis a protracted conflict over wages erupted with about three hundred workers, many of whom subsequently "left." In spite of these difficulties, management did not consider feminizing again.

Still, since both men and women worked at Bekasi Motor, gendered innovations in the labor process were far more likely than at the large firms. Most instances of feminization begin as accidents or experiments. Managers try out women to see if they can do certain jobs before displacing men. The very presence of both men and women on the shop floor practically guarantees that supervisors will have the chance to see them doing each other's jobs: in everyday practice, men fill in temporarily for women, and women for men. For example, when a woman is sick, a man in the section may cover for her. During Friday prayers, which most men attend, women perform the men's work. Supervisors who make assessments about how the labor process is functioning evaluate these day-to-day events through a gendered lens. If male workers are not satisfying production requirements for quality, this deficiency may be attributed to their gender rather than to them as individuals. A woman filling in for a man during his lengthy illness and performing exceptionally well, even better than the man, could prod the supervisor to consider whether *women* (not just this particular woman) might be better at the job than men, after all. At Bekasi Motor, for example, managers conducted a three-month productivity study that compared men and women on the same machines. They found that on particular machines men averaged 10 percent more production than women, and women performed only 0.5 percent better on quality. If women had not been present on the shop floor, management would probably never have thought to conduct this experiment.

Although Bekasi Motor feminized in the early 1990s, it masculinized several years later. Competitive sectors and firms show higher rates of gendered changes because the pressure to innovate in the labor process is more intense. In particular, when investment in more efficient technology is not feasible or brings limited returns, employers tinker with the labor process to elicit more production from workers. This high rate of innovation around the margins means a higher probability of gendered innovations, such as feminization. The combination of a more intense competitive situation and a tighter bottom line forced Bekasi Motor to be far more concerned with squeezing out small improvements in productivity through changing the labor process.

Ironically, the highly male-intensive and capital-intensive sectors—the sectors that could cut their wages the most by switching to a female workforce—are the least likely to adopt gendered innovations in the labor process. It is not simply a matter of the structural features of capital-intensive sectors but a function of the absence of women: management does not have the opportunity to compare men and women side by side. Comparisons do not guarantee that changes in the gender division of labor will occur, but they increase the likelihood. Of course, factories that employ mostly men do alter the labor process in order to enhance efficiency and productivity, but feminization is unlikely to be the path that they choose. Since capital-intensive firms often start with few women in their workforces, they are likely to remain that way, so there is a path-dependent quality to these intensely masculine industries.

Although the two variables highlighted here, competitive situation and the presence of women, do not appear to be influenced by gendered discourses of work, the presence of women itself is influenced deeply by gendered discourses of work. For example, when I asked supervisors and managers at the large firms why there were no women in production jobs. I heard a range of responses, from the banal—"We don't have bathrooms for women," or "The men won't pay attention to their work because they'll flirt with the women"—to simply "We just never thought about it," "It's too dangerous," "The work is not suitable for women," and "Yeah, why?" Responses generally fell into three categories: ruling out the employment of women on grounds that all the work was too heavy and dirty; rationalizing that "women never applied;"[11] and admitting openness to the idea of using women in jobs deemed to be relatively light, such as quality control and inspecting. One remarkable aspect of managers' responses was that most had never even considered employing women, and this showed in their automatic response that the work was too heavy or too dirty for women. Even those managers open to employing some women were careful to specify that they had to be placed in areas with "light" work. Some managers also voiced concern about pregnancy leave and the associated absences, as well as the difficulty of finding appropriate jobs for women during their pregnancies. The managers amenable to employing women in a narrow range of jobs, however, usually acknowledged strong cultural barriers to the employment of women in the auto factories. One director of an assembly plant observed, "The vast majority of jobs are really not too dirty and heavy for women; besides, the work that women do in the rice fields is quite heavy. But there are big cultural obstacles to hiring women in automobile factories."

The main difference between Bekasi Motor and the big firms was not the content of the gendered discourses of work but the linking process between the gendered discourse and particular jobs. Management at Bekasi Motor had hired many women in the early 1990s not only because they had the necessary educational requirements and were easier to manage but also because some jobs had been classified as relatively light and simple. In contrast to the large automobile factories, where each operator was responsible for mounting the heavy molds called dies, Bekasi Motor assigned a male worker to change the dies and set the machines.[12] Operators therefore did not require high levels of technical knowledge and did not have to do any heavy lifting, making it possible, in management's mind, to place women in these jobs. Women were employed only on the small presses, which managers described as light and requiring more care, but not on the large presses, where they considered the work to be too heavy for women. Most managers believed that women were as productive as men on the small presses but less productive on the larger presses. Women also did machining work that managers considered less dangerous but requiring more attention to detail. "Women's hands are more nimble [*luwes*], and they are more careful than men," asserted one supervisor. He added, "The work on the large presses requires the workers to pick up large pieces of metal, which results in lower productivity for women." The large automobile employers used exactly the same argument to justify excluding women from all presswork, even that which produced small components and that Bekasi Motor considered to be light.

## Linking Gendered Discourses of Work to Gendered Outcomes

The focus on competitive markets and the absence or presence of women explains some cross-sectoral and intrasectoral variation in the gendered practices in manufacturing work, including why gendered innovations in the labor process are more likely in some firms than in others. But what about variations in gendered practices among firms in similar competitive situations that already have some women in their workforce—the situation in all the garment, plywood, and textile firms in the sample? Gendered discourses of work shape the way that managers conceive of running a factory profitably, yet the consonance of the content of the gendered discourses of work between factories did not result in homogeneous divisions of labor on the shop floor. That would seem to indicate that gendered discourses are irrelevant. In positivistic social science, ideas and material variables are important only if it can be shown that a particular idea results in a specific outcome; otherwise, the discourse has no *predictive* value. Social science is not simply about prediction but about understanding, however, and interpretive frameworks shed light on *how* social processes work. Gendered discourses of work therefore provide an interpretive lens through which to see and understand better the process whereby work is allocated to men or women.

The consonance of the discourse and the variance in the outcome are less contradictory if the process through which gendered discourses of work become translated into actual gender divisions of labor on the shop floor are examined. Although women (or men) may be regarded as similar types of workers, machines and jobs vary. The key is to link the ideal worker to the task, since a good pairing improves efficiency, productivity, and thus profitability. The linking process, however, can have multiple outcomes. Running a carding machine, for example, is not inherently "light" or "heavy" work, since all descriptions are relative. Management must ascribe characteristics to this machine and match it to the gendered worker, in effect gendering the machine or the job. But this process of linking varies from factory to factory, so in one place operating the carding machine may be considered light and therefore regarded as women's work, whereas at another it may be designated as heavy and thus more suitable for men. This process of association between the gendered worker and the job is critical, as the actual content of the gendered discourses of work is remarkably similar between factories. The classification of jobs as being either high or low on the range of factors in which the genders differ (degree of carefulness, lightness/heaviness, etc.) is weighed against other factors that managers perceive as distinguishing men from women, such as strike propensity, discipline, and absenteeism.

Although I found a relatively consistent pattern of gendered discourses of work in Indonesia, Leslie Salzinger's (1997, 2003) research in the Mexican *maquiladoras* has uncovered much more variation. Her work is a necessary antidote to the generic portrayal of women factory workers in the developing world, and she shows that as female labor shortages forced employers to hire more men, a wide array of gendered organizing principles emerged in the *maquiladoras*. Salzinger emphasizes how new gendered meanings develop within a common discursive context, whereas my research in Indonesia shows how different gender divisions of labor arise without necessarily changing the larger gendered meanings. Managers in different factories held relatively consistent gendered ideas across factories, but the translation of these meanings into the allocation of actual work assignments varied considerably.[13]

But why do these gendered translations change? Since gender is a key organizing principle in the factory, managers sometimes attribute less than optimal productivity to a wrong-gendered worker in the job. Gendered innovations in the labor process involve *re*linking gendered workers to particular jobs, and feminization and masculinization usually result in the redrawing of the line between men's and women's work. For example, if work of poor quality is coming out of a predominantly male section, managers may conclude that the jobs require more care and patience than men possess, and they solve the problem by replacing the men with women. If male workers give supervisors trouble, management might attribute the difficulty to their gender rather than to the supervisor's management style or to the stress or monotony of work in that particular section.

Management described gendered innovations in the labor process as improving efficiency and productivity. Feminization, however, was only one possible outcome of these innovations; masculinization or a simple reallocation of work without changing the overall ratio of women to men on the shop floor could also take place. The structural imperative to remain competitive does not result automatically in specific gendered changes in the labor process. Rather, a process of *translation* must occur, whereby managers assess, given the resources at their disposal, how best to fulfill the imperative. Since the shop floor is a gendered terrain, managers view the workforce in highly gendered terms, and feminization is one possible outcome of the translation from profit to practice. In some factories, management never ultimately challenged the specific link between gender and jobs, and the gender division of labor remained ossified for decades.

It is impossible to determine a priori which firms will adopt a particular gendered translation. Managers pursue profit with great vigor, yet the particular path of action that will lead to the greatest profit is never obvious. Their explanations for the gendered changes they made to the labor process were not simply post hoc rationalizations for decisions taken for other reasons. Unless gender was a relevant category to managers, they would not adopt a *gendered* choice as the solution to their productivity problems. Gendered discourses of work not only explain why gendered innovations in the labor process take place but also why employers are so selective in the jobs that they shift from men to women. Demonstrating the mechanics of gendered innovations at the factory level requires comparisons *within* sectors and between factories that adopt distinct gendered solutions to organizing production in pursuit of profit.

## Feminization and Gendered Innovations in the Labor Process

Whereas the automobile case study showed how differences in competitive situation and in the presence of women resulted in distinct gendered outcomes, other case studies demonstrate the independent effect of gendered discourses of work when these variables are held constant. If structure is the determining factor in causing feminization, then the factories within a given sector should move in the same gendered direction. Yet when labor intensity is controlled for, factories are seen to adopt radically different gendered practices. In some cases, the gendered outcome flies in the face of the feminization literature, with export-oriented factories retaining male workers and inward-oriented factories feminizing. By comparing factories that face similar competitive environments within their sectors and that employ a significant number of women in their workforces, it is possible to see more clearly the effect of gendered discourses of work.

### Garments

In the garment industry, all the firms in the sample either feminized or began production with an overwhelmingly female workforce, yet factories enacted distinct gendered patterns of organization, as can be seen by the comparison of two factories, Indogarment and Bogorama.

Indogarment began production in 1980 on the outskirts of Jakarta. It employed only about 100 people when it began production, but over the years the owner added additional sewing lines, and by 1999 some 1,500 operators toiled on sixteen assembly lines, and about 87 percent of these workers were women. In the first five years of production, however, approximately half the workforce was male, and men were involved in most areas of production, including sewing.

Sewing is often assumed to be a female endeavor, but in Indonesia many men sew. A stroll down almost any street in Jakarta reveals small sewing shops with men at the machines, and men are present in large numbers in the small- and medium-scale firms of the garments sector throughout Java. Supervisors at Indogarment observed that in the early 1980s, most of those hired with sewing skills were men, not women. As a former supervisor explained, "A lot of local men were skilled sewers and produced good quality garments." Wages for men and women were the same, so hiring women did not convey wage savings. Men and women worked side by side. The personnel director remarked that "at first we did not really have a good idea of what kind of work was appropriate [cocok] for men and women, so everything was mixed. Over time we learned from our mistakes."

The process of learning led to gendered innovations in the labor process—in this case, feminization. The managing director observed that feminization was a conscious policy of management: "We are intentionally doing this. Why? Because what we found out [was that with] . . . the male workers, the increase of productivity was very fast . . . but after reaching the maximum, or what is supposed to be the maximum, then they are stagnant and quickly go down. While the female worker is quite slow, reaching . . . their productivity . . . but stable for a very long, long period of time." According to the managing director, men's productivity peaked at six months, stagnated for six months, and then dropped; women's productivity increased slowly but steadily over the same period of time. Management concluded that men were getting bored because the work was unsuitable to their character, and bored men were difficult to control on the shop floor.

The line leaders put less emphasis on productivity and more on women's being easier to control. Again, this was primarily an issue of work discipline rather than of propensity to strike. Both male and female supervisors regarded men as "naughty" and as more likely to steal.[14] Men left their work stations more frequently to smoke and go to the bathroom and were more likely to give supervisors a hard time when asked to perform tasks other than their primary job. One supervisor observed, "Women follow instructions, but men are more likely to want to do things their own way." Another supervisor commented vehemently: "Men are naughty [*bandel*], so they are only accepted for the jobs for which women are not appropriate [*cocok*]. Women are patient, obey instructions [*turut*], and are easily controlled [*gampang diatur*]. Even though women's absenteeism is a little bit higher, they make up for it because they are not naughty like men." Supervisors complained that men had to be asked several times to do something but that women usually followed orders after being told just once or twice. Moreover, most supervisors observed that although men's and women's productivity was roughly similar, women's sewing was of higher quality, which led them to prefer women.[15] These explanations complement those of Indogarment's managing director—if men had poorer work discipline than women, then it would not be surprising if their productivity fell. As they "got bored" with the job, they took breaks more frequently, especially since their targets became easier to fulfill as they became more adept at their jobs.

The point, however, is not whether men's productivity was really falling or whether men were actually less obedient workers. Rather, the fascinating part of these discussions is that supervisors and top management readily attributed individual traits—whether positive or negative—to the *gender* of the worker. Instead of developing general ways to make workers more disciplined, management phased men out of the sewing lines. Their assessment was that the ill fit between men and sewing work reduced productivity, so the solution was to replace men with women. Managers carried out feminization quickly at Indogarment. As the factory expanded, they shifted men to other areas of production, and women replaced male sewers who quit. A few men remained on the sewing lines, but most were hangers-on from the 1980s. The personnel director occasionally considered hiring a man, but men had to undergo a grueling interview with her before she would put them on the sewing lines, and they had to know how to sew already.

According to top management, the positive features of female labor more than offset some of the disadvantages associated with women workers: namely, maternity and menstruation leave. Managers diminished the impact of these "problems" in a number of ways. Although they did not forbid women to take menstruation leave, a group incentive worked as a powerful stimulus not to take it, as an absence negatively affected the wages of all members in the group, and the incentive was substantial, averaging about 29 percent of base pay.[16] In addition, recall that the average median tenure in the garments industry was low, and at Indogarment the median tenure was three to four years. Since the factory hired relatively young workers, paid maternity leave only after a year of employment (following the trial period, so really fifteen months), and provided birth control (pills and injections) at the factory clinic, they kept paid maternity leave down to about 4.4 percent of the female workforce (3.6 percent of the overall workforce) per year. As in most garment concerns, Indogarment adopted a turnover-inducing wage regime, with few promotion opportunities and heavy overtime.

A final word about labor strife will counter an obvious alternative explanation. There were protests and strikes at Indogarment, and some workers and management recalled a strike that occurred around 1985, but feminization had begun before that. Management blamed men, and men's alleged coordination of the strike merely confirmed the positive evaluation of female labor and negative perception of male labor. There were two additional strikes in 1994, the year that the company introduced the group incentive, but in spite of women's participation in these strikes, Indogarment's enthusiasm for employing women did not wane.

While Indogarment feminized, Bogorama masculinized. Located in a suburb of Jakarta and established in 1990, Bogorama was a joint venture between a Japanese company and a locally owned textile group. The firm employed about 90 percent women when it began production, a decision influenced partially by the demands of the Japanese partner, which strongly preferred female labor. Indonesian managers were also inclined to employ women, as they reasoned that women were easier to control and less likely to protest. In addition, they considered women to be more careful, patient, and neat and thus better suited to most of the work in the factory. Men worked primarily in the cutting section, where work was considered heavy. In 1996, however, the production manager decided to experiment by introducing men at strategic points on one of the sewing lines. "We noticed that there were some bottlenecks on the sewing line. Since men are faster sewers, we placed men in certain places on the line so that they could push production. We used to use all women, but now we produce more with the mixed line. I prefer to use all women, but in order to increase production it is better to mix in some men." By placing men only at these key points, she reasoned, she could increase production without seriously compromising quality. Her experiment succeeded, and men moved into the selected positions on all the lines. The share of men in the production workforce grew from about 10 percent to 17 percent. Since men received the same wages as women, wage costs did not increase as a result of masculinization. The manager has considered experimenting with an all male line but hesitates because she fears that quality would suffer and that higher management, in particular the Japanese, would be opposed.

Pairing these two cases in garments illustrates how firms with similar production processes and virtually identical structural features—high labor and export intensity—have come to different gendered conclusions about the best way to improve productivity. Although both factories employed primarily women, Indogarment used a higher ratio of women than Bogorama. Indogarment feminized; Bogorama masculinized. In each case, however, gendered discourses of work deeply influenced the way managers chose to increase productivity.

## Plywood

Plywood factories began on one of two tracks in the early 1980s. Some employed mostly men, others mostly women, and most remained on the track where they began. Nevertheless, some changes in the gender division of labor took place in the sampled firms.

Indoplywood was one of the two plywood firms in the sample that feminized. Founded in 1978 in East Kalimantan, the factory began production in 1979 and was female-intensive from the beginning. Political difficulties forced the company to shut down in 1985, and when it reopened in 1986, management decided to increase the proportion of women in the workforce. As one manager observed: "Women are easier to control and are less likely to strike, and we figured out that there were actually a lot of jobs in the factory that women could probably do better than men. We discussed it with the directors, and they really supported us." According to one high-level production manager, the aim of feminization was to facilitate labor control and to improve the quality of the final product, since women were more careful in their work habits. The leadership in production surveyed the jobs performed by men and considered many of them to be light enough for women to execute. They began to move the men out of these jobs in stages and to replace them with women. The labor control issue had special poignancy at this time: although this particular factory had no publicized instances of strike activity, another factory run by the same group and located just down the river had a persistent problem after the firing of six labor activists in 1982.

Even though the firm expanded its female workforce, men still constituted about 30 percent of the workers—over two hundred men, which was more than enough to stir up "trouble." Avoiding strikes was one factor among many, but feminization would not have occurred unless management had found work in the factory deemed appropriate for women; otherwise, feminization would have been thought to jeopardize productivity and perhaps endanger women's physical safety. Supervisors had clear recollections about why certain jobs could be transferred to women and others could not: "We replaced men with women on the hoist, center lock, and in unreeling to facilitate control and improve quality (since women were more careful). These jobs were also light and not dangerous." Sometimes they tried women in a job as an experiment—for example, as operators on the glue-spreading machine or the double-sizer/sander—but switched back to men when the women did not perform as well as they had hoped. When a few women did stick it out in male sections, management attributed their success to the tomboyish nature of these particular women.[17] In sum, management faced a situation in which they thought they could improve efficiency by transferring women to jobs that they could do as well as or better than men.

Korply, a Korean joint venture established in 1983 in East Kalimantan, employed primarily men from the beginning, but in 1997 the new manager in the front half of production began to shift women into previously male jobs. Two main factors drove this feminization. First, the quality of wood had declined precipitously, so Korply hired more women for the detail-oriented repair sections of production. Second, the new manager, who was transferred from another factory in the group, surveyed the gender division of labor and determined, on the basis of his experience, that women could do some of the jobs assigned to men. He had a well-developed notion of why men and women should be placed in distinct jobs: "Men and women each have special characteristics and jobs have special characteristics, too. You have to place each in the jobs that are in line with these distinctive traits." Besides, he preferred to manage women: "Women are not crass, they clean up their work areas, and they don't take as many breaks because they seldom smoke."

Lower-level supervisors recalled that a decade earlier the firm had paid women slightly lower wages than men. Yet the firm feminized not when there was a clear wage advantage but in 1997, when minimum wage regulations had equalized male and female pay. The manager also wanted to decrease the number of men in order to reduce lost time on Fridays, when male workers demanded a longer lunch period in order to attend Friday prayers. He suspected that male workers, who tended to smoke, used daily prayers as an excuse to take more breaks.

Like garment firms, plywood factories adopted a turnover-inducing, low-wage regime. Women seldom took menstruation leave because they would lose overtime pay by doing so, and since most plywood factories ran twelve-hour shifts, women earned at least five hours of overtime a day. In fact, overtime pay exceeded base pay.[18] Women's median tenure was five years at Korply and Indoplywood, and at Korply about 4 to 4.7 percent of the female workforce (1.7 to 2.0 percent of the total workforce) was on maternity leave each month. Each firm hired relatively young women, twenty-four to twenty-six being the oldest ages they would consider, and there was a strong preference for unmarried women. Thus the companies reduced high absenteeism through strong monetary incentives and decreased the chances that women would be employed long enough to claim maternity benefits by selecting a wage regime that encouraged turnover with its long hours.

Although Korply and Indoplywood feminized, many firms that began with male majorities eschewed feminization. Machoply, established in 1980 in East Kalimantan, employed primarily men from the beginning. In 1999 women made up only 35 percent of the workforce, and the male share of employment had increased by about 3 percent over the previous five years. The gendered discourses of work at Machoply were virtually identical to those at other firms, but production managers placed greater emphasis on the weight of the work. Even though women could do most of the work, supervisors agreed, it was better to use men because they were more appropriate for jobs that were deemed to be heavy. "We use men on all of the jobs in the rotary section because workers rotate between jobs, and many of the jobs are too heavy for women. In assembling, we mix men and women in feeding the veneer into the machine and stacking it on the way out, as we require the strength that men possess but also the care and patience of women." The plywood firms I surveyed utilized similar technology and production processes, and all exported virtually 100 percent of production, yet they adopted different gendered organizational patterns. As in the garment cases, gendered discourses of work played an integral role in how managers chose to organize production and increase productivity.

## Textiles

The textile industry was similar to plywood in that there were wide disparities between firms in women's share of employment. Some factories employed mostly women, others mostly men, and yet others roughly half men and half women. In addition, some firms feminized, some masculinized, and others made no notable gendered innovations in the labor process.

Indotex, an Indonesian-owned weaving factory in Bandung, began production in 1968. At the time, the factory employed primarily men as weavers. As in other factories, managers at Indotex espressed the opposition between female and male in a series of binary oppositions—easy to control/rebellious, light/heavy, patient/impatient, careful/careless— and managers placed women and men in jobs that they thought best matched the workers' respective gendered attributes. Managers also thought that gender affected the way workers responded to different wage systems, with men working faster than women under piece-rate conditions and women putting in a relatively consistent level of effort regardless of the payment system.

As in all weaving factories, the loom operation absorbed the most labor. Work on even the semiautomatic looms required some physical stamina, and since the weaver had to carry the finished product to the warehouse, managers considered work on the looms to be heavy and thus more appropriate to men. In addition, since pay was based on a piece-rate system, management favored hiring men, as under this method of payment they believed that men would produce more than women.[19] The piece-rate system, however, generated high levels of conflict between workers and management, since the pay was cut for product that did not meet quality standards. Management developed extremely negative opinions about male workers; the factory manager noted that "men cut work, are naughty, aggressive, and more likely to strike." But as long as the factory used both semiautomatic and manual looms, with payment based on a piece-rate system, managers were reluctant to employ women on the looms.

In 1973 the introduction of new automatic weaving machines opened the door for a gendered solution to management's labor control problem. The historical literature on gender and labor processes points out that the introduction of new machinery is a perfect opportunity for would-be feminizing employers to make their move (de Groot and Schrover 1995), and so it was at Indotex. The quantity of production on automatic looms depended less on the diligence and stamina of the operator, so the company abolished the piece-rate system and initiated a daily wage. Under that system, managers thought that women would be more consistent workers than men, and the automatic looms required less physical strength. After weighing their options, management concluded that replacing men with women would probably not negatively affect productivity and that labor control would be easier. As the factory manager stated: "Men's production is more than women's, but not by much, and the quality is about the same. But men are naughty, so we put women on the new machines and replaced the men in stages on the old machines." Management therefore readily attributed problems of labor control to the gender of the workers filling the jobs, even though shifting work from men to women carried some significant short-term costs. Since men had more experience than women in operating looms, hiring women required investing time and resources in training a new workforce. Moreover, managers did not consider the possibility that much of the labor conflict was a product of the piece-rate system of payment, rather than the gender of the workers, and that men might have been more docile had their pay not been tied directly to the amount they produced.

Still, the belief that men were more troublesome and women easier to control did not lead to a wholesale replacement of men with women. As stated by the head of the weaving section, "The most important thing is that women be placed in work that is in line with their *kodrat*." Management considered women to be appropriate only for work that was light and that required patience and attention to detail. Feminization was therefore selective and occurred only in areas of production in which management regarded women to be equally or more productive than men. For example, management never feminized the sizing section, and they continued to use men to carry things between sections of production, because they thought this work was too heavy for women to perform as well as men.

In the 1980s, however, management did feminize an additional section of production—warping: "Men's work performance was poor, so we replaced them with women, and the results were better." A supervisor further explained that "warping work requires patience and care, so it is really more appropriate to women." Whether women are really more productive or obedient or patient than men is beside the point. Rather, the dynamic that merits attention is that management attributed individual traits—whether positive or negative—to the *gender* of the worker. When productivity in warping declined, instead of developing ways to make all workers more disciplined and productive in their respective jobs, management replaced men with women. In the early 1970s, women were only 20 percent of workers at Indotex, but by the end of the 1980s, women claimed about 75 percent of the production jobs.

While Indotex produced for the local market, Solotex, an Indonesian-owned spinning mill in Central Java, exported some of its production. The factory underwent feminization through a process similar to that at Indotex, although the labor control issue was less salient. When it started to manufacture yarn in 1983, at least half and maybe more of the workforce was male. The company hired men to install the spinning machines from Taiwan and did not want to fire them once the project was completed. At first, men worked on almost all the machines, but after a few years the production head began to replace the men with women. According to the manager of this spinning plant: "We used men in all sections of production, but there were women as well. We evaluated women's abilities and they were good workers, and sometimes it was difficult to find men. But women were also more diligent [*rajin*], easier to work with [*gampang kerja sama*], and supervisors in the field began to ask for women." The head of production echoed the factory manager's rationale: "We began to replace the men with women a few years after beginning production. It's better to use women on the machines because they are careful and patient. If the work is not rough [*kasar*], then it is better to use women." Management began to replace men with women around 1986, and by 1999, 65 percent of the production workers were women. Women operated almost every machine in the factory; men were relegated mostly to doffing and transporting material between production sections.

In contrast to both Indotex and Solotex, Jayatex enacted few if any changes in the gender division of labor in its units of production, which included multiple spinning, weaving, and dyeing and finishing mills in a large factory complex west of Jakarta. Jayatex was locally owned and established in 1974; it exported a large share of its production. In late 1998 it employed an average of 29 percent women in the spinning mills and 36 percent women in the weaving factories, and over the years this percentage did not change. Like managers at the other textile factories, those at Jayatex considered women to be more appropriate for light work that required patience and attention to detail, and men to be better suited for heavy work. They were less insistent than managers at Indotex about the rebelliousness of male workers; most managers simply highlighted women's tendency to follow orders more quickly than men and greater flexibility about doing work outside of their job description. The main difference was thus not the gendered discourses themselves but the linking process between these discourses and the jobs in the factory.

Managers at Jayatex classified machine work as either heavy or light, and within the jobs categorized as light they distinguished between those requiring greater attention to detail and those that demanded less intensity of concentration. They then assigned the appropriately gendered worker to the job. This linking process led to a dramatically different gender division of labor: unlike the managers at Indotex, those at Jayatex considered work even on fully automatic looms to be heavy, since the operator had to stand for long periods of time and supervise a number of machines that ran continuously. They therefore preferred to hire men as loom operators. Women were overwhelmingly concentrated in the inspecting, warping, and reaching jobs, all of which were considered to be light and to require great attention to detail. When I mentioned to one manager that many factories used women on the looms, he nodded but replied that he would do so only if "forced" to by upper management.

Managers at Jayatex were also reluctant to hire more women because they doubted that women were cheaper to employ than men. Menstruation leave and higher premiums on the night shift made women more costly to employ, and since pregnant women were not allowed to work at night, pregnancies caused scheduling problems in the rotating shift system. Yet management was more than willing to put up with these draw-backs in sections where they deemed that women's special talents resulted in significant productivity advantages in comparison with men: "Women do have more costs associated with employing them, but we weigh that against their strengths, such as patience and attention to detail." Given the view that women were more expensive to employ, it is unsurprising that on occasion management experimented with using men in women's jobs but regarded all these experiments as failures. In the inspecting section, one manager recalled, "We tried out men . . . but a lot of flawed material got through, so we decided to stick with women, who are more patient and better at catching defective fabric." Another supervisor experienced the same disappointing results when he tried out men on the sectional warper: "The results were unsatisfactory because men are just not careful [*teliti*] enough." The failure of these particular men to perform well in these jobs was immediately attributed to the gender of the worker rather than to the individual worker's shortcomings.

Since management deemed the experiments with placing men or women in different job classifications to be failures, they did not consider feminization—or masculinization—as a measure that would improve pro-ductivity. The gender division of labor thus remained ossified for more than twenty years at Jayatex. A necessary precondition for feminization, then, is that managers identify hiring women for particular job categories as improving productivity and/or labor control, and this decision is pro-foundly shaped by gendered discourses of work. Although intense com-petition, especially in labor-intensive sectors, increases the probability that feminization will occur, employers that face cutthroat competition do not necessarily conclude that hiring women will give them a competitive edge. Feminization is only one conceivable solution to the problems of produc-tivity and labor control that employers face.

The single recorded strike at Jayatex in 1993, in which almost 5,000 of the 7,000 workers walked out, did not persuade managers to increase women's presence in the workforce. When the conglomerate opened a new spinning location in another Jakarta suburb, it transferred management from the established factory complex to the new production site, and managers ap-plied exactly the same gender division of labor there, employing an aver-age of 29 percent women. The production manager at the new location explained: "It would be inhumane to put women in jobs in front spinning.

The work requires a lot of pushing and lifting. In general, we are not enthusiastic about employing women because pregnancies make things tough. Pregnant women cannot work at night, which makes things difficult because we use a rotating shift system. On top of that, pregnant women get three months off for maternity leave." Still, management thought it necessary to put up with these drawbacks in sections where women's special talents were needed. The production manager observed that Japanese technicians had encouraged them to use women in the carding-drawing-roving (CDR) section: "In Japan, they use women in CDR. The technicians brought along some Japanese women—they were big!— to demonstrate that women were up to the job." The Indonesian managers stuck with men, however, because they thought that Indonesian women were not as big and strong as these Japanese "superwomen."

Contrary to the expectations of feminization theory, the most export intensive of the three factory complexes, Jayatex, employed the fewest women, while the most inward-oriented, Indotex, relied most on women workers. All the producers in this sample faced competitive markets, and all the factories were labor intensive, yet they adopted distinct gendered labor processes and showed different gendered trends over time. Significantly, even in those factories that feminized, feminization was selective: some jobs were feminized, while others were not. Gender divisions of labor were reconfigured rather than obliterated. Gendered discourses of work played a definitive role in how managers made decisions about increasing productivity.

## Conclusion

A shop-floor view of the feminization process in Indonesia shows how gendered discourses of work illuminate employers' reasons for adopting various gendered labor practices, with some opting for feminization and others sticking with men or masculinizing. Competitive markets and the presence of women in the workforce help to explain why factories in labor-intensive sectors are more likely to adopt gendered innovations in the labor process than are capital-intensive industries. Competition creates constant pressure for factories to increase efficiency and quality, so firms in competitive industries tinker with the production process in order to squeeze more productivity from their workers, and gendered innovations in the labor process are considered one means of raising productivity. Sectors and firms that face less competitive markets will not innovate around the margins to the same degree as the more competitive sectors and firms, reducing the likelihood of gendered innovations in the labor process and hence of feminization.

Another reason why labor-intensive sectors feminize more strongly than capital-intensive industries is not merely that labor-intensive sectors are driven to hire women to gain wage savings but that employers in these sectors are also impelled to make small adjustments to the production process in order to get more productivity from their workers. In addition, since gendered innovations in the labor process grow out of shop-floor experiments, the absence of women on the shop floor in capital-intensive sectors makes feminization even less likely.

These two variables do not explain the gendered variations among and within the labor-intensive sectors, however. To better understand the different gendered outcomes in these sectors requires an interpretive approach showing how managers link gendered discourses of work to particular jobs or machines. Gendered discourses of work, which are tied to larger gendered discourses in Indonesia via the concept *kodrat*, shed light on the process through which managers make gendered innovations in the labor process. Presenting the cases as comparisons within sectors shows how varying outcomes are produced out of similar structural locations and production processes. Introducing gendered discourses of work reveals how an interpretive and gendered approach complements conventional political economic analysis and offers a better understanding of how feminization unfolds in specific settings. Case studies offer examples of how structural forces were translated into gendered innovations in the labor process, sometimes resulting in feminization and sometimes not.

Integrating gendered discourses of work into the analysis helps otherwise puzzling practices become intelligible. For example, why did managers at Indotex, when adopting feminization as a gendered innovation in the labor process, not feminize the entire workforce, given that men were considered to be more troublesome than women? Instead, they limited the scope of feminization to jobs that they believed women performed as well as or better than men; even though men were considered to have many negative characteristics, these disadvantages had to be tolerated in jobs in which men's productivity was thought to be much higher than women's.

Why did factories facing intense exposure to global competition, such as Jayatex, eschew hiring more women? Because they thought women were more expensive employees than men, that women were not significantly easier to control than men, and that much of the work was too heavy for them to perform as well as men. Why did employers that preferred to employ men hire some women, even though they considered women workers more costly than men? They hired women in the job categories in which women were thought to be more productive than men. In sum, the gendered cost-benefit analysis that managers engaged in was far more complex than is conveyed by the current theorizing of feminization.

# 6

# Gendered Paths of Industrialization

## A Cross-Regional Comparative Analysis

Although feminization is widespread, many countries have proved immune to it. In fact, countries exhibit different gendered trajectories of industrialization, with the proportion of women in the workforce increasing in some countries, decreasing in others, and changing little in yet others. Moreover, even in countries that have followed similar gendered paths, women's share of manufacturing employment varies widely. Even when sector is controlled for, national variations remain. How can varying gendered paths and patterns of industrialization be explained? This chapter both describes and explains gendered paths and patterns of industrialization across twenty-seven sectors and ten countries in three regions: Argentina, Brazil, and Mexico in Latin America; Singapore, South Korea, and Taiwan in East Asia; and Indonesia, Malaysia, the Philippines, and Thailand in Southeast Asia.[1] I chose these ten countries because gendered employment data were available for them over a long period of time; they represent major industrializing countries in the three regions; and they have experienced a variety of gendered patterns of manufacturing employment.

The cross-national comparative analysis confirms many of the insights developed in the case study of Indonesia and shines additional light on the ways in which supply variables affect feminization. The growth of employment in labor-intensive sectors relative to capital-intensive sectors, as expected, explains much of the cross-national variation in gendered trends in industrialization over time. Employment growth has also had a positive effect on women's share of employment, with women claiming more of the newly created jobs than men. Strong labor unions have a negative impact on women's share of employment. In countries with strong unions, feminization has been less impressive and women have had lower shares of employment. Reductions in fertility, in contrast, have had a positive effect on both feminization and women's share of employment. Education and labor force participation rates have had mixed effects.

Latin America presents a stark contrast to East and Southeast Asia, in both industrialization paths and union strength, which had profound consequences for women's employment opportunities. The Latin American countries in the analysis employed far fewer women than the Asian countries, a result not only of differences in the industrialization paths they pursued but also of distinct patterns of labor incorporation. Populism in Latin America created relatively strong unions, whereas the systematic exclusion and repression of labor by authoritarian regimes in Asia produced weak unions. The varying forms of labor incorporation had gendered consequences that are still evident today and suggest that docile unions facilitated the absorption of women into manufacturing work.

## Trends in Feminization and the Employment of Women in Manufacturing

Patterns of feminization and women's share of employment in manufacturing show sharp interregional differences as well as intriguing intraregional variations. Although feminization has taken place in all three regions, it has been weakest in the Latin American cases (see Figure 6.1). Brazil began a mild trend of feminization in the 1970s, with women's employment increasing from about 20 percent in 1970 to around 25 percent in 1985. Of the three Latin American countries, Mexico has experienced the strongest feminization. In 1960 women claimed less than 15 percent of manufacturing jobs; their share of employment increased slowly until about 1985, reaching just over 20 percent; and by 1993 the female share of manufacturing employment had increased to 30 percent. Argentina remains stubbornly masculine, having masculinized modestly from a female share of employment of about 27 percent in 1964 to only 18 percent in 1994.

In contrast to the Latin American cases, all the East Asian countries underwent a strong wave of feminization in the 1960s and 1970s (see Figure

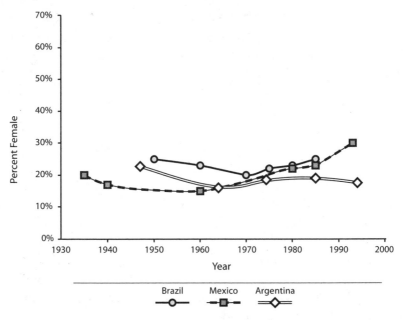

**Figure 6.1.** Women's share of manufacturing employment—Latin America. *Source:* See Statistical Appendix.

6.2). South Korea feminized until about 1975, with female employment reaching 49 percent; the trend in Taiwan lasted until around 1980, with female employment peaking at 50 percent. Thereafter, both countries masculinized. South Korea in particular experienced a precipitous decline: by 1990, women held only 37 percent of manufacturing jobs. Though less dramatic, women's employment in Taiwan shrank to 45 percent in 1990. Singapore revealed a similar pattern of feminization, but after a brief masculinization dip in 1980 it resumed feminization. Southeast Asia also underwent impressive feminization (see Figure 6.3). The Philippines showed a marked feminization trend, with a slow but steady increase in female employment from 19 percent in 1967 to 40 percent in 1993. Indonesia, Malaysia, and Thailand feminized at about the same rate as the Philippines.

In addition to variations in trends over time, the ten countries also differ in terms of women's *share* of employment. The Latin American countries remain the most masculine, with women claiming at most 30 percent of manufacturing jobs. East Asia is in the middle, showing high levels of

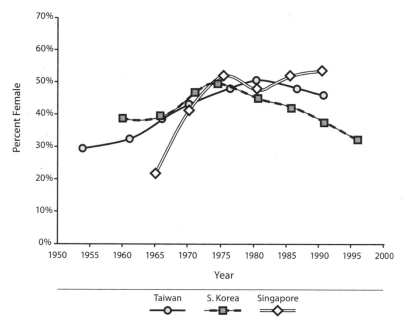

**Figure 6.2.** Women's share of manufacturing employment—East Asia. *Source:* See Statistical Appendix.

female employment at the end of the feminization trend—about 50 percent—and lower but still respectable percentages after masculinization, roughly 32 to 45 percent. Women claim the largest share of manufacturing work in Southeast Asia, with the Philippines being the lowest at around 40 percent and Thailand the highest with over 60 percent.

## The Gendered Logic of Industrialization

Although most of the countries included in this study engaged in both export-oriented and import-substitution industrialization (EOI and ISI) strategies, the balance between them varied markedly. The Latin American countries pursued a course of industrialization that relied more heavily on ISI; East Asia, though having a potent ISI dimension, put more emphasis on EOI; and Southeast Asia was more similar to East Asia, although ISI and EOI did not deepen to the same degree. The timing of industrialization also differed markedly, with Latin America's industrialization taking off sharply during the Depression and World War II and East Asia's (re)start-

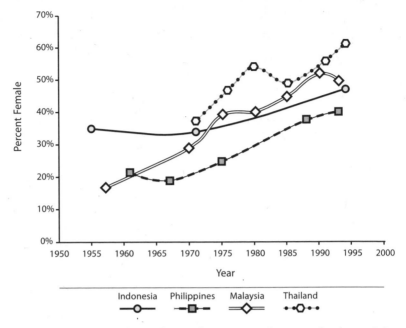

**Figure 6.3.** Women's share of manufacturing employment—Southeast Asia. *Source:* See Statistical Appendix.

ing after World War II.[2] Southeast Asia presents a more varied picture, although its period of impressive economic growth for the most part began in the 1970s or later.

The decade of the 1930s was a key historical juncture in Latin America, with the Depression and World War II acting as catalysts for the development of local industries to produce goods that could no longer be imported. Argentina, Brazil, and Mexico underwent primary ISI from the 1930s and 1940s until the mid-1950s and then proceeded to secondary ISI in the mid-1950s (Gereffi 1990; Kaufman 1979). Since employment growth was concentrated in capital-intensive industries, a masculinization trend was notable in the region during the 1950s and 1960s.

In the 1970s, Mexico and Brazil began to feminize.[3] Feminization was directly related to shifts in sectoral employment, which was in turn produced by changes in industrialization policy. In 1968, Brazil complemented its ISI program with diversified export promotion (Gereffi and Wyman 1990; Haggard 1990), and employment in labor-intensive sectors such as garments, footwear, and food processing expanded sufficiently to generate some feminization. The degree of feminization was modest, however, because employment in many capital-intensive industries—iron and steel, transport, and nonelectrical machinery—expanded as well. Labor-intensive sectors were a more significant component of Mexico's industrialization, in contrast to Brazil's, in the 1970s, 1980s, and 1990s. Although employment in some capital-intensive sectors such as transport and nonelectrical machinery grew sharply as well, the Border Industrialization Program fostered the development of the infamous *maquiladoras*, and many of the industries that produced for export there were labor intensive. The combined effect of the North America Free Trade Agreement (NAFTA) and the devaluation of the peso in the wake of financial crisis in 1994 led to a skyrocketing of the *maquiladora* share of manufacturing employment from 7 percent in 1985 to 27 percent in 1996 (Cooney 2001). Mexico's feminization has therefore been much more dramatic than Brazil's. Unlike Brazil and Mexico, Argentina experienced deindustrialization in the 1970s, with industrial employment falling 26 percent between 1975 and 1980 (Drake 1996). Labor-intensive sectors that employed women stagnated or shrank, and as a result, women's share of employment declined in the 1970s and 1980s.

In contrast to the Latin American cases, South Korea, Taiwan, and Singapore pursued a more consistently export-oriented strategy of industrialization. South Korea and Taiwan engaged in ISI, but they began to focus on manufactured exports earlier than Latin America and combined secondary ISI with a strong export orientation. Both South Korea and Taiwan pursued primary ISI in the 1950s, but they aborted this industrialization strategy in the 1960s and shifted to primary EOI. Primary EOI lasted until the early 1970s, when both countries moved to secondary EOI and secondary ISI (Gereffi and Wyman 1990; Haggard 1990; Woo 1991). The trajectory of gendered employment in South Korea and Taiwan mirrored these changes in the industrialization strategies pursued (see Figure 6.2).

In South Korea the explosion of employment in labor-intensive sectors led to a wave of feminization from 1965 until 1975. With the shift from primary to secondary EOI in the 1970s, however, employment grew most rapidly in the more capital-intensive sectors, and a steady trend of masculinization ensued. Labor-intensive sectors continued to be important in the 1970s and even into the 1980s, dampening the degree of masculinization that occurred. In the 1980s, however, Korean manufacturers began to export their labor-intensive industries to countries with cheaper labor costs, in particular to Southeast Asia (Lee 1994; Lindblad 1997; Wie 1991). Women's share of employment subsequently declined to 37 percent. A similar pattern occurred in Taiwan, but the masculinization trend in the 1980s was weaker there, as Taiwan did not push the development of capital-intensive sectors as aggressively as South Korea (Haggard 1990). As in South Korea, labor-intensive industries moved offshore to Southeast Asia in the late 1980s: between 1985 and 1990, Taiwan lost more than 150,000 jobs in textiles and garments, although employment continued to be generated in more capital-intensive sectors.

Singapore was the only country in the sample that followed an exclusively export-oriented path. Its employment growth was most impressive in labor-intensive industries, and as expected, women began to claim a larger share of manufacturing work. The shift from primary EOI to secondary EOI in the mid-1970s weakened the feminization trend, but Singapore did not settle into a pattern of masculinization, because electronics continued to be the engine of employment growth (Rodan 1997). Consequently, feminization was stronger and more sustained than in South Korea and Taiwan.

Whereas the East Asian countries shifted from primary ISI to primary EOI fairly quickly, the Southeast Asian countries persisted with primary ISI for a longer period of time and began primary EOI later. Malaysia initiated primary ISI in the 1950s and commenced EOI in the late 1960s (Rasiah 1997). Between 1957 and 1970 women's share of manufacturing employment expanded by 11 percent. The absence of gendered employment data in the 1960s makes assessing the precise starting moment of the feminization trend impossible, but the steep slope of the feminization curve between 1970 and 1975 lends credence to the claim that the majority of the increase between 1957 and 1970 occurred after the export promotion program began. In the 1980s, Malaysia embarked on some secondary ISI and EOI, which led to the expansion of employment in some capital-intensive industries. Employment growth in electronics, however, dwarfed all other sectors, so feminization continued.

In the Philippines, primary ISI took place in the 1950s and 1960s, and under Marcos some primary EOI began in the early 1970s (Hutchison 1997). The beginning of the feminization trend cannot be pinpointed precisely, given the absence of a data point between 1967 and 1975, but between 1961 and 1967 women's share of employment decreased, which suggests that the modest feminization occurring between 1967 and 1975 was a result of the expansion of employment in labor-intensive export industries in the early 1970s. Marcos never fully implemented the export promotion policy (Hawes 1992), however, so the degree of feminization was moderate in comparison to that of Malaysia. Between 1975 and 1988, feminization continued apace, as employment increased at a higher rate in labor-intensive sectors than in the capital-intensive sectors.

Indonesia and Thailand, beginning primary EOI later than Malaysia and the Philippines, pursued ISI (mostly primary but some secondary in the 1970s) from the 1950s until the mid-1980s, when both shifted to primary EOI (Hewison 1997; Jomo 1997). Thailand's gendered trajectory is surprising, as women's share of manufacturing employment increased about 20 percent during the ISI period, but it is less shocking once the overwhelming dominance of textiles, a labor-intensive sector, is taken into account. By 1980, almost half of employment in manufacturing was in textiles, and over half of the total increase in jobs between 1970 and 1980 occurred in textiles. Textiles went through a lean period in the early 1980s which led to some masculinization, but from the mid 1980s, feminization resumed as other labor-intensive sectors took off with the onset of primary EOI. Indonesia was similar to Thailand, since textiles generated much of the new employment between 1971 and 1980, although much less so than in Thailand, which accounts for the more modest slope of its feminization curve. Most of the feminization in Indonesia occurred from the early 1980s onward, when the country began to promote a variety of labor-intensive export industries.

## Explaining Sectoral Variations: Unions and Supply Factors

The type of industrialization affects gendered trends in the manufacturing sector as a whole through its effects on the expansion and contraction of sectoral employment. But if labor intensity and capital intensity are the only factors affecting women's employment, levels of female employment in a sector should be relatively constant across nations. As suggested in previous chapters, these variations in sectoral levels of female employment require incorporating into the analysis factors other than the balance of employment in labor- and capital-intensive sectors—such as the potential impact of labor unions and labor supply factors.[4]

### The Gendered Impact of Unions

Why do unions have a gendered impact? Simply put, unions are gendered institutions, as is evident in their memberships, their leaderships, and the policies that they pursue. Feminist labor historians have documented numerous instances of male workers striking to prevent the influx of female labor, and unions were at the forefront of many struggles to implement protective legislation for women. Protective legislation makes it more expensive and difficult (and sometimes impossible) for employers to hire women.[5] The motivations behind male opposition to women workers varied, but the most common included fear of downward pressure on wages, a sense of threatened masculinity, a fear that women would "pollute" and reduce the prestige of male occupations (Goldin 2002), and quite simply the desire to defend union members' jobs. Since battles over the gendering of work are often about the deskilling of jobs, the redefinition of job classifications, and maintaining jobs for members, male-dominated unions have obstructed feminization. The absence of strong unions removes a potential barrier to feminization, while strong unions have the potential to impede feminization.[6]

The impact of unions depends not only on their capacity to disrupt employer efforts to feminize but also on bargaining institutions. If wages are set through industry-wide bargains, especially if they apply to all workers regardless of their membership in a union, employers have less incentive to hire women instead of men, since women will receive the same wages as men for the same work. Some feminization may take place even in countries with strong unions if the sector is relatively new (and hence unorganized) or if employment growth takes place primarily through the establishment of new factories rather than the expansion of existing ones. Moreover, when industry is expanding rapidly, employers that previously relied primarily on men are more likely to tap into female labor as the supply of male labor at a particular level of education and wage rate diminishes. When employment is growing, strong unions slow down the pace at which women are integrated into the manufacturing workforce. Unions may have a negative impact on female employment also when employment is contracting: that is, women may be laid off at a higher rate than men, resulting in masculinization.

To test these propositions statistically, it is necessary to devise an index that measures the relative power of unions in the ten cases. The union index combines three indicators. The first is the dominant *level at which collective bargaining takes place,* and the second is *union density.* Although both are common measures of union strength (McGuire 1999), union density on its own can be a misleading indicator of labor's power in developing countries (Rudra 2002); high levels of union density (as well as union concentration and centralization) may be a result of exclusionary corporatist policies and a poor indicator of union power. I therefore add a third indicator, *political inclusion,* which takes into account the extent to which the state embraces or permits labor mobilization.[7] Figures 6.4, 6.5, and 6.6 illustrate how union strength, as measured by this index, has changed over time.

Of the ten countries, the strongest unions are in Latin America. Populist leaders in an array of Latin American countries completed the initial in-

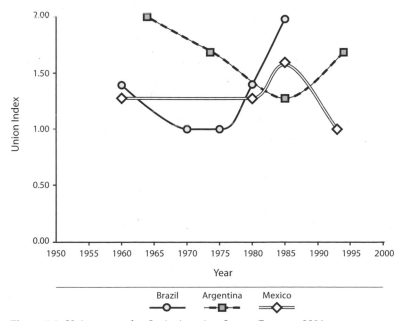

**Figure 6.4.** Union strength—Latin America. *Source:* Caraway 2006.

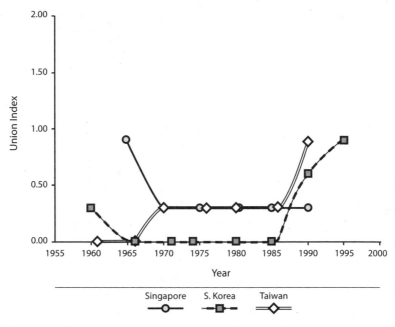

**Figure 6.5.** Union strength—East Asia. *Source:* Caraway 2006.

corporation of labor in the 1930s and 1940s. In Argentina and Brazil, this incorporation took place in the 1940s, and in Mexico, Lázaro Cárdenas brought the labor movement under his wing in the 1930s (Collier and Collier 2002). The level of inducements and constraints that the state offered to labor varied from country to country, but the common thread was that repression was no longer the primary means of controlling labor (Collier and Collier 1979). This model of incorporation corresponds to what Stepan (1978) referred to as inclusionary corporatism. The combination of the production of relatively high value-added goods with protected local markets sustained the populist bargain between the state, capital, and labor for many years. Although these populist coalitions later broke apart in Argentina (1966) and Brazil (1964), and the military dictatorships that came to power moved to exclude labor (O'Donnell 1973), the crucial point is that populism resulted in high levels of unionization, compared with those of other developing countries (Rama and Artecona 2002). In addition, the level at which bargaining is conducted is higher than in other developing countries (International Labor Office 1997; Kuruvilla 1996).

With respect to political inclusion, Argentine unions remained a political force even under repressive regimes. Although military governments in Argentina prohibited links between unions and Peronist parties and tried to weaken single-union bargaining, unions continued to be a political presence and were "unusually powerful" between 1955 and 1983 (Drake 1996; James 1988; McGuire 1997, 270–71). Unions were initially in a weaker position in Brazil. Although prohibited from having links to political parties for most of the period, electoral competition between 1945 and 1964 gave unions some leverage in the political arena (Kaufman 1979). After the military coup in 1964, as government intervention increased and collective protests became riskier, labor maintained its position to some extent because the "dictatorship promoted industrialization, maintained corporatist unions, and allowed limited political party and electoral activity" (Drake 1996, 31; Mericle 1977). In the late 1970s and 1980s the labor movement became more assertive and fostered the formation of the Workers' Party (Keck 1992). In Mexico, the labor movement developed a close relationship with the ruling party, the PRI, and received a variety of socioeconomic benefits in exchange for backing the regime during crises and for supporting the PRI in elections (Middlebrook 1995). From the 1980s on, however, union power eroded steadily as the PRI distanced itself from unions (Cook 1995).

Union density has also been relatively high in the Latin American cases. Argentine unions began with the highest levels of union density, but over time density decreased from about 40 percent in the late 1960s to just over 20 percent in the 1990s (Rama and Artecona 2002). In Brazil, union membership grew even after the dictatorship came to power, although it remained relatively constant at around 25 percent of the economically active population. In the late 1970s and 1980s union density began to rise (Keck 1992). Mexico's relatively high union density peaked in the 1980s at about 35 percent and then declined significantly in the 1990s (Rama and Artecona 2002).

Bargaining institutions are relatively centralized, although the extent of centralization varies, in the three Latin American countries. In Argentina, collective bargaining was conducted nationally at the industry level between employers and one officially recognized union as the bargaining agent, with bargaining agreements applicable to all workers in the industry, whether unionized or not, for most of the period under consideration

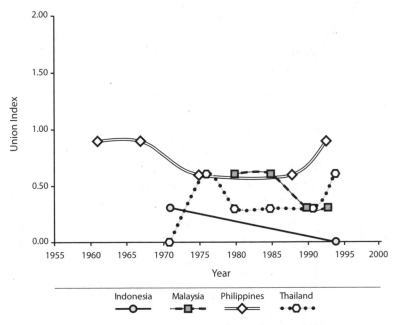

**Figure 6.6.** Union strength—Southeast Asia. *Source:* Caraway 2006.

(1950 to early 1990s) (Córdova 1984b; James 1988). Unions in Brazil, banned from having direct links to other unions, were structured by craft and industry within each state, so they were more fragmented than in Argentina. Although there was no unifying confederation to bring together disparate elements of the labor movement, unions were given a monopoly over representation of workers in their industry within a given geographic territory (Mericle 1977). The law prohibited enterprise (plant-level) unions, and with the exception of the years between 1964 and 1977, most negotiations took place on an industry-wide basis; collective bargains applied to all workers in the industry in the geographic unit, whether organized or not; and all workers in the industry or profession were required to pay a union tax. In Mexico, plant-level bargaining predominated, although some agreements covered entire branches of the economy, such as metallurgy and textiles, and coordination in bargaining between plants in the same federations resulted in highly centralized bargaining outcomes in sectors such as steel and automobiles (Bronstein and Córdova 1984; Córdova 1984b; O'Connell 1999; Roxborough and Bizberg 1983). Unions also frequently inserted security clauses in collective agreements which gave unions control over recruitment (Córdova 1984a), with obvious implications for feminization.

In contrast to Latin America, East Asian governments have always excluded labor: the political environment in East Asia has been far more hostile to labor than in Latin America, and unions have had less room to maneuver politically. In Taiwan the Kuomintang implanted an exclusionary regime before the popular sector mobilized, but in Korea and Singapore the state repressed leftist labor movements (Deyo 1989, 1990; Koo 2001). Although the intensity and level of repression varied both across time and between countries, "labor has always been an object of control and exclusion and has never been considered a major political ally or constituency" (Koo 2001, 5–6). During most of the period from World War II to the late 1980s, state-backed unions had a monopoly of representation in Taiwan and Singapore and a near monopoly in South Korea. South Korea is unique in that a dynamic independent labor movement emerged in the 1980s and played an important role in the democratic transition. Democratization in South Korea and Taiwan in the 1980s and 1990s softened but did not overturn labor's relative exclusion (Chu 1996; Koo 2001, 2000). Union density presents a mixed picture in East Asia. Although union density was much higher in Singapore and Taiwan than in South Korea, this is because the ruling regimes chose a more corporatist method of controlling labor.[8] In Taiwan in particular, increases in density reflected rising membership from self-employed craftspeople who joined unions in order to obtain insurance.[9] Bargaining in all three countries took place primarily at the enterprise level, and in Singapore the range of issues subject to bargaining was extremely narrow.

Once again, Southeast Asia presents a more varied picture. In the worst periods of repression, labor exclusion was just as severe as in the East Asian cases. Even in the cases where labor was relatively free to mobilize, it was in a weak political position (Deyo 1997). For the most part, labor movements in the region were isolated from political parties. Union density was low, with unions in Malaysia and the Philippines organizing about 10 percent of the labor force, and in Indonesia and Thailand less than 5 percent (Rama and Artecona 2002). Collective bargaining took place primarily at the enterprise level, was weakly institutionalized, and covered few workers. Southeast Asian unions have much in common, but there have been important differences in the extent of political repression, both between countries and over time within countries.

In the Philippines the left was crushed in the 1950s, but an active and independent labor movement persisted in the 1950s and 1960s (Lambert 1990; Wurfel 1959). Ferdinand Marcos repressed the remaining elements of the labor movement after the declaration of martial law in 1972, adopting an exclusionary form of corporatism (West 1997). By the mid-1980s, however, the Philippines had developed the most radical and dynamic labor movement in Southeast Asia, and after Corazon Aquino came to power in 1986, formal restrictions on labor in the Philippines eased (Dejillas 1994). Labor unions in Indonesia in the 1950s and 1960s had close relationships to political parties (Tedjasukmana 1959), but the Suharto regime eviscerated the leftist unions in the late 1960s and forced all remaining unions into a state-backed federation in 1973. This exclusionary form of corporatism remained in place until Suharto's fall in 1998 (Hadiz 1997). In Malaysia the colonial regime killed off leftist leaders in the 1940s and 1950s, and after independence in 1957 the state neither embraced nor repressed the remaining moderate unions until it began to tighten controls over labor in the mid-1960s, making strikes more difficult and imposing strict limitations on the content of collective agreements (Grace 1990; Jomo and Todd 1994). In electronics, unionization was banned entirely until the late 1980s, and even then, only enterprise unions were permitted. In Thailand, unions were banned for most of the 1950s and 1960s, and political repression was especially severe under the regime of Field Marshal Sarit Dhanarajata, 1958–63 (Brown and Frenkel 1993). During a brief political opening in the early 1970s, labor organization exploded, but a military coup in 1976 resulted in a brief bout of repression, and conservative forces took over the labor movement. Since the 1980s, Thai governments have not had close relations with unions, but with the exception of a brief period following the 1991 coup, neither has the state cracked down on them (Hewison and Brown 1994; Mabry and Srisermbhok 1985).

## A Statistical Test of the Impact of Union Strength and Supply Factors

To assess the impact of union strength on gendered patterns of industrialization, I conducted a series of statistical tests. The data set has 1,154 observations, spanning the late 1950s to the mid-1990s. Each observation corresponds to an industrial sector $j$ for a particular year $t$ in a country $i$. The models presented explain changes in women's employment or the female share of employment in sector $j$ as a function of union strength, capital intensity, and country-level controls. The dependent variable, the share of female employment and feminization, is operationalized as the percent of female employment in a sector or the log of total female employment. The main independent variables include union strength, capital intensity1, capital intensity2, total employment, and sector dummies.[10]

In addition to these independent variables, I ran specifications that included variables affecting the supply of female labor. Cultural differences between countries could adversely affect women's capacity to participate in work outside the home, either directly through outright prohibition or indirectly through poor education and high fertility. I thus ran the model with three additional variables: fertility, measured as the total fertility rate; female labor force participation (FLFP), measured as the percentage of women in the labor force; and education, measured as the average years of schooling for women aged fifteen.[11] Fertility is expected to have a negative effect on feminization, since higher fertility makes women less appealing employees and limits the number of years that they are available to work. Conversely, education should make women more attractive to employers and encourage feminization. Female labor force participation rates are also expected to have a positive impact on feminization, since higher participation rates indicate that fewer cultural obstacles prevent women's involvement in economic activities. Fertility rates were in decline and education levels were improving in all of the countries, although the levels of fertility and education varied considerably among them. In most of the countries, female labor force participation rates also revealed a steady upward trend, though again, the rates differed from country to country.

Model I tests the various hypotheses with a simple OLS regression of the natural log of the share of female employment in a sector on union strength, the supply variables, and sectoral dummies to control for sector-specific effects. The model explains 65 percent of the variation in women's share of employment, and unions have a negative and statistically significant impact (see Table 6.1). All the supply variables are statistically significant and have an impact in the expected direction, with the exception of education. Although statistically significant, the coefficient for education is negative. The model confirms all the hypotheses except that for education.

Another estimation strategy takes advantage of the cross-sectional panel structure of the data to explain the changes in patterns of women's em-

**Table 6.1.** Model I: Determinants of women's employment

| Variable | Without supply variables | | With supply variables | |
|---|---|---|---|---|
| | Coefficient | S.e. | Coefficient | S.e. |
| Union strength | −0.103*** | 0.007 | −0.073*** | 0.007 |
| Female labor force part. | | | .212*** | 0.04 |
| Fertility | | | −0.039*** | 0.003 |
| Years of education | | | −0.014*** | 0.003 |
| Constant | 0.391*** | 0.018 | 0.524*** | 0.032 |
| R-square | 0.659 | | 0.723 | |
| Adjusted R-square | 0.652 | | 0.716 | |
| F-test | F (24, 1129) = 91.07 | | F (27, 1126) = 108.85 | |
| N | 1,154 | | 1,154 | |

*Source:* See Statistical Appendix.
*Note:* Unstandardized coefficients; $p$ values indicated by *, **, and *** for values less than 0.1, 0.05, and 0.01 respectively.

ployment. Table 6.2 presents two cross-sectional time series models with random effects for country and year which test the relationship between union strength and feminization. The models use the natural log of total female employment as the dependent variable. In Model II the independent variables are total employment, capital intensity, union strength, lagged (past) female employment, and the square of the lagged variable. The auto-regressive lag and the quadratic term were included, since past levels of female employment could have a strong impact on future female employment, and that effect might be nonlinear. Again, the coefficients for union strength and capital intensity (both measures) are negative and statistically significant. Total employment is also significant and has a strongly positive impact on women's employment. The coefficient for lagged female employment is negative but significant in only one of the specifications, while the quadratic term is positive and consistently significant. This indicates strong resistance to initial feminization but more rapid incorporation afterward—although that conclusion must be treated with caution, given the low significance of lagged female employment. Both fertility and education are statistically significant. The coefficient for fertility is negative, as expected, but the coefficient for education is negative as well, contrary to expectations. The FLFP rate changes signs and is significant only when the first capital-intensity measure is used.

Although Model II is helpful to an understanding of the impact of unions when employment is increasing, assessing the impact of unions when em-

**Table 6.2.** Models II and III: Determinants of women's employment

| | Model II | | | | Model III | | | | |
|---|---|---|---|---|---|---|---|---|---|
| Total employment | 0.716*** (.023) | 0.713*** (.023) | 0.721*** (.021) | 0.710*** (.02) | 1.142*** (.016) | 1.13*** (.017) | 1.142*** (.016) | 1.142*** (.016) | 1.132*** (.016) |
| Capital intensity1 | -0.143*** (.028) | -0.145*** (.028) | -0.153*** (.029) | | -0.069*** (.018) | -0.074*** (.018) | -0.069*** (.018) | -0.074*** (.018) | |
| Capital intensity2 | | | | -0.184*** (.026) | | -0.065*** (.016) | | -0.065*** (.016) | -0.087*** (.016) |
| Lagged female employment | -0.102* (.06) | -0.095 (.060) | -0.096 (.061) | -0.083 (.061) | 0.302*** (.039) | 0.294*** (.038) | 0.302*** (.039) | 0.305*** (.039) | 0.306*** (.038) |
| Lagged female emp squared | 0.028*** (.004) | 0.028*** (.004) | 0.027*** (.004) | 0.027*** (.004) | 0.069*** (.006) | 0.070*** (.006) | 0.069*** (.006) | 0.071*** (.006) | 0.070*** (.006) |
| Lagged total employment | | | | | -0.393*** (.061) | -0.372*** (.062) | -0.393*** (.061) | -0.349*** (.063) | -0.348*** (.063) |
| Lagged total emp. × lagged fem emp. | | | | | -0.067*** (.008) | -0.068*** (.008) | -0.067*** (.008) | -0.071*** (.008) | -0.070*** (.008) |
| Union | -0.313*** (.066) | -0.277*** (.069) | -0.311*** (.041) | -0.291*** (.041) | -0.05** (.025) | -0.044 (.033) | -0.05** (.025) | -0.029 (.026) | -0.023 (.026) |
| FLFP rate | | .729** (.231) | -0.026 (.249) | | | | | 0.054 (.141) | -0.297* (.152) |
| Total fertility rate | | | -0.065*** (.024) | -0.144*** (.026) | | | | -0.035** (.014) | -0.073*** (.016) |
| Years of education | | | -0.067*** (.014) | -0.086*** (.014) | | | | -0.023*** (.009) | -0.033*** (.009) |
| Constant | 0.507 (.324) | 0.408 (.329) | .804** (.332) | 1.342*** (.332) | -0.828** (.334) | -0.851** (.341) | -0.851** (.342) | -0.845** (.342) | -0.561 (.343) |
| R-square (within) | 0.852 | 0.852 | 0.851 | 0.851 | 0.944 | 0.944 | 0.944 | 0.944 | 0.944 |
| R-square (between) | 0.9 | 0.92 | 0.944 | 0.972 | 0.991 | 0.992 | 0.992 | 0.993 | 0.997 |
| R-square (overall) | 0.871 | 0.872 | 0.877 | 0.880 | 0.955 | 0.955 | 0.955 | 0.955 | 0.956 |
| N | 918 | 918 | 918 | 918 | 918 | 918 | 918 | 918 | 918 |

*Source:* See Statistical Appendix.
*Note:* Unstandardized coefficients, standard errors in parenthesis; $p$ values indicated by *, **, and *** for values less than 0.1, 0.05, and 0.01 respectively.

ployment is contracting is also important, and Model III captures this dynamic. Model III introduces a lag term of total employment and an interaction term between lagged total employment and lagged female employment, which permits speculation about the potential impact of a contraction of employment. The coefficients for both lagged total employment and the interaction term between lagged total employment and lagged female employment are negative and statistically significant regardless of the capital-intensity measure used in the analysis, indicating that a contraction in employment results in a loss of female employment. The decline in women's employment is smaller than the increases secured when employment expanded, however, which suggests that although women lose jobs during an economic contraction, their incorporation is resilient. In this model, the coefficients for lagged female employment and the square of lagged female employment are both positive and statistically significant, showing that the larger the share of women employed in the past, the larger it will be in the future. In other words, there is some path dependence at work in determining women's overall shares of employment. Yet the union variable is significant in only one of the four specifications of this model. The supply variables achieve good levels of statistical significance, with the exception of the FLFP rate when the first capital-intensity measure is used. Fertility and education have negative coefficients, and the coefficient for the FLFP rate switches signs between the two specifications.

The findings related to unions, fertility, and education were robust across the three models. The impact of FLFP rates was mixed because it was highly sensitive to the specification of the models, and substantively, its impact vacillated between positive and negative. The negative relationship between education and feminization is surprising and suggests that higher levels of education do not necessarily facilitate women's entry into manufacturing work. It is likely that education is a threshold variable—employers seek out a certain minimal level of education, but more education beyond that does not make women workers more appealing employees. Of course, women with higher levels of education are better equipped to find more remunerative employment in other parts of the economy and may choose to avoid the drudgery of a factory job in favor of less taxing work elsewhere.

The effect of the union variable was strongest in Model I and Model II and weaker in Model III. Part of the reason for this weakness may be related to a hierarchical modeling problem. Union strength was assessed at the country level rather than at the sectoral level, since union data rarely correspond precisely to the ISIC categories for classifying employment in manufacturing. Data for the three indicators in the union index could be found for some sectors but not for others. The differences between country and sectoral measures of union strength for most of the Asian countries are minimal during the bulk of the period under examination, but for the Latin American cases, especially Mexico, the differences could be substantial. Sectoral measures of union strength would probably have produced stronger results for the union variable in these cases. For example, the textile industry in Mexico was surprisingly masculine—women's share of employment was only 25 percent in 1985—given that strong feminization had occurred in other labor-intensive sectors. This fact becomes less puzzling, however, when the strength of unions in the sector is taken into account. The textile sector is one of the most highly unionized in Mexico and has negotiated collective agreements that cover the entire industry (Zazueta and de la Peña 1984).[12] The sectors that feminized most strongly were in the *maquilas,* where unions were comparatively weak.

To assess further the robustness of the union variable, I ran Models II and III using employment in all manufacturing rather than sectoral employment. In the previous analyses, each case was one sector in one year in one country. In these models, each case is one year in one country. Since the union variable is no longer tied to sectoral employment data, these models are not affected by a hierarchical modeling problem. Models IV and V are identical to Models II and III except for the omission of the capital-intensity variable, which was tied to sectors. In spite of the much smaller sample size (fifty-one cases), the coefficients for the union variable are statistically significant and the effect remains negative (see Table 6.3). The coefficient for union strength is also larger than in the sectoral model.

## Conclusion

Differences in gendered patterns of industrialization can be explained by the balance of employment between labor-intensive and capital-intensive sectors, employment growth, the strength of labor unions, and fertility. The trend over time—feminization versus masculinization—is best explained

**Table 6.3.** Models IV and V: Determinants of women's employment, county-based

| Variable | Model IV | Model V |
|---|---|---|
| Total employment | 1.13*** | 1.13*** |
| | (.038) | (.033) |
| Lagged female employment | −0.153 | .851 |
| | (.467) | (.826) |
| Square or lagged female employment | .006 | -0.076 |
| | (.019) | (.079) |
| Union | −0.552*** | −0.325*** |
| | (.076) | (.083) |
| Lagged total employment | | −1.928* |
| | | (1.117) |
| Lagged total employment × lagged female employment | | 0.111 |
| | | (.089) |
| Constant | −1.47 | 5.972 |
| | (2.812) | (3.961) |
| R-square (within) | 0.965 | 0.963 |
| R-square (between) | 0.967 | 0.989 |
| R-square (overall) | 0.954 | 0.971 |
| N | 51 | 51 |

*Source:* See Statistical Appendix.
*Note:* Unstandardized coefficients, standard errors in parentheses; $p$ values indicated by *, **, and *** for values less than 0.1, 0.05, and 0.01 respectively.

by the balance of employment between sectors. Since primary EOI encourages employment growth in labor-intensive sectors relative to capital-intensive sectors, there is a strong relationship between EOI and feminization. As EOI matures, however, masculinization usually ensues, since employment usually expands more rapidly in capital-intensive sectors. ISI, in contrast, usually, but not always, leads to masculinization, since it tends to generate more employment in capital-intensive sectors. In addition, the data demonstrate that employment growth has consistent and dramatic positive effects on women's share of employment.

This finding about the positive impact of employment growth ties in nicely with the arguments about stickiness, spillover, and snowballing made in Chapter 4. Employment growth not only increases demand for labor but also facilitates the unsettling of established gender divisions of labor. Employers that expand production can shift women into previously male jobs without firing male workers, and when job growth occurs in new industries, employers have far more flexibility in determining the gendered allocation of work. They can hire women without displacing men—though the extent to which they can do so depends on the strength of unions as well.

Although the overall trend of gendered employment can be explained by the type of industrialization pursued, women's share of sectoral employment varied considerably between countries. Union strength and fertility explained some of these differences, and both variables had consistent and substantively interesting effects on cross-national patterns in women's employment. Strong unions resulted in lower shares of female employment and slowed the pace of feminization, and a high fertility rate negatively affected feminization and women's share of employment.

Perhaps most important, the analysis offers support for the contention that demand-based explanations and labor market institutions have a stronger overall effect on feminization than cultural factors do. The weakness of the female labor force participation variable in particular suggests that cultural limits on such participation are malleable. In other words, increased demand for female labor, combined with weak unions, allows women to be pulled rapidly into the labor market in spite of cultural obstacles. Labor-excluding authoritarian developmental states in Asia and inclusionary populist politics in Latin America created distinct gendered legacies. Latin America had lower shares of female employment in manufacturing not only because it followed a different path of industrialization but also because it had stronger unions.

# Conclusion

Industrialization in developing countries since World War II has created millions of manufacturing jobs in economies previously dominated by agriculture and extractive industries. What is often overlooked by the scholars who focus on this economic transformation is that industrialization not only produces manufacturing jobs but also generates distinct opportunities for men and for women. The gendered character of industrialization is evident not only in the demand for labor but also in labor market outcomes. Since capitalists conceive of labor as a gendered input and match available jobs to *gendered* workers—not abstract labor—their hiring practices not only affect whether men or women are given opportunities to work but also construct gendered labor markets. The gendered construction of labor markets has immense consequences not only for whether men and women have access to jobs but also for the kinds of jobs that they can hope to attain. This book has explored the movement of the tectonic plates in global capitalism which generated feminization in many parts of the world, and it has examined the ways whereby domestic political economies and social structures mediate the extent to which capitalists can hire men and women. By shedding light on these processes, it not only illuminates the causal forces behind different gendered paths of development; it also offers explanations for why the massive incorporation of women into formal-sector work in manufacturing has had such a limited effect on diminishing gender inequalities in labor markets.

## Industrialization as a Gendered Process

Industrialization, through its effects on the balance of sectoral employment in the economy, dramatically affects the mobilization of male and female labor, with some types of industrialization leading to feminization and others to masculinization. My analysis partially confirms the claim by feminization scholars that EOI is strongly associated with feminization. EOI encourages the growth of employment in labor-intensive sectors in its early stages, and it is this rapid expansion of employment in labor-intensive rather than capital-intensive sectors that prompts feminization. Since EOI becomes more capital intensive as it matures, however, masculinization followed on the heels of feminization in the East Asian NICs as well as the Mexican *maquiladoras*. In contrast, ISI in its early and later stages tends to be more capital-intensive than primary EOI and therefore leads to higher shares of male employment and little if any feminization.

Yet countries that pursue similar kinds of industrialization are not mere carbon copies of one another with respect to women's presence in manufacturing work, and this is true even in comparisons of the same sector across national contexts. Thus, although there is a strong association between the path of industrialization and gendered trends over time—whether women's share of employment rises or falls—actual shares of female employment vary widely across countries that have pursued similar industrialization policies.

My study explains this diversity in gendered outcomes in two ways. First, there are mediating institutions in national political economies which shape the gendered effects of the sectoral shifts in employment generated by industrialization. This book has placed particular emphasis on the impact of unions in reducing the incorporation of women into manufacturing work. The relationship between labor strength and more masculine manufacturing workforces suggests that it is not so much the alleged docility of women that drives feminization but rather the docility of unions. Feminization was strongest and women's shares of sectoral employment were highest in countries where labor was organizationally weak and excluded from political power. In contexts where organized male workers are feeble and unions pose little threat to employers, women's docility, whether real or imagined, is not an especially important added benefit. Indeed, the impact of women's docility should be greater in contexts where organized male labor is relatively strong.

The gendered political economy approach shows that attention should be placed on the gendered impact of the mediating institutions that impede the flow of women to factory work. When male-dominated unions are weak, there are fewer obstacles to feminization, as employers have a freer hand to hire and fire, to organize production as they see fit, and to set wages. Thus, an unintended consequence of labor-excluding authoritarian regimes in Asia has been to facilitate feminization. Conversely, the populist legacy of relatively strong unions in much of Latin America has resulted in lower shares of manufacturing work for women. The Latin American countries in my cross-national analysis had lower shares of female employment and feminized less not only because labor-intensive sectors tended to constitute a lower proportion of total employment than in the Asian cases but also because unions were stronger.

Second, this study shows how a host of other mediating institutions and labor supply factors facilitated feminization. Institutionally, the case study of Indonesia revealed how the authoritarian state demobilized unions, political parties, and religious organizations and how it only weakly enforced protective legislation, which assured that employers could hire women. Improvements in education, reductions in fertility, and increased labor force participation rates also made women more available and appealing workers. The cross-national statistical analysis further demonstrated that of these supply factors, fertility had the most direct effect on feminization: reductions in fertility led to increases in women's participation in manufacturing work.

The gendered political economy approach thus offers insights that help to explain notable variations in the gendered development trajectories between countries. In the Philippines, for example, there are lower shares of female employment than in the other Southeast Asian countries in this study. Part of the reason for this outcome is that the Philippines moved more weakly, and later, into EOI than the rest of the region, but these lower levels of female employment are also related to the existence of stronger unions and the relatively high fertility levels of Filipino women. Because of the influence of the Roman Catholic Church, the Philippines may be the only country in the region that never implemented a comprehensive family planning program. Although fertility rates declined from 6 to 3.6 percent between 1965 and 2000, this is a slower rate than in the rest of the region; and of the five Southeast Asian countries studied in this book, fertility rates in the Philippines remain the highest (Hirschman 2002).

Taiwan and South Korea, while pursuing similar industrialization paths, also had somewhat different gendered outcomes. Although both feminized, women's share of employment was and remains higher in Taiwan than in South Korea. Once again, this difference can be partially but not entirely explained by subtle differences in industrialization policies: South Korea moved much more vigorously into capital-intensive investments than Taiwan did in the 1970s. But this difference in industrialization policy cannot explain sectoral-level differences in women's share of employment. Differences in mediating institutions are probably not at the root of this disparity, as both countries were led by authoritarian developmental states that repressed labor during most of the time under consideration. Rather, some important differences in the supply characteristics of women probably slowed the pace of feminization in South Korea and consequently led to lower shares of female employment. Married women in South Korea have far lower labor force participation rates than those in Taiwan, partly because of different industrial structures. Small, geographically dispersed enterprises in Taiwan have enabled married women to continue to hold jobs more easily than their counterparts in South Korea, where large enterprises concentrated in large cities prevail (Brinton, Lee, and Parish 1995). The organizational features of industries therefore have a strong influence on women's continued participation in work, and as labor markets tighten, married women's participation becomes crucial for sustaining levels of female employment.

I am cautious, however, about making overly bold claims of a direct relationship that holds across national contexts between supply factors and women's share of employment. The analysis of Indonesia, for example, stressed improvements in women's education rather than the actual level of women's education, and the cross-national statistical analysis found that higher levels of education did not positively affect women's share of employment. Although a certain minimal level of education is a prerequisite for employment in modern factories, and although improved education for women would also make them more attractive to potential employers, countries with higher educational levels for women do not have higher shares of female employment in manufacturing. Thailand, which has perhaps the highest share of female employment in manufacturing in the world, does not have the highest level of female education. Since much industrial employment requires fairly low levels of education, it may be a threshold variable: employers in many sectors may require a minimal level of education but may not wish to hire workers with higher educational credentials because they would be more expensive.

Female labor force participation rates also had inconsistent effects across countries in the sense that higher rates were not associated with higher levels of female employment in manufacturing. FLFP rates are important to the extent that women's engagement in work is sufficient to satisfy increased demand by capital. Of course, higher female FLFP rates are more propitious for feminization than low ones, but feminization could occur even when FLFP rates are low, although they would slow down feminization if growth in demand for female labor is rapid. Fertility, in contrast, was found to have a more direct effect. Given the costs associated with maternity leave, lower fertility makes women more attractive to hire. In Southeast Asia the fastest feminization and the highest shares of female employment occurred in the countries with the lowest fertility rates.

## The Dynamics of Feminization

Through analysis of the interaction among labor supply, mediating institutions, and capital's demand for gendered labor, my study of Indonesia highlighted the dynamics of the feminization process. By showing how structural forces are mediated through features of the domestic political economy, it provided a richer understanding of the gendered dynamics of industrialization and illuminated a series of gendered processes at work in global capitalism. What are the the processes through which feminization was enacted?

First, although changes in labor supply and mediating institutions were important, the stimulus for feminization in Indonesia was the change in capital's demand for women workers. Once feminization takes off, the potential for feedback effects arises (Pierson 1993; Thelen 1999). These feedback effects could be both positive and negative. In Indonesia, demand for women's labor expanded; fertility rates continued to decline; education levels continued climbing; and women's labor force participation rates more than kept up with demand. Feedback effects were largely positive in Indonesia, which explains the sustained nature of feminization there.

Second, foreign capital has the potential to alter national gendered practices. Much of the research on feminization has focused on multinational corporations and their strong preference for hiring women workers. In Indonesia I found mixed support for this contention. In some sectors, such as textiles, there was not a noticeable difference between domestic and foreign capital, and some foreigners, in particular the Japanese, employed far more men than local factories. In other sectors, such as footwear, garments, and some electronics subsectors, foreign capital did indeed rely more on female labor than did Indonesian capital. In these sectors, both domestic and foreign capital preferred to hire female labor, but women's share of employment in the foreign firms was higher. When foreign capital flooded into the garment, footwear, and electronics industries in the late 1980s and early 1990s, this stronger preference for female labor increased the degree of feminization that occurred in Indonesia. In cases where foreign capital accounts for a large proportion of employment in a sector, and if that foreign capital has a stronger preference for female labor than local capital does, then the entry of foreign investors into an industrial terrain can generate dynamics that increase the degree of feminization taking place.

Third, sectoral feminization heightens the degree of feminization that occurs. In Indonesia, feminization in manufacturing as a whole was not simply the result of the expansion of labor-intensive sectors; in fact, many of the labor-intensive sectors that spurred EOI actually relied more on male labor in the 1970s than in the 1990s. Rather, many employers in labor-intensive sectors that had employed fairly large proportions of men in their workforces began to change their gendered hiring preferences. Sectoral feminization involved two processes: first, the shift of jobs from men to women in old factories; second, the establishment of new factories that hired many women from the beginning. The most labor-intensive sectors feminized most strongly—conceivably the result of the greater level of competition in these sectors, but this explanation fails to account for the timing of the change. These sectors had always been labor intensive, and since labor-intensive sectors are generally competitive because of ease of entry, employers had long faced competitive markets.

To understand sectoral feminization, one must take into account the specific logic behind employers' decisions to hire men or women—which brings us to the fourth dynamic: the impact of gendered discourses of work on gendered innovations in the labor process. Employers hold well-developed views about the relative talents and benefits of male versus female labor, and these beliefs shape the way they organize production. The association of gender, jobs, and productivity means that in efforts to get more output from their workers, managers resort to gendered innovations in the labor process. Gendered innovations are more likely to occur in sectors that are competitive and in which women make up more than a marginal share of the production workforce. Consequently, labor-intensive sectors are far more likely to feminize than capital-intensive sectors. The highly male-intensive and capital-intensive sectors are on a path that is extremely unlikely to lead to feminization.

Finally, stickiness and spillover dynamics highlight the interconnections across the different waves of feminization that occurred in Indonesia. Since gender divisions of labor on the shop floor are "sticky," established firms face higher barriers to feminization than new employers. For this reason, growth in employment is crucial, as it allows existing employers to hire women without firing men, and new firms can simply employ women from the start. Spillover effects, in contrast, push the feminization process forward. The expansion of women's employment in previous waves positively influenced women's employment in later waves as domestic investors copied successful feminizers, both domestic and foreign.

The dynamics outlined here are important not only for what they reveal about how feminization takes place but because they have implications for the potential of feminization to overturn or lessen gender inequalities in employment.

## In/Equality

Gender-based pay inequalities in manufacturing generally take two forms. The first and most blatant is the payment of lower wages to women than to men performing the same or similar work. The second is the denial to women of the more highly remunerated jobs, either through job segregation on the shop floor or through exclusion from employment in capital-intensive sectors. Feminization, as a process that expands women's integration into waged labor, should ameliorate some of these inequalities. Indeed, Marx fully expected that the gender division of labor and the gender inequalities that resulted from it would diminish as more and more women were drawn into the workforce. Similarly, neoclassical economic theory predicts that as the demand for female labor increases, as it does during feminization, the price of female labor should also increase relative to male labor.

In contrast to these optimistic projections, most feminist theorists are more pessimistic. Feminization theorists place a great deal of emphasis on the importance of women's lower wages in driving export-oriented and labor-intensive sectors to seek out women workers. One implication of this explanation of feminization is that women are likely to make few inroads into capital-intensive sectors. Another implication is that if feminization leads to an equalization of male and female wages in labor-intensive sectors, employers will diminish their reliance on women workers.[1] Whereas Marx and neoclassical economists argued that the mobilization of women workers would lead to a diminishment of gender inequalities, feminists countered that since only highly competitive sectors that needed to reduce wage costs would hire women, gender inequalities would not be reduced, because women enter feminized ghettos in the labor market rather than the high-pay sectors. How does Indonesia's experience bear out these contrary expectations?

Perhaps the place to start is with the assertion by feminists that the key dynamic driving feminization is the wage impulse. While finding some support for the argument that women's lower wages can explain why labor-intensive sectors are more likely to hire women, I found the causal weight given to wages questionable. Women in Indonesia, as in all countries, receive lower average wages than men, even when human capital and occupational categories are controlled for (Manning 1998). Average wage differences are wide for two reasons: first, women are concentrated in low-pay sectors; and second, within sectors, firms that employ high ratios of men to women tend to pay higher average wages than those that employ high ratios of women to men. Although women's average wages in Indonesia are indeed lower than men's average wages, one notable finding of this study has that many Indonesian employers in labor-intensive firms—where the wage pressures should be the strongest—paid men and women the same wages. Wage differences between male-intensive and female-intensive firms were much smaller in labor-intensive than capital-intensive sectors, which means that labor-intensive firms saved little by shifting to women.

Under these circumstances, one would expect employers in labor-intensive industries to shift to a male workforce, yet many of these employers continued to prefer to employ women, even though the array of benefits that women were entitled to receive made them more expensive employees than men. Thus, if only wages are considered, the continued employment of women in labor-intensive sectors in Indonesia is quite puzzling. My study suggests that gendered discourses of work help to explain why labor-intensive firms are willing to employ women at the same wages as men. Since employers attribute a host of positive features to women, and since these ascribed characteristics are believed to result in higher productivity in certain jobs, employers believe that it is more profitable to hire women, even if they are paid the same wages as men.

Nevertheless, the reluctance by employers in capital-intensive sectors to hire women and the consequences of continued wage inequality for men and women at first glance seem to be evidence against the optimism of Marx and neoclassical economists regarding the positive effects of waged work on gender inequalities. But Marx was vague about the time horizon he had in mind for this process, so as long as the wage gap narrows over time, it could be argued that given enough time, his predictions would be borne out. Did feminization in Indonesia result in a narrowing of male-female wage differentials?

Unfortunately, the industrial survey does not collect gender-differentiated wage data. Nevertheless, some inferences can be based on firm-level data and on the industrial survey by comparing male-intensive and female-intensive sectors. The comparison of male-intensive and female-intensive sectors is not the ideal way to proceed because of the ecological fallacy: the distribution of wages between men and women cannot be directly assessed. If there are wage gains within a sector, it is unclear whether men and women shared equally in those gains. Given the high demand for female labor in many sectors and the use of the minimum wage as the standard for base pay, however, it is unlikely that women were excluded from all the wage gains, in particular given that the firm-level data that I collected revealed little wage discrimination between men and women in labor-intensive firms.

Manning's (1998) study of manufacturing wages found that wage inequality between sectors increased during the 1980s. In 1980, with 100 taken as the mean production worker's wage, the difference between the highest and lowest pay sectors (215 for car and car components, and 45 for *kretek* cigarettes), was 170, and by 1992 this figure rose to 267. Manning's study therefore bears out the expectations of feminization theorists. Using a slightly different measure, however, yields different results. I calculated an unweighted mean wage for manufacturing, so each sector was given equal weight regardless of the number of workers employed. This measure is less precise in assessing overall levels of wage inequality, but it is a better measure for evaluating sectoral inequalities. Using the unweighted mean wage, I found a narrowing of sectoral wage differentials. Between 1985 and 1990, the difference between the lowest wage sector, tobacco, and the highest wage sector, industrial chemicals, declined from 214 to 179 to 176. To break down the data even further, I also calculated the ratio of sectoral wages per capita to the unweighted mean for 1985, 1990, and 1995. I then separated the sectors by the level of female intensity—sectors employing 0 to 25 percent women, those employing 25 percent to 50 percent women, and those employing over 50 percent women (see Table C.1). If the ratio increases, it indicates that the sector's wages have improved relative to the mean wage, but if the ratio decreases, the sector's wages have lost ground relative to the mean wage. The ratio of sectoral wages per capita to the unweighted mean wage increased between 1985 and 1995 in six of nine of the most female-intensive sectors, in two of seven of the moderately feminine sectors, and in four of the seven masculine sectors. Of seven of the eight moderately and highly feminine sectors that showed increases in the ratio, the majority of the change occurred between 1990 and 1995.

This analysis should be treated with some caution, as it assumes that women workers have shared the wage gains equally with male workers. Despite their shortcomings, the data do provide some indication that feminization has modestly reduced gender-based wage inequalities in some sectors. Moreover, while most sectors that experienced progress were female intensive, the least impressive gains were in the sectors where men made up 50 to 75 percent of the workers. In fact, most sectors in the middle category underwent a deterioration of relative wages. Tzannatos's (1997) analysis of labor force survey data, which shows an overall increase (i.e., for all economic activities) in women's wages relative to men's wages from 55.6 in 1986 to 60.0 in 1992, supports the analysis as well.

Before concluding that feminization has caused these changes, however, one must consider the independent effect of the minimum wage policy. In 1989 the government passed a minimum wage law, and beginning in 1990 the government began to pay more attention to the implementation of the

**Table C.1.** Ratio of sectoral wages per capita to unweighted mean wage (all manufacturing)

| Sector | 1985 | 1990 | 1995 | Change 1985–1995 |
|---|---|---|---|---|
| 0–25% female | | | | |
| Paper (medium high) | 1.03 | 1.10 | 1.39 | 0.36 |
| Industrial chemicals (high) | 2.56 | 2.25 | 2.12 | −0.44 |
| Rubber (medium low) | 0.81 | 0.76 | 0.70 | −0.12 |
| Nonferrous metals (high) | 0.86 | 1.71 | 1.51 | 0.65 |
| Fabricated metal (medium low) | 1.12 | 0.92 | 1.07 | −0.05 |
| Nonelectrical machinery (medium high) | 1.02 | 1.20 | 1.29 | 0.27 |
| Transportation (high) | 1.49 | 1.42 | 1.59 | 0.09 |
| 25%–50% female | | | | |
| Food (medium high) | 0.73 | 0.73 | 0.87 | 0.14 |
| Beverages (medium high) | 1.32 | 1.23 | 1.09 | −0.23 |
| Leather (low) | 0.63 | 0.53 | 0.64 | 0.01 |
| Wood processing (medium low) | 0.82 | 0.81 | 0.73 | −0.09 |
| Wood products (low) | 0.66 | 0.52 | 0.53 | −0.14 |
| Printing (medium low) | 1.19 | 1.20 | 1.10 | −0.09 |
| Nonmetallic minerals (medium low) | 1.50 | 0.78 | 1.04 | −0.46 |
| >50% female | | | | |
| Tobacco (medium high) | 0.42 | 0.46 | 0.36 | −0.06 |
| Textiles (medium low) | 0.57 | 0.56 | 0.66 | 0.10 |
| Garments (low) | 0.60 | 0.56 | 0.61 | 0.01 |
| Footwear (low) | 0.97 | 1.68 | 0.66 | −0.31 |
| Other chemicals (medium high) | 1.66 | 1.49 | 1.50 | −0.17 |
| Plastic (low) | 0.59 | 0.56 | 0.67 | 0.08 |
| Electronics (medium high) | 1.17 | 1.17 | 1.40 | 0.23 |
| Prof/scientific equip. (medium low) | 0.67 | 0.79 | 0.86 | 0.19 |
| Other manuf. (low) | 0.59 | 0.56 | 0.63 | 0.03 |

*Source:* Biro Pusat Statistik, *Statistik Industri Besar dan Sedang* (various years).
*Note:* Level of each sector's capital intensity is indicated in parentheses.

minimum wage legislation in establishments with twenty-five or more workers. The new legislation required the regular revision of regional minimum wages, with the goal of raising the wage over time to fulfill the minimum physical needs (*kebutuhan fisik mimimal,* or KFM) of a single worker. Real wages began to rise in the early 1990s, which is in part due to the more stringent enforcement of minimum wage legislation. The government took court action against several firms that refused to pay the minimum wage; although the fines were laughably small, the embarrassment and inconvenience of going to court acted as incentives to comply with the law (Manning 1998). In addition, workers began striking in record numbers in the early 1990s, and the main cause of strikes was employers' noncompliance with the minimum wage (Kammen 1997), so over time more employers abided by the legislation rather than deal with the inevitable strike that would result from their violation of the law. Real minimum wages in Jakarta rose 25 percent between 1988 and 1992 and 24 percent between 1992 and 1994. The increase in the legal minimum wage resulted in real gains for workers. Although their pay still did not fulfill the government-defined KFM, by 1994 the minimum wage was 85 percent of the KFM (Manning 1998). In large firms, the addition of incentives, subsidies for food and transportation costs, and overtime would have brought most workers over the KFM standard.

Has feminization or the minimum wage law caused the wage gains experienced by women? Minimum wages tend to benefit the weakest and most poorly paid workers, and as Manning notes (1998, 225), "Minimum wages have probably mainly affected establishments which pay wages at the lower end of the earnings distribution." Female as well as male workers in low-wage sectors should therefore have benefited the most from the implementation of the minimum wage law. Market intervention produced these gains, and it is doubtful that market dynamics (i.e., feminization without the minimum wage policy) would have caused the same level of improvement.

Although on average, women have benefited, they have not shared equally in these wage gains. Tobacco, one of the largest employers of women, has not improved its position relative to either the unweighted mean wage or the highest-paying sector; those working in the electronics industry, which requires higher educational levels, experienced by far the strongest growth in relative wages. And in spite of the wage gains for women, it is important to emphasize that in all but two female intensive sectors (electronics; other chemicals), women's wages are far lower than average wages. The main reason, of course, is the continued closure to women of many capital-intensive industries.

On this count, feminization has ambiguous effects on women. Although employers absorbed female labor with great alacrity and gave women new job opportunities in the formal sector, these opportunities were concentrated in the labor-intensive, low-wage sectors of manufacturing. Most of the higher-paying sectors in Indonesia feminized only modestly if at all. And even though women often earned wages equal to men's wages in the low-pay sectors, men's average wages continued to be higher than women's average wages, since women were excluded from the high-pay sectors. This resistance by capital-intensive firms is puzzling, as the capital-intensive employers could significantly reduce their wage bill by replacing men with women.

Although some of this resistance to hiring women by capital-intensive sectors may have been a result of a belief in women's greater instability as workers, my study has shown that the differences between men's and women's stability were overstated and that many such differences could be explained by sector-specific labor practices and limited promotion tracks for women. Similarly, skill-based explanations were unpersuasive, since men's and women's jobs required similar amounts of training. Differences in worker stability were far greater between sectors than between men and women, and the sectoral case studies demonstrated that given the right kind of labor practices, women had long job tenures. Most employers in labor-intensive sectors adopted turnover-inducing labor practices that resulted in higher turnover for all workers but especially for women. Higher levels of turnover allowed employers to juggle women's maternity leave more effectively than low levels, since employers could safely hire a replacement during the leave and reabsorb the returning worker without bloating the workforce. In contrast, the capital-intensive sectors that adopted turnover-reducing labor practices had far more difficulty cycling women who took maternity leave in and out of the workforce. Women would respond to the incentives for long tenure in the same way as men, and many would undoubtedly return to work after maternity leave. It was women's potential stability rather than their instability that was the real obstacle to employing them in these industries. Given that these sectors paid high wages, employers simply hired men.

It is notable that when capital-intensive sectors do seek out women, they implement turnover-inducing employment practices quite similar to those utilized in labor-intensive sectors. Thus, gender has an independent impact on how employers organize production, and once women are selected as the preferred workforce, employers purposely adopt labor practices that result in shorter work tenures. In addition, as shown in Chapter 5, path dependence is in play in the capital-intensive sectors. Since they employ few women and face less competition, they are far less likely than labor-intensive sectors to adopt feminization as a gendered innovation in the labor process.

Feminization therefore had a decidedly mixed effect on inequality in

Indonesia. Studies of other countries come to similarly disappointing conclusions. While gender-based wage differences in manufacturing narrowed slightly in South Korea, they widened in Hong Kong and Singapore.
Empirical studies show mixed results for Taiwan: some found that the gender pay gap widened others, that it narrowed (Seguino 1997a, 1997b; Berik
2000). In Indonesia the implementation of a minimum wage policy accounts for much of the decrease in the gender wage gap in manufacturing.
The largest reduction in wage inequalities took place between 1990 and
1995, which corresponds perfectly with the first five years of the minimum
wage policy. Women have made few inroads into the capital-intensive sectors that pay high wages, and additional reductions in the gender gap in
wages will depend on women's gaining entry into those sectors. My findings thus lead to fairly pessimistic projections about the potential for
women to break down such barriers. Capital-intensive sectors are less
likely to feminize because of the lower level of competition, the absence
(or scarceness) of women on the shop floor, and the challenges that maternity leaves present to managing the size of the workforce. And capital-
intensive sectors that do hire women tend to adopt turnover-inducing
rather than turnover-reducing strategies. Women in capital-intensive industries thus usually work under conditions similar to those experienced
by women in labor-intensive industries. Gender is so deeply embedded in
the daily practices of production that market mechanisms are unlikely to
remedy these inequalities. In other words, integration into waged work is
necessary but insufficient to overturn the gendered hierarchies present in
the relations and structures of production.

## Further Comparative Implications

In addition to the implications already outlined, I conclude with three
additional and more explicitly comparative implications of this work. The
first is related to cross-national differences in wage inequality between men
and women, the second to how differences in economic growth help to explain gendered patterns of industrialization, and the third to the impact of
culture on women's employment.

My finding that factories in Indonesia paid men and women equal
wages inevitably causes gasps from other scholars. So much of the literature is driven by the causal link between cheap female labor and femi-

nization that this finding is, to say the least, surprising. Yet a closer look at wage studies shows that Indonesia and perhaps Southeast Asia in general exhibit a pattern of wage differentiation unlike that of East Asia, where male-female pay disparities can be extremely large. For example, the research of Bai and Cho (1995) shows that gender-based wage differentials were much sharper in East Asia than in Southeast Asia. Similarly, Standing (1996) compared wages in the Philippines and Malaysia and found that wage disparities for similar classifications of workers were not always severe, though differences were greater in Malaysia than in the Philippines, where the wage gap between men and women in large firms was extremely small. The difference between men's and women's wages in South Korea, however, was one of the widest in the world (Amsden 1989; Standing 1999).

Since the degree of wage discrimination varies across national contexts, the strength of the wage impulse should vary as well. Feminization theorists would lead us to believe that the greater the gender wage gap, the greater the degree of feminization. Given the wider wage disparities between men and women in East Asia, therefore, one would expect employers to hire more women workers there than in Southeast Asia, yet the opposite is the case. To return to a point emphasized repeatedly in this book, there are features in addition to women's lower wages that make them appealing as workers; a careful analysis of national-level institutions and supply factors is also needed to explain variations in women's participation in manufacturing work.

These cross-national differences in gendered paths of industrialization may be partially attributable to variations between countries in the rate of employment growth. The cross-national statistical analysis pointed to the importance of employment growth for feminization. Strong growth in sectoral employment is associated with feminization, but women's share of employment in a sector tends to decline when sectoral employment shrinks. Argentina is a laggard in terms of women's employment in manufacturing not only because capital-intensive sectors are larger and unions are strong but also because industry has stagnated. The case study of Indonesia suggests a number of reasons why employment growth has a positive effect on women's share of employment. It is not simply that employers are forced to hire women because labor markets are tight (Indonesia was and is a labor surplus economy), but rather that when sectors are expanding and hiring new workers, employers have the flexibility to alter gendered divisions of labor on the shop floor. They can hire women without firing men, and new employers can simply start off by hiring primarily women. Rapid expansion of employment, while having positive effects for the employment of all workers, is especially good for women.

The impact of employment growth on the expansion of women's employment in manufacturing, perhaps surprisingly, casts some doubt on cultural explanations for wide disparities between countries in women's share of employment. It is tempting to explain lower shares of female employment in some parts of the world by pointing to cultural practices that restrict women's participation in the workforce. Countries in the Middle East, for example, tend to have very low shares of female employment in manufacturing, and an obvious explanation would be that Islam as practiced in the Middle East restricts women's role in the economy. Certainly this is one important factor in explaining the masculine nature of manufacturing in the region. Yet women's low share of employment there could also be a result of feeble growth in manufacturing employment and the kind of industrialization pursued. As noted by Moghadam (1995, 2), "The limited nature of Middle Eastern women's industrial employment has another cause, and that is the relatively limited depth and scope of industrialization in most of the region, including relatively little foreign direct investment in manufacturing."

One important finding of the Indonesian case study is that foreign manufacturers often relied more heavily on female labor than did local manufacturers, and it was EOI that led to a major burst in employment in labor-intensive sectors and in foreign investment in these industries. It is perhaps unsurprising, then, that the Middle Eastern countries that have experienced employment growth in labor-intensive sectors have the highest shares of female employment in manufacturing in the region. Morocco (36.2 percent in 1982), Tunisia (43.3 percent in 1989), and Turkey (25.2 percent in 1992) have all promoted labor-intensive export manufacturing and have shares of female employment in manufacturing that are comparable to non-Muslim countries (Moghadam 1995, table 8). It is not coincidental that these countries are not major oil exporters and have therefore had to rely more on other engines of growth, suggesting that oil hinders not only democracy (Ross 2001) but also women's access to manufacturing employment. Culture is important, of course—Islam as practiced in Indonesia, for example, has been far more permissive of women's economic participation than in Arab countries. But the experience of Morocco, Tunisia, and Turkey in the Middle East, as well as Bangladesh (Feldman 1992) in South Asia, suggest that structural shifts in the economy can break down cultural barriers to women's employment quite rapidly, which opens the door to other kinds of changes in gender relations in society and politics.

# Statistical Appendix

National statistical agencies in many countries publish industrial surveys with gendered employment data only sporadically, which made it impossible to collect data for the same years in the different countries. When I could, I collected data once for every five years; when I could not, I used whatever was available. Unless otherwise noted, employment data for the cross-national analysis comes from the following years and sources:

## Argentina 1947, 1964, 1974, 1984, 1994

### Sources

> 1947: *IV Censo General de la Nación año 1947,* vol. 2. Buenos Aires: Instituto Nacional de Estadística y Censos.
>
> Remaining years: *Censo Nacional Economico.* Buenos Aires: Instituto Nacional de Estadística y Censos.

## Brazil 1950, 1960, 1970, 1975, 1980, 1985

### Sources

> All years: *Censo Industrial.* Rio de Janeiro: IBGE–Serviço Nacional de Recenseamento.

## Indonesia 1955, 1971, 1993

Sources

All years: *Statistik Industri Besar dan Sedang*. Jakarta: Biro Pusat Statistik.

## Malaysia 1957, 1970, 1975, 1980, 1985, 1990, 1993

Sources

1970, 1980: *Laporan Am Banci Penduduk Malaysia*. Kuala Lumpur: Department of Statistics.

1957, 1975, 1985, 1990: Jamilah Ariffin, "Economic Development, Industrial Trends, and Women Workers in Malaysia." In *Economic Development and Women in the World Community*, ed. K. Roy, C. Tisdell, and H. Blomquist, 59–77. Westport, Conn.: Praeger, 1996.

1993: *ILO Yearbook of Labor Statistics 1996*. Geneva: ILO.

## Mexico 1940, 1960, 1980, 1988, 1993

Sources

All years for national data: *Censo Industrial*. Mexico City: Direccion General de Estadística (INEGI).

For *maquiladora* data: *Estadística de la Industria Maquiladora de Exportación* (1974–1982, 1979–1989, and 1990–1994). Mexico City: INEGI.

## Philippines 1961, 1967, 1975, 1988, 1993

Sources

1961, 1967: *Economic Census of the Philippines*. Manila: Bureau of the Census and Statistics.

1975, 1988: *Census of Establishments*. Manila: National Census and Statistics Office.

1993: *Industry Yearbook of Labor Statistics*. Manila: Bureau of Labor and Employment Statistics.

## Singapore 1965, 1970, 1975, 1980, 1985, 1990

### Sources

1965, 1970, 1975, 1980: *Annual Report of the Ministry of Labor*. Singapore: Ministry of Labor.

1985, 1990: *Yearbook of Labor Statistics 2000*. Geneva: ILO.

## South Korea 1960, 1966, 1971, 1974, 1980, 1985, 1990, 1995

### Sources

1960, 1966: *Census of Mining and Manufacturing*. Seoul: Ministry of Commerce and Industry.

Remaining years: *Year Book of Labor Statistics*. Seoul: Office of Labor Affairs.

## Taiwan 1954, 1961, 1966, 1970, 1976, 1980, 1986, 1990

### Sources

1954, 1961, 1966, 1976, 1986: *General Report on Industry and Commerce Census*. Taipei: Committee of Second Industrial and Commercial Census of Taiwan Province

1970 (October): *Establishment Survey on Employment, Hours, Earnings, and Labor Turnover in Secondary Industries*. Taipei: Taiwan Provincial Labor Force Survey and Research Institute.

1980, 1990: *Yearbook of Earnings and Productivity Statistics*. Taipei: Directorate-General of Budget, Accounting, and Statistics.

## Thailand 1971, 1976, 1980, 1985, 1991, 1994

### Sources

All years: *Report of the Industrial Census (Whole Kingdom)*. Bangkok: National Statistical Office.

# Notes

## Introduction

1. The exceptions are studies of India and the Southern Cone in Latin America, where manufacturing work is more male intensive and EOI has been less significant. Salzinger's (2003) work is another important exception.

2. Medium and large firms include all establishments with more than twenty employees.

3. Much neoclassical economics literature uses women's behavior as the explanation for persistent inequalities and gender divisions in labor markets; the classic text is Becker (1981). Some neoclassical economists prefer to highlight "tastes for discrimination" or statistical discrimination, but ultimately these practices should be weeded out through the market mechanism. See Blau and Ferber (1992) for a useful discussion. In a similar vein, recent attempts to use the "varieties of capitalism" approach (Hall and Soskice 2001) attribute gender segregation in labor markets to statistical discrimination by employers and women's lack of investment in particular types of skills, which is presented as a rational response to their future role as childbearers and caregivers (Estévez-Abe 2005; Estévez-Abe, Iversen, and Soskice 2001).

4. The specific definition of patriarchy varies among theorists, but for my purposes the main point is that it is a system based on dynamics that are distinct from those of capitalism, in which men dominate women.

5. See Barrett (1988), Miles (1986), and Vogel (1995) for useful overviews of this literature. The Marxist-feminist literature is vast, and this discussion by necessity elides some of the important differences between various approaches in order to make the larger point.

## 1. The Gendered Political Economy Approach

1. The literature here is too extensive to discuss in detail, but for important book-length studies about women workers in export industries, see Chant and McIlwaine (1995), Cravey (1998), Diamond (1979), Elias (2004), Fernandez-Kelly (1983a), Heyzer (1988), Joekes (1982), Kim (1997), Kothari and Nabasing (1996), Kung (1994), Lee (1998), Ong (1987), Salaff (1981), Salzinger (2003), Sklair (1993), Tiano (1994), Wolf (1992), and Yelvington (1995).

2. Even explanations of feminization that are not explicitly feminist, such as those of

Standing (1989) and Wood (1991), highlight the importance of the export orientation and labor intensity of manufacturing work in propelling feminization.

3. The database allows the choice of local currency or 1990 dollars. I use the dollar figures, since doing so permits comparisons across countries and across time.

4. The capital-intensity and wage groupings correspond to sizable gaps between ranked sectors. Some categories have far more sectors than others, which is to be expected, given that Indonesia has pursued a labor-intensive path of industrialization in recent years.

5. A study by the Asian-American Free Labor Institute in the early 1990s compared wage rates of men and women in the textiles, garments, footwear, electronics, food, and wood products industries and found that the average wage earned by women was 22 percent lower than that of men (Tjandraningsih 2000). Without proper controls factored in (for sector, tenure, overtime pay), however, it is difficult to assess these figures.

6. In most cases, these calculations include basic wages, incentive payments, and all other wage additions *except* overtime.

7. Women received overtime pay after six hours, whereas men received overtime only after the seventh hour.

8. To get a sense of how gendered discourses of work appear in the various studies of women factory workers, see Banerjee (1995), Chant and McIlwaine (1995), Charoenloet and Soonthorndhada (1988), Chhachhi and Pittin (1996), Ecevit (1991), Garnsey and Paukert (1987), Hirata (1989), Humphrey (1987), Kelly (1986), Lie and Lund (1994), and Ong (1987). Elias (2004) is perhaps the most careful analysis of how gendered discourses of work shape hiring practices and gender divisions of labor on the shop floor.

9. Other scholars who have found similar gendered discourses of work in their research in Indonesia include Andriyani (1989), Saptari (1995), Tjandraningsih (1991), and Yusuf (1991).

10. I emphasize perceptions, since supervisors had extremely unsophisticated ideas about absenteeism. When asked who had higher absenteeism, they answered, "Women," and then explained that this was so because most of the employees were women!

## 2. Feminized Ghettos?

1. Labor market segmentation theory has many similarities to dual labor market theory, especially in its use of the terms primary and secondary markets, but segmentation theorists also highlight distinct modes of labor control. Both theories argue that secondary work has low skill levels, but segmentation theorists are more skeptical about instability as a characteristic of the worker rather than as an effect of working in the secondary labor market. Segmentation theorists also agree that women prevail in the secondary market, so this approach is subsumed under dual labor market theory for my purposes. These authors also acknowledge more openly that gender complicates the analysis and have admitted that their approach cannot fully explain racial and gender divisions within the workforce; Edwards (1979) suggests that they require a separate analysis. Labor market segmentation theorists such as Gordon, Edwards, and Reich (1982) also argue that capital segregates workers in order to keep them divided politically. One study that empirically tested the theory in Hong Kong found that women were not more likely to predominate in secondary firms but that regardless of where women worked, they received lower pay, suggesting that women are confined to lower-paying occupations in both labor markets (Lee 1997).

2. One textile firm had two factories on site, and I obtained data for both, so four factories provided data. I also obtained multiple years of data for several of the firms.

3. These high figures on the top end (12.6 and 9.7) are a result of obtaining only one month of data at one factory, and this period overlapped with the annual leave given for

the Muslim holiday, Idul Fitri, when employers generally let workers off for a week to two weeks. Annual leave accounted for 10.7 percent of male absences and 5 percent of women's absences. Even if annual leave is excluded from the figures, women's rates are lower at this firm, since men skipped and missed work because of illness much more often than women.

4. Vacation is not included. All figures include sick leave, unexcused and excused absences, menstruation leave, and maternity leave.

5. Salzinger (2004) reached similar conclusions in her research in the *maquiladoras* in Mexico.

6. In my interviews with personnel managers and supervisors, I found a widespread impression that married women with children were more likely than other women to be absent. Wolf (1992) found the same preconceptions in her work in Central Java. A number of studies show that some employers—some that had employed single women but then hired married women when forced to do so by labor market constraints—conclude that older married women are actually more dependable than younger single women (see Canning 1996; and Lee 1988; Tiano 1994). In a fascinating study, Brinton, Lee, and Parish (1995) show that married women in South Korea and Taiwan have markedly different patterns of labor force participation and rates of pay, in spite of having had similar patterns when industrialization began: employers in Korea employ fewer women across the board, and there is a stronger push by families for women to quit work after marrying. This pressure on women to quit would be expected to lead Korean employers to be especially careful about selecting young and single workers.

7. Since firms rarely hired married women, it might be surprising that one-quarter to one-half of the female workers in the factories that I visited were married, which suggests that women were reluctant to quit after marrying because finding alternative industrial employment would be difficult. Being married and having children significantly altered a woman's job prospects, even though she might still be in her early to mid-twenties. In her study of electronics workers in Malaysia, Aihwa Ong (1983) found that many women quit voluntarily out of exhaustion after three to four years but that an increasing number of women stayed on after marriage. Employers nevertheless attempted to keep their workforces young, not only because of the lower wages that could be paid but because they knew the work took a toll on employees and their productivity. Kim (1997) also found that in South Korea it was difficult for women to return to the best factories after marrying; only the factories offering lower wages and worse working conditions would hire them.

8. Women may be paid less even when their work is graded as skilled, or the difference in pay for a woman in an unskilled versus a skilled job may be small. See Bai and Cho (1995), Banerjee (1991), Elias (2004), Hirsch (1986), and Roldan (1996).

9. Andriyani's (1989) study of a textile factory in the 1980s came to similar conclusions.

10. *Tukang* means "skilled craftsman" in Indonesian, and *otot* means "muscle." Thus the men's only skill was said to reside in their muscles.

11. The same authors also discuss "industrial skills," but this category does not play a significant role in their explanation of gender segregation in labor markets.

12. In order to retain about 5,000 out of 24,000 cases that employed no female workers (there is not a natural log of zero), I used Percent Female rather than the natural log of Percent Female. I did so for substantive reasons—if one in five firms employs no women, an important part of the story is missed by their omission. In addition, since wage data are not broken down by gender in the survey, I can capture the gender effect only by regressing the share of female employment on wages per capita. My assumption is that if women are paid dramatically lower wages than men, then factories that employ mostly women in a sector will have lower wages per capita than those that employ mostly men.

13. Industrial Standard Industrial Classification (ISIC) 353 and ISIC 354 were combined because there were so few cases of each.

14. Elias (2004) notes a similar situation in the employment of rural Malay married women with children in Malaysia.

## 3. Appealing Women and Permissive Institutions

1. Islamic organizations do not inevitably aim to constrain women's public roles, but religious organizations and parties often have conservative views about women's role in society. I focus on Islam because it is the main religion in Indonesia.

2. Such campaigns could be extremely effective. Robinson (1989) reports that a campaign in 1983 in Nuha district in South Sulawesi resulted in two hundred women being fitted with IUDs, and eighty more women in 1984.

3. The extent to which the program would have been successful in a context of slow economic growth and stagnant educational levels is a matter of debate, however.

4. It is relatively rare for single women to have children (unless divorced or widowed) in Indonesia, and those who do are ostracized. If a young woman becomes pregnant out of wedlock, the families concerned put strong pressure on the couple to marry.

5. Vreede-de Stuers (1976) has noted that the desire of the government to reduce the birthrate was the primary rationale behind the 1974 marriage law.

6. The measurement of trends in ownership and access to land using national statistics is perilous because of definitional concerns. For a thorough discussion, see Pincus (1996), who, though he does not present changes in land ownership over time in the three villages he surveyed in West Java, found high levels of landlessness, both in ownership of land and in access to it via sharecropping arrangements.

7. One statistical note: problems with the comparability of labor force statistics in the 1971 and 1980 censuses are due to differences in the minimum number of hours or days individuals had to have worked during the previous week to be classified as economically active: in 1971, individuals had to have worked two days; in 1980, only one hour. Since the work requirement for 1980 is lower, the level of decline must be sharper than presented above. It should also be mentioned that women's involvement in agriculture, as measured by agriculture's share of total female employment, rose slightly in the 1980s, from 53.8 percent in 1980 to 55.6 percent in 1987; this only partially reversed the declines of the 1970s, however. See Oey-Gardiner (1991).

8. Light skin is highly valued, and rural Indonesians are conscious of having relatively dark skin as a result of working outdoors. Working in the factory also provides young women with a way to leave the village and mix with other people, in particular with men from outside their villages.

9. Legislation also banned women's work in the mines, but this did not affect the manufacturing sector. Laws regarding maternity leave, menstruation leave, and higher premiums for working the night shift (when permitted) created added costs for hiring women but did not prohibit women's employment.

10. The extent to which employers actually provide transportation is unclear, although there are certainly many cases in which they do not. Wolf (1992) found that in the rural area where she conducted fieldwork, only one of the several factories employing women at night supplied transportation.

11. The highly mechanized firms are the most likely to require night work, as they need to run the machines twenty-four hours a day. Manning (1979) also found that employers believed there was much local opposition to the employment of women on the night shift. The highly mechanized weaving firms employed a much lower percentage of women than the less mechanized factories, with the most mechanized employing only 21 percent women as loom operators (foreign-owned firms, which were all highly mechanized, were even

lower—13 percent), whereas women constituted 58 percent of all loom operators in non-mechanized firms.

12. The religious leaders did not prevent managers from employing young women, but they urged them to hire women from the neighboring hamlet and to have them work under the supervision of a respected man from their community. Religious leaders considered these steps necessary to protect the morality of the young female workers (Mather 1985).

13. Kammen (1997) links the genesis of this form of bureaucratic "entrepreneurialism" to the rentierist nature of early import-substitution industrialization. In addition to the union, officials from the Ministry of Manpower (formerly the Ministry of Labor) and military units also became enmeshed in clientelistic webs. Kammen's review of estimates of illegal fees as a percentage of costs of production average about 30 percent, and his survey of firms in East Java support these estimates; see his chaps. 3 and 5.

14. The evidence is anecdotal but comes up frequently in accounts of labor relations in Indonesia, and several of the factories where I conducted research had retired military men in the personnel department. Wolf (1992) also found former army and police officials as personnel managers in her research sites. Likewise, it was common to see men in military uniform sitting with the security guards or hanging around the factory premises. Even when military men are not directly involved, the threat of bringing in the police can be enough to deter a worker from protesting unfair treatment.

15. Stories of the interrogation, arrest, and firing of strike leaders are pervasive in newspaper accounts. See INDOC and YLBHI reports, as well as Kammen's (1997) dissertation for a host of evidence drawn from newspapers and legal cases. In the 1990s the targeting of leaders led some striking workers to refuse to negotiate with employers, partially because they believed that those chosen as representatives would be fired.

16. The most famous case was the 1994 murder and rape of Marsinah, an East Javanese woman who was a strike leader at a watch factory.

17. For example, a 1987 regulation (Peraturan Menteri Tenaga Kerja No. Per-05/Men/87) required that in order to register, unions have branches in twenty provinces and one hundred districts, and one thousand factories. This would have required would-be unions to establish branches in twenty of the twenty-seven provinces, a difficult goal for a nascent organization. On the formation of independent unions, see Hadiz (1997) and Bourchier (1994).

18. Papanek and Schwede (1988), for example, compare women's labor force activity in Indonesia to that of women in Bangladesh, also a majority-Muslim country. In 1974 only 4 percent of women in Bangladesh were in the workforce, compared with about one-third in Indonesia.

19. Stoler (1977) is contrasting the pattern of colonial exploitation in Southeast Asia with that described by Boserup (1970) in Africa, where colonial powers relied more heavily on male labor for export agriculture, leaving subsistence production to women. The impact of Dutch rule on elite (*priyayi*) women, however, seems to have been more dramatic, at least in the case of Central Java. See Carey and Houben (1987).

20. NU was not just a political party. The organization included a network of religious schools as well as an exclusively religious arm that interpreted Islamic texts and recommended proper religious practices for its members. Its grassroots strength came from its schools and the involvement of local religious leaders, especially in East and Central Java.

21. On *abangan* and *santri*, see the classic text by Geertz (1976). *Abangan* refers to Javanese Muslims who combine a mix of animist, Hindu-Buddhist, and Islamic beliefs and practices. *Santri*, in contrast, are "purer" or more orthodox Muslims. On the modernist and traditionalist split, see Wertheim (1986).

22. On the emasculation of the political parties in the early 1970s, see Crouch (1978) and Wertheim (1986). The nationalist and Christian parties were also combined to form the *Partai Demokrasi Indonesia* (PDI), or Indonesian Democratic Party.

23. Under the chairmanship of H. J. Naro, a Suharto stooge, the PPP accepted Pancasila as its ideological basis in 1984, and soon thereafter NU withdrew from the PPP and from formal politics (Wertheim 1986). A common Suharto tactic in dealing with the parties was to arrange for a change in leadership if they showed signs of becoming a threat to his regime.

## 4. Spillover, Stickiness, and Waves

1. In Indonesia, ISI was not an organized and well-conceived strategy similar to that in the developmental states in East Asia; however, production in manufacturing was sold overwhelmingly on the internal market.

2. This categorization is my own. For a more detailed analysis of the changing structure of Indonesian industry, see Hill (1990a, 1990b, 1992).

3. For an overview of the development of the garment and textile industries, see Hill (1991). The impact of export certificates is doubted by some, but a number of garment producers told me that these incentives were an important part of their decision to invest.

4. Before 1986, the *Statistik Industri Sedang dan Besar* series suffered from underenumeration, so the figures for the number of employees for the 1970s and for 1980 in Table 4.1 may underestimate actual employment. The 1985 figures are from the *Sensus Ekonomi*, which rectified the underenumeration problem. For a discussion of some of the problems with the *Statistik Industri,* see Hill (1990a).

5. For a brief list of the various liberalization measures, see Winters (1996, 156-57).

6. Three sectors—refineries/coal, iron and steel, and nonferrous metals—are not included in the analysis of gendered trends over time because the 1971 industrial survey reported no employment in them.

7. In East Java, Willner (1961) found that men held 98 percent of the jobs on the looms in the late 1950s. In West Java, mechanized firms in the 1970s also referred to jobs on the looms as men's work (Manning 1979), and Harjono (1990) found that in the Majalaya area near Bandung, looms had long been regarded as men's work. In the spring of 1999, when I visited a number of small textile concerns in Majalaya, the vast majority of the old shuttle looms were still run by men.

8. At one firm, none of the interview subjects had worked in the factory in the 1970s, so the gender division of labor in effect during that period could not be determined. In the 1980s, women were on the looms.

9. Hardjono's (1990) article involves research in 1987, but the author presents the gender division of labor as a long-established pattern.

10. Investment figures underestimate Japanese influence in textiles today. Some major textile groups have intimate ties to Japanese textile firms and trading companies, and Japanese textile machinery is used extensively. On Japanese investment in Indonesia, see Wie (1984) and Kinoshita (1986); for data on the foreign presence in textiles, see Hill (1991).

11. In the Japanese textile industry, women were 64 percent of employees in 1970. See Japanese Bureau of Statistics (1973).

12. Before 1995, these data were not computerized, and collecting them involved spending an afternoon in the office that compiled the data and wading through a huge stack of old monthly reports. I included all years for which I could obtain at least three months of data. For 1984 and 1992, I obtained none, and for 1994, I found data only for the month of April (5,043 men; 11,922 women).

13. *Sinar Harapan,* July 18, 1980; *Sinar Pagi,* February 25, 1984.

14. *Pikiran Rakyat,* November 4, 1981; *Angkatan Bersenjata,* January 9, 1981; *Sinar Pagi,* December 2, 1983; *Merdeka,* December 12, 1983; *Pikiran Rakyat,* February 14, 1984; *Sinar Pagi,* February 20, 1984.

15. *Kedaulatan Rakyat*, May 6, 1982, and November 9, 1983. There is a long history of Javanese migration to other islands. During the colonial period Javanese were used in the plantations on Sumatra because the local populace would not work in them. See Stoler (1985). Employers in East and West Kalimantan no longer need to bring in recruits from Java, as there is a ready supply of East Javanese transmigrants.

16. The same argument is made by two excellent studies of the Bandung area by the Akatiga research group. My research in garments was primarily in the Jabotabek area (see note 22), and the same pattern they describe in Bandung is evident around Jakarta. For Bandung, see Grijns et al. (1992) and Yusuf (1991). In my sample, all the firms that had relied on a significant male workforce were established either during ISI or in the early transition years. Establishments founded in later years hired primarily women from the beginning.

17. The information about production in workshops and medium-sized factories is based largely on an interview with the subcontracting manager. The manager traveled in West Java and parts of Central Java.

18. I say almost always because one Japanese-run plywood mill in East Java employed an extremely high ratio of men to women; it was well known within plywood circles because its hiring practices were considered unusual.

19. See, for example, Charoenloet and Soonthorndhada (1988), Kuniko (1988), Lim (1978), Ong (1987), Salih and Young (1989), and Smith (1984).

20. This holds true even when timing is controlled for. For example, women were a higher proportion of workers in NIC firms established under EOI than in Indonesian firms that began production during EOI.

21. The stickiness phenomenon applies regardless of the origin of investment. In firms that began production before 1980, both foreign and domestic investors tend to employ fewer women than those established after 1986.

22. Jabotabek is an acronym for Jakarta and vicinity—Jakarta, Bogor, Tangerang, and Besaki. I treat these areas together, even though Bogor, Tangerang, and Besaki were part of West Java.

23. These varying levels of labor force participation probably link to cultural differences as well. The Sudanese constitute the majority of the population in West Java; Jabotabek has a heterogeneous population; and Central Java's is primarily Javanese. See Grijns et al. (1992) for some cursory observations along these lines.

## 5. From Profit to Practice

1. The immense diversity in gendered practices and discourses in Indonesia is analyzed by Atkinson and Errington (1990).

2. I use Brenner's (1995, 21) definition of a hegemonic discourse of gender: "models that support the claims of a particular category of people to superior status and power, models which are most likely to be invoked in formal discourse and which are most often accorded a position of supremacy among other, potentially competing models."

3. Kartini Day is a national holiday, and girls and women across the archipelago dress up like Javanese princesses for the occasion.

4. *Ibu* means mother but in current usage also encompasses mature women with no children.

5. Female civil servants are therefore thrown into the same category as wives and in essence become the wives of the state.

6. For a discussion of Sukarno's views on the role of women, see Brown (1981).

7. Management might try out a man in a women's section, either out of curiosity or because of short-term labor shortages, but according to managers, unless the man was "ef-

feminate," he would usually complain or quit. Managers speculated that the men who quit in these situations were embarrassed to do women's work. Other managers observed that men thought they were above doing women's work and would refuse to do it. The word usually used in this context in Indonesian was *gengsi* (literally, prestige; in slang, to put on airs). Others noted that men doing "women's work" risked being ridiculed and teased by other men. Masculinization, then, usually proceeds in big leaps, since enough men need to be placed in a section to give male workers a basis of solidarity. Elias (2004) also found that men who performed "women's work" were stigmatized and ridiculed.

8. To protect the anonymity of my sources, I am not using the actual names of any factories.

9. It is unwise to read too much into immediate postfinancial crisis figures in the automobile industries because the workforce shrank so dramatically. Before the crisis, Bekasi Motor had more than 700 production workers, but in 1999 the workforce had dwindled to 314.

10. Thanks to Douglas Kammen, who shared data from his strike database. Unless otherwise noted, all strike data is from this database.

11. This response is a rationalization because if they had wanted to hire women, they could simply have put up signs asking women to apply, requested women from their closest Department of Manpower office, or engaged an independent labor recruiter.

12. The dies inserted into the stamping machine are extremely heavy and usually require the use of lifting tools to install. The dies must be changed in order to produce a different component.

13. In Indonesia there was an abundant supply of female labor while I was conducting my research, which may explain why I found far more consistency than did Salzinger (1997). Necessity is the mother of invention, including the invention of new gendered meanings on the shop floor.

14. The reaction of female supervisors was often far more intense than that of the male supervisors, however.

15. Supervisors are concerned about quality because product that does not meet quality standards does not count toward the production quota, and their bonus is determined largely by the fulfillment of this quota.

16. The average for many sections was as high as 40–50 percent. The overall average is pulled down because new employees undergoing training did not receive premiums, bonuses, or incentives.

17. The managers actually used the word *tomboi* (and masculine adjectives) to refer to women who did work deemed more suitable to men. Women in men's jobs were thus incorporated into the binary discourse as "mannish women."

18. Women received higher overtime pay on the night shift than men because regulations stipulated that overtime began after six hours for women and after seven hours for men.

19. It is commonly believed in Indonesia that men work faster under piece-rate conditions. In cases where quality standards are low, managers prefer to hire men, since they believe that men will produce more. If quality is important, men's speed becomes a liability.

## 6. Gendered Paths of Industrialization

1. Singapore is actually part of Southeast Asia but is usually grouped with the East Asian newly industrializing countries (NICs), since it posted consistent and impressive gross domestic product (GDP) growth earlier than the rest of Southeast Asia.

2. Cumings (1984) has noted that Japanese colonization resulted in the establishment of a significant industrial base in Korea and Taiwan; however, much of that base was damaged

during World War II and the Korean War, and most heavy industry in Korea was located in the north.

3. In Figure 6.1, Mexico appears to have begun its feminization trend in 1960, but this appearance is due largely to a twenty-year gap in the statistical record between 1960 and 1980.

4. I considered including protective legislation as well but could not obtain cross-national data on its enforcement. To some extent, though, the union variable will also capture some of the impact of protective legislation. If unions are strong, protective legislation is more likely to be enforced. If unions are weak, the chances are greater that protective legislation will be ignored.

5. The literature on this subject is extensive. For a few examples, see Rose (1992), Milkman (1987), Cockburn (1983), and Hartmann (1979). The most common legislation limited the hours women could work each day, controlled night work, and excluded women from employment in certain areas such as underground work in mines.

6. Unions are not inherently hostile to women. Rather, as historically male-dominated institutions, they act to defend the interests of their members.

7. Each of the three indicators is scored 0, 1, or 2, with union density and political inclusion receiving a weight of 0.3 each and the level of collective bargaining 0.4. For the collective bargaining indicator, enterprise-level bargaining receives a 0; national, industry, or branch (or combination thereof) bargaining receives a 2; and cases that are mixed or in which industry-level bargaining has been suspended or significantly weakened (e.g., during much of the dictatorship in Brazil) receive a 1. Union density is measured as the percentage of union members in the economically active population and is scored 0 if union density is less than 10 percent, 1 if union density is between 10 and 25 percent, and 2 if it is greater than 25 percent. Political inclusion is scored 0 in cases in which labor is not an accepted political actor and in which states actively repress or demobilize labor as a potential force (e.g., by forcing all organizing to take place within state-sanctioned peak federations in which the leadership is unrepresentative of members). A score of 1 is given to countries in which serious restrictions on organizing and mobilization exist but independent unions form and take some actions to defend member interests. Cases in which the state actively engages with labor or in which labor is relatively free to pressure the government politically (i.e., in a democracy) receive a 2. These rankings of political inclusion do not mesh perfectly with regime type. Although all countries scored 0 were authoritarian, and most countries scored 1 either were undergoing political transitions or were semidemocracies (e.g., Malaysia), authoritarian regimes that practiced inclusionary corporatism (e.g., Mexico), as well as democracies, were scored 2. For further details on the construction of the index, including the scores assessed for each indicator, see Caraway (2006).

8. Union density in Singapore was relatively high in the early 1960s, at almost 30 percent, but declined steadily thereafter, to about 14 percent in the early 1990s. In Taiwan, union density increased from about 8 percent in the 1960s to 35 percent in the 1990s, with most of the increase occurring from the 1980s to the present. Until the 1990s, union density in South Korea was below 10 percent and hovered around 10 percent in the early 1990s (Rama and Artecona 2002).

9. Big jumps in union density took place in the 1980s, from just 14.9 percent in the late 1970s to 24.6 percent at the end of the decade (Lee 2000).

10. For capital intensity1, I took the natural log of value-added per capita for each sector in each country and divided it by the mean value-added per capita (unweighted) for all of manufacturing in the country. This variable measures the relative capital intensity of each sector in each country. Capital intensity2 measures how capital intensive the sector is in global terms. I used the natural log of value-added per capita for each sector in each country and divided it by the mean value-added for all manufacturing in the world. The world

figure is an unweighted average of all sectors of manufacturing that were used in the analysis (ISIC 353 and 354 were excluded because coverage is spotty). The value-added data were taken from the UNIDO's Industrial Statistics Database (1998, 3-digit ISIC), and I chose the values from 1986 when available; for Brazil, I used 1985, and for Singapore 1987. Cross-national value-added data are sparse before the 1980s, but as long as the relative ranking of sectors has not changed significantly, the results should not be affected dramatically. Value added in footwear, for example, undoubtedly increased over time, but remained a relatively labor-intensive sector when compared with other sectors.

11. Female labor force participation and total fertility rates were obtained from the World Bank's World Development Indicators (WDI), with the exception of Taiwan (Freeman, Chang, and Sun 1994; Li 1973; Republic of China National Statistics 2005). WDI is the most extensive source for cross-national labor force data, but the data to calculate labor force participation rates for the female population aged fifteen years and above are not in the database, so I used the rate for all women. For Taiwan, I was able to secure labor force participation data only for women fifteen and above (Chang 1978; Chow 2001; Wu and Chuang 2002), so I estimated these figures by comparing the difference between the fifteen-and-above and the all-ages participation rates for South Korea, the country in the sample most similar to Taiwan. Education data were obtained from the Barro-Lee Data Set of International Measures of Schooling Years and Schooling Quality, available at http://www.worldbank.org/research/growth/ddbarle2.htm, accessed on February 6, 2005. Some data had to be estimated from this source, since it provides data for only every five years from 1960 through 1990 (estimations available upon request).

12. The unionization rate in textiles was 50.4 percent in the late 1970s, the fifth highest rate among the twenty industries listed.


## Conclusion

1. Ghosh (2004) not only states this explicitly but goes further to argue that decreases in wage inequality have led employers to stop hiring women. The empirical support for that argument is mixed, however, as the decreases in women's presence in formal-sector employment in manufacturing, where firms are more likely to pay minimum wages and abide by protective legislation for women, are not as large as Ghosh suggests.

# Works Cited

Acero, Lillian. 1995. "Conflicting Demands of New Technology and Household Work: Women's Work in Brazilian and Argentinian Textiles." In *Women Encounter Technology: Changing Patterns of Employment in the Third World*, ed. Swasti Mitter and Sheila Rowbotham, 70–92. New York: Routledge.

Amsden, Alice H. 1989. *Asia's Next Giant: South Korea and Late Industrialization*. New York: Oxford University.

Andriyani, Nori. 1989. "Pembagian Kerja Secara Seksual pada Kerja Upahan." B.A. thesis, University of Indonesia, Jakarta.

Anker, Richard. 1998. *Gender and Jobs: Sex Segregation of Occupations in the World.* Geneva: International Labour Office.

Anker, Richard, and Catherine Hein. 1985. "Why Third World Urban Employers Usually Prefer Men." *International Labour Review* 124 (1): 73–90.

———. 1986. *Sex Inequalities in Urban Employment in the Third World.* London: Macmillan.

Armstrong, Pat, and Hugh Armstrong. 1987. "Feminist Marxism." In *The Politics of Diversity: Feminism, Marxism, and Nationalism*, ed. Roberta Hamilton and Michele Barrett, 208–237. London: Verso.

Armstrong, Peter. 1982. "If It's Only Women It Doesn't Matter So Much." In *Work, Women, and the Labour Market*, ed. Jackie West, 27–43. London: Routledge & Kegan Paul.

Arrigo, Linda Gail. 1980. "The Industrial Work Force of Young Women in Taiwan." *Bulletin of Concerned Asian Scholars* 12 (2): 25–38.

Atkinson, Jane Monnig, and Shelly Errington, eds. 1990. *Power and Difference: Gender in Island Southeast Asia.* Stanford: Stanford University Press.

Bai, Moo Ki, and Woo Hyun Cho. 1995. *Women's Wages and Employment in Korea.* Seoul: Seoul National University.

Banerjee, Nirmala. 1991. "The More It Changes, the More It Is the Same: Women Workers in Export Oriented Industries." In *Indian Women in a Changing Industrial Scenario*, ed. Nirmala Banerjee, 237–298. Newbury Park, Calif.: Sage.

———. 1995. "Something Old, Something New, Something Borrowed . . . the Electronics Industry in Calcutta." In *Women Encounter Technology: Changing Patterns of Em-*

*ployment in the Third World,* ed. Swasti Mitter and Sheila Rowbotham, 233–255. New York: Routledge.

Baried, Baroroh. 1986. "Islam and Modernization of Indonesian Women." In *Islam and Society in Southeast Asia,* ed. Taufik Abdullah and Sharon Siddique, 139–154. Singapore: Institute of Southeast Asian Studies.

Baron, Ava. 1991. "Gender and Labor History: Learning from the Past, Looking to the Future." In *Work Engendered: Toward a New History of American Labor,* ed. Ava Baron, 1–46. Ithaca: Cornell University Press.

Barr, Christopher M. 1998. "Bob Hasan, The Rise of APKINDO, and the Shifting Dynamics of Control in Indonesia's Timber Sector." *Indonesia* 65 (April): 1–36.

Barrett, Michele. 1988. *Women's Oppression Today: The Marxist/Feminist Encounter.* London: Verso.

Becker, Gary. 1981. *A Treatise on the Family.* Cambridge: Harvard University Press.

Beechey, Veronica. 1987. *Unequal Work.* London: Verso.

Benjamin, Dwayne. 1996. "Women and the Labour Market in Indonesia during the 1980s." In *Women and Industrialization in Asia,* ed. Susan Horton, 81–133. New York: Routledge.

Berik, Gunseli. 2000. "Mature Export-Led Growth and Gender Wage Inequality in Taiwan." *Feminist Economics* 6 (3): 1–26.

Biro Pusat Statistik. 1975. *Sensus Penduduk 1971, Seri D.* Jakarta: BPS.

———. 1983. *Sensus Penduduk 1980, Seri S.* Jakarta: BPS.

———. 1988. *Sensus Ekonomi 1985: Statistik Industri Besar dan Sedang.* Jakarta: BPS.

———. 1992. *Sensus Penduduk 1990, Seri S2.* Jakarta: BPS.

———. Various years. *Statistik Industri Besar dan Sedang.* Jakarta: BPS.

Blackwood, Evelyn. 1995. "Senior Women, Model Mothers, and Dutiful Wives: Managing Gender Contradictions in a Minangkabau Village." In *Bewitching Women, Pious Men: Gender and Body Politics in Southeast Asia,* ed. Aihwa Ong and Michael G. Peletz, 124–158. Berkeley: University of California Press.

Blau, Francine D., and Marianne A. Ferber. 1992. *The Economics of Women, Men, and Work.* Englewood Cliffs, N.J.: Prentice-Hall.

Boomgaard, Peter. 1981. "Female Labor and Population Growth on Nineteenth-Century Java." *Review of Indonesian and Malayan Affairs* 15 (2): 1–31.

Boserup, Esther. 1970. *Woman's Role in Economic Development.* New York: St. Martin's Press.

Bourchier, David. 1994. "Solidarity: The New Order's First Free Trade Union." In *Indonesia's Emerging Proletariat: Workers and Their Struggles,* ed. David Bourchier, 52–63. Clayton, Victoria, Australia: Centre of Southeast Asian Studies, Monash University.

Bradley, Harriet. 1989. *Men's Work, Women's Work.* Minneapolis: University of Minnesota Press.

Brenner, Johanna, and Maria Ramas. 1984. "Rethinking Women's Oppression." *New Left Review* 144 (March–April): 33–71.

Brenner, Suzanne. 1995. "Why Women Rule the Roost: Rethinking Javanese Ideologies of Gender and Self-Control." In *Bewitching Women, Pious Men: Gender and Body Politics in Southeast Asia,* ed. Aihwa Ong and Michael G. Peletz, 19–50. Berkeley: University of California Press.

———. 1998. *The Domestication of Desire: Women, Wealth, and Modernity in Java.* Princeton: Princeton University Press.

Brinton, Mary C. 1993. *Women and the Economic Miracle: Gender and Work in Postwar Japan.* Berkeley: University of California Press.

Brinton, Mary C., Yean-Ju Lee, and William L. Parish. 1995. "Married Women's Employment in Rapidly Industrializing Societies: Examples from East Asia." *American Journal of Sociology* 100 (5): 1099–1130.

Bronstein, Arturo S., and Efrén Córdova. 1984. "Collective Bargaining." In *Industrial Relations in Latin America: A Study of the Parties Involved, the Theory and Practice of Their Interactions and Procedures in Disputes, with Special Reference to the Private Sector*, ed. Efrén Córdova, 87–108. New York: Praeger.

Brown, Andrew, and Stephen Frenkel. 1993. "Union Unevenness and Insecurity in Thailand." In *Organized Labor in the Asia-Pacific Region: A Comparative Study of Trade Unionism in Nine Countries*, ed. Stephen Frenkel, 82–106. Ithaca: ILR Press of Cornell University Press.

Brown, Colin. 1981. "Sukarno on the Role of Women." *Review of Indonesian and Malayan Affairs* 15 (1): 64–92.

Bureau of the Census (Economics and Statistics Administration). 1992. *Population Trends: Indonesia*. Washington, D.C.: U.S. Department of Commerce.

Cagatay, Nilufer, and Gunseli Berik. 1991. "Transition to Export-Led Growth in Turkey: Is There a Feminisation of Employment?" *Capital & Class* 43 (Spring): 153–177.

Canning, Kathleen. 1996. *Languages of Labor and Gender: Female Factory Work in Germany, 1850–1914*. Ithaca: Cornell University Press.

Caraway, Teri L. 1998. "Perempuan dan Pembangunan: Sejarahnya Sebagai Lapangan Studi dan Ideologi Pemerintah Indonesia." *Jurnal Perempuan* 5 (November–January): 4–14.

———. 2006. "Gendered Paths of Industrialization: A Cross-Regional Comparative Analysis." *Studies in Comparative International Development* 41 (1): 26–52.

Carey, Peter, and Vincent Houben. 1987. "Spirited Srikandhis and Sly Sumbadras: The Social, Political, and Economic Role of Women at the Central Javanese Courts in the 18th and Early 19th Centuries." In *Indonesian Women in Focus: Past and Present Notions*, ed. Elsbeth Locher-Scholten and Anke Niehof, 12–42. Providence, R.I.: Foris.

Carver, Terrell. 1996. *Gender Is Not a Synonym for Women*. Boulder, Colo.: Lynne Rienner.

Catanzarite, Lisa M., and Myra H. Strober. 1993. "The Gender Recomposition of the Maquiladora Workforce in Ciudad Juarez." *Industrial Relations* 32 (1): 133–147.

Chang, Ching-hsi. 1978. "Female Labor Force Participation in Taiwan." Ph.D. diss., Ohio State University, Columbus.

Chant, Sylvia, and Cathy McIlwaine. 1995. *Women of a Lesser Cost: Female Labor, Foreign Exchange, and Philippine Development*. East Haven, Conn.: Pluto Press.

Chapkis, Wendy, and Cynthia Enloe. 1983. *Of Common Cloth: Women in the Global Textile Industry*. Washington, D.C.: Institute for Policy Studies.

Charles, Maria. 2005. "National Skill Regimes, Postindustrialism, and Sex Segregation." *Social Politics* 12 (2): 189–316.

Charles, Maria, and David B. Grusky. 2004. *Occupational Ghettos: The Worldwide Segregation of Women and Men*. Stanford: Stanford University Press.

Charoenloet, Voravidh, and Amara Soonthorndhada. 1988. "Factory Management, Skill Formation, and Attitudes of Women Workers in Thailand: A Comparison between an American and a Japanese Factory." In *Daughters in Industry: Work, Skills, and Consciousness of Women Workers in Asia*, ed. Noeleen Heyzer, 209–236. Kuala Lumpur: Asian and Pacific Development Center.

Chhachhi, Amrita, and Renee Pittin. 1996. "Multiple Identities, Multiple Strategies." In *Confronting State, Capital, and Patriarchy: Women Organizing in the Process of Indus-*

*trialization*, ed. Amrita Chhachhi and Renee Pittin, 93–130. The Hague: Institute of Social Studies.

Chow, Peter C. Y. 2001. *Social Expenditure in Taiwan (China)*. Washington, D.C.: World Bank.

Chu, Yin-Wah. 1996. "Democracy and Organized Labor in Taiwan: The 1986 Transition." *Asian Survey* 36 (5): 495–510.

Cockburn, Cynthia. 1983. *Brothers: Male Dominance and Technological Change*. London: Pluto Press.

Cohn, Samuel. 1985. *The Process of Occupational Sex-Typing: The Feminization of Clerical Labor in Great Britain*. Philadelphia: Temple University Press.

——. 2000. *Race and Gender Discrimination at Work*. Boulder, Colo.: Westview.

Collier, Ruth Berins, and David Collier. 1979. "Inducements versus Constraints: Disaggregating 'Corporatism.'" *American Political Science Review* 73 (4): 967–986.

——. 2002. *Shaping the Political Arena: Critical Junctures, the Labor Movement, and Regime Dynamics in Latin America*. Notre Dame, Ind.: University of Notre Dame Press.

Collins, Jane L. 2002. "Mapping a Global Labor Market: Gender and Skill in the Globalizing Garment Industry." *Gender & Society* 16 (6): 921–940.

——. 2003. *Threads: Gender, Labor, and Power in the Global Apparel Industry*. Chicago: University of Chicago Press.

Connell, R. W. 1987. *Gender and Power*. Stanford: Stanford University Press.

Cook, Maria Lorena. 1995. "Mexican State-Labor Relations and the Political Implications of Free Trade." *Latin American Perspectives* 22 (1): 77–94.

Cooney, Paul. 2001. "The Mexican Crisis and the Maquiladora Boom: A Paradox of Development or the Logic of Neoliberalism?" *Latin American Perspectives* 28 (4): 55–83.

Córdova, Efrén. 1984a. "The Latin American Picture." In *Industrial Relations in Latin America: A Study of the Parties Involved, the Theory and Practice of Their Interactions and Procedures in Disputes, with Special Reference to the Private Sector*, ed. Efrén Córdova, 3–24. New York: Praeger.

——. 1984b. "Other Features of Labor Relations at the Undertaking Level." In *Industrial Relations in Latin America: A Study of the Parties Involved, the Theory and Practice of Their Interactions and Procedures in Disputes, with Special Reference to the Private Sector*, ed. Efrén Córdova, 129–146. New York: Praeger.

Coulson, Margaret, Branka Magas, and Hilary Wainwright. 1975. "'The Housewife and Her Labour under Capitalism'—a Critique." *New Left Review* 89 (January–February): 59–71.

Coyle, Angela. 1982. "Sex and Skill in the Organisation of the Clothing Industry." In *Work, Women, and the Labor Market*, ed. Jackie West, 10–26. London: Routledge & Kegan Paul.

Cravey, Altha J. 1998. *Women and Work in Mexico's Maquiladoras*. Lanham, M.D.: Rowman & Littlefield.

Crouch, Harold A. 1978. *The Army and Politics in Indonesia*. Ithaca: Cornell University Press.

Cumings, Bruce. 1984. "The Origins and Development of the Northeast Asian Political Economy: Industrial Sectors, Product Cycles, and Political Consequences." *International Organization* 38 (1): 1–40.

Dalla Costa, Mariarosa. 1973. "Women and the Subversion of the Community." In *The Power of Women and the Subversion of the Community*, ed. Mariarosa Dalla Costa and Selma James, 21–56. Bristol: Falling Wall Press.

de Groot, Gertjan, and Marlou Schrover. 1995. "General Introduction." In *Women*

*Workers and Technological Change in Europe in the Nineteenth and Twentieth Centuries,* ed. Gertjan de Groot and Marlou Schrover, 1–16. Bristol, Pa.: Taylor & Francis.

Dejillas, Leopoldo J. 1994. *Trade Union Behavior in the Philippines, 1946–1990.* Manila: Ateneo de Manila University Press.

Deyo, Frederic C. 1989. *Beneath the Miracle: Labor Subordination in the New Asian Industrialism.* Berkeley: University of California Press.

——. 1990. "Economic Policy and the Popular Sector." In *Manufacturing Miracles: Paths of Industrialization in Latin America and East Asia,* ed. Gary Gereffi and Donald L. Wyman, 179–204. Princeton: Princeton University Press.

——. 1997. "Labour and Industrial Restructuring in South-East Asia." In *The Political Economy of South-East Asia: An Introduction,* ed. Garry Rodan, Kevin Hewison, and Richard Robison, 205–224. New York: Oxford University Press.

Diamond, Norma. 1979. "Women and Industry in Taiwan." *Modern China* 5 (3): 317–340.

DiMaggio, Paul J., and Walter W. Powell. 1991. "The Iron Cage Revisited: Institutional Isomorphism and Collective Rationality in Organizational Fields." In *The New Institutionalism in Organizational Analysis,* ed. Walter W. Powell and Paul J. DiMaggio, 63–82. Chicago: University of Chicago Press.

Djajadiningrat-Nieuwenhuis, Madelon. 1987. "Ibuism and Priyayization: Path to Power?" In *Indonesian Women in Focus: Past and Present Notions,* ed. Elsbeth Locher-Scholten and Anke Niehof, 43–51. Providence, R.I.: Foris.

Doeringer, Peter B., and Michael J. Piore. 1971. *Internal Labor Markets and Manpower Analysis.* Lexington, Mass.: Heath Lexington Books.

Downs, Laura Lee. 1995. *Manufacturing Inequality: Gender Division in the French and British Metalworking Industries, 1914–1939.* Ithaca: Cornell University Press.

Drake, Paul W. 1996. *Labor Movements and Dictatorships: The Southern Cone in Comparative Perspective.* Baltimore: Johns Hopkins University Press.

Dutch East Indies. 1933–1936. *Volkstelling 1930.* Batavia: Department van Economische Zaken.

Ecevit, Yildiz. 1991. "Shop Floor Control: The Ideological Construction of Turkish Women Factory Workers." In *Working Women: International Perspectives on Labor and Gender Ideology,* ed. Nanneke Redclift and M. Thea Sinclair, 56–78. New York: Routledge.

Economic and Social Commission for Asia and the Pacific. 1987. *Young Women Workers in Manufacturing: A Case Study of Rapidly Industrializing Economies of the ESCAP Region.* Bangkok: United Nations.

Edwards, Richard. 1979. *Contested Terrain: The Transformation of the Workplace in the Twentieth Century.* New York: Basic Books.

Eisenstein, Zillah R. 1979. "Developing a Theory of Capitalist Patriarchy and Socialist Feminism." In *Capitalist Patriarchy and the Case for Socialist Feminism,* ed. Zillah R. Eisenstein, 5–40. New York: Monthly Review Press.

Elias, Juanita. 2004. *Fashioning Inequality: The Multinational Company and Gendered Employment in a Globalizing World.* Burlington, Vermont: Ashgate.

Elliot, Janet. 1997. "Equality? The Influence of Legislation and Notions of Gender on the Position of Women Wage Workers in the Economy: Indonesia 1950–58." In *Women Creating Indonesia: The First Fifty Years,* ed. Jean Gelman Taylor, 127–155. Clayton, Victoria, Australia: Monash Asia Institute.

Elson, Diane, and Ruth Pearson. 1981a. "'Nimble Fingers Make Cheap Workers': An Analysis of Women's Employment in Third World Export Manufacturing." *Feminist Review* 7 (Spring): 87–107.

———. 1981b. "The Subordination of Women and the Internationalization of Factory Production." In *Of Marriage and the Market,* ed. Kate Young, Carol Wolkowitz, and Roslyn McCullagh, 18–40. New York: Routledge.

England, Paula. 1992. *Comparable Worth: Theories and Evidence.* New York: Aldine de Gruyter.

———. 2005. "Gender Inequality in Labor Markets: The Role of Motherhood and Segregation." *Social Politics* 12 (2): 264–288.

Estévez-Abe, Margarita. 2005. "Gender Bias in Skills and Social Policies: The Varieties of Capitalism Perspective on Sex Segregation." *Social Politics* 12 (2): 180–215.

Estévez-Abe, Margarita, Torben Iversen, and David Soskice. 2001. "Social Protection and the Formation of Skills: A Reinterpretation of the Welfare State." In *Varieties of Capitalism: The Institutional Foundations of Comparative Advantage,* ed. Peter A. Hall and David Soskice, 145–183. New York: Oxford University Press.

Feldman, Shelley. 1992. "Crisis, Islam, and Gender in Bangladesh: The Social Construction of a Female Labor Force." In *Unequal Burden: Economic Crises, Persistent Poverty, and Women's Work,* ed. Lourdes Beneria and Shelley Feldman, 105–130. Boulder, Colo.: Westview.

Ferguson, Ann, and Nancy Folbre. 1981. "The Unhappy Marriage of Patriarchy and Capitalism." In *Women and Revolution: A Discussion of the Unhappy Marriage of Marxism and Feminism,* ed. Lydia Sargent, 313–338. Boston: South End Press.

Fernandes, Leela. 1997. *Producing Workers: The Politics of Gender, Class, and Culture in the Calcutta Jute Mills.* Philadelphia: University of Pennsylvania Press.

Fernandez-Kelly, Maria Patricia. 1983a. *For We Are Sold, I and My People: Women and Industry in Mexico's Frontier.* Albany: State University of New York Press.

———. 1983b. "Mexican Border Industrialization, Female Labor Force Participation and Migration." In *Women, Men, and the International Division of Labor,* ed. June Nash and Maria Patricia Fernandez-Kelly, 205–223. Albany: State University of New York Press.

Fligstein, Neil. 2001. *The Architecture of Markets: An Economic Sociology of Twenty-First-Century Capitalist Societies.* Princeton: Princeton University Press.

Ford, Michele. 1999. "Testing the Limits of Corporatism: Industrial Relations in Suharto's Indonesia." *Journal of Industrial Relations* 41 (3): 372–392.

Foucault, Michel. 1990. *The History of Sexuality: An Introduction.* New York: Vintage.

Fox, Julia D. 1993. "Transformations in the Labor Process on a World Scale: Women in the New International Division of Labor." In *The Labor Process and Control of Labor,* ed. Berch Berberoglu, 137–151. Westport, Conn.: Praeger.

Fraser, Nancy. 1989. "What's Critical about Critical Theory? The Case of Habermas and Gender." In *Unruly Practices: Power, Discourse, and Gender in Contemporary Social Theory,* ed. Nancy Fraser, 113–143. Minneapolis: University of Minnesota Press.

Freeman, Ronald, Ming-Cheng Chang, and Te-Hsiung Sun. 1994. "Taiwan's Transition from High Fertility to Below-Replacement Levels." *Studies in Family Planning* 25 (6): 317–331.

Frobel, Folker, Jurgen Heinrichs, and Otto Kreye. 1980. *The New International Division of Labor.* New York: Cambridge University Press.

Fuentes, Annette, and Barbara Ehrenreich. 1983. *Women in the Global Factory.* Boston: South End Press.

Gardiner, Jean. 1975. "Women's Domestic Labour." *New Left Review* 89 (January–February): 47–58.

———. 1976. "Political Economy of Domestic Labour in Capitalist Society." In *Depen-*

*dence and Exploitation in Work and Marriage,* ed. Diana Leonard Barker and Sheila Allen, 109–120. New York: Longman.

Garnsey, Elizabeth, and Liba Paukert. 1987. *Industrial Change and Women's Employment: Trends in the New International Division of Labour.* Geneva: International Institute for Labour Studies.

Geertz, Clifford. 1976. *The Religion of Java.* Chicago: University of Chicago Press.

Geografia e Informatica Instituto Nacional de Estadística. 1983. *Estadística de la Industria Maquiladora de Exportacion, 1974–1982.* Mexico: Instituto Nacional de Estadística, Geografia e Informatica.

Gereffi, Gary. 1990. "Paths of Industrialization: An Overview." In *Manufacturing Miracles: Paths of Industrialization in Latin America and East Asia,* ed. Gary Gereffi and Donald L. Wyman, 3–31. Princeton: Princeton University Press.

Gereffi, Gary, and Donald L. Wyman, eds. 1990. *Manufacturing Miracles: Paths of Industrialization in Latin America and East Asia.* Princeton: Princeton University Press.

Gertler, Paul J., and John W. Molyneaux. 1994. "How Economic Development and Family Planning Programs Combined to Reduce Indonesian Fertility." *Demography* 31 (1): 33–63.

Ghosh, Jayati. 2004. "Globalization, Export-Oriented Employment for Women, and Social Policy: A Case Study of India." In *Globalization, Export-Oriented Employment, and Social Policy: Gendered Connections,* ed. Shahra Razavi, Ruth Pearson, and Caroline Danloy, 91–125. New York: Palgrave Macmillan.

Goldin, Claudia. 2002. "A Pollution Theory of Discrimination: Male and Female Differences in Occupations and Earnings." National Bureau of Economic Research Working Paper 8985. Available at http://papers.nber.org/papers

Gordon, David M. 1972. *Theories of Poverty and Underemployment: Orthodox, Radical, and Dual Labor Market Perspectives.* Lexington, Mass.: Lexington Books.

Gordon, David M., Richard Edwards, and Michael Reich. 1982. *Segmented Work, Divided Workers: The Historical Transformation of Labor in the United States.* New York: Cambridge University Press.

Grace, Elizabeth. 1990. *Shortcircuiting Labour: Unionising Electronics Workers in Malaysia.* Kuala Lumpur: INSAN.

Grijns, Mies. 1987. "Tea-Pickers in West Java as Mothers and Workers: Female Work and Women's Jobs." In *Indonesian Women in Focus: Past and Present Notions,* ed. Elsbeth Locher-Scholten and Anke Niehof, 104–119. Providence, R.I.: Foris.

Grijns, Mies, et al. 1992. *Gender, Marginalisation and Rural Industries: Female Entrepreneurs, Wage Workers, and Family Workers in West Java.* Bandung, Indonesia: PSP-IPB, ISS, and PPLH-ITB. Published for the Institute of Social Studies (Netherlands) by Akatiga Foundation, Centre for Social Analysis.

Grossman, Rachel. 1978. "Women's Place in the Integrated Circuit." *Southeast Asia Chronicle—Pacific Research* 9 (5–6): 2–17.

Hadiz, Vedi R. 1997. *Workers and the State in New Order Indonesia.* New York: Routledge.

Haggard, Stephan. 1990. *Pathways from the Periphery: The Politics of Growth in the Newly Industrializing Countries.* Ithaca: Cornell University Press.

Hall, Peter A., and David Soskice, eds. 2001. *Varieties of Capitalism: The Institutional Foundations of Comparative Advantage.* New York: Oxford University Press.

Hanchard, Michael. 1999. "Black Cinderella? Race and the Public Sphere in Brazil." In *Racial Politics in Contemporary Brazil,* ed. Michael Hanchard, 59–81. Durham, N.C.: Duke University Press.

Hardjono, Joan. 1990. *Developments in the Majalaya Textile Industry.* Bandung: ISS-Bandung Research Project.

Hartmann, Heidi. 1979. "Capitalism, Patriarchy, and Job Segregation by Sex." In *Capitalist Patriarchy and the Case for Socialist Feminism,* ed. Zillah R. Eisenstein, 206–247. New York: Monthly Review Press.

Harvey, David. 1999. *The Limits to Capital.* New York: Verso.

Hawes, Gary. 1992. "Marcos, His Cronies, and the Philippines' Failure to Develop." In *Southeast Asian Capitalists,* ed. Ruth McVey, 145–160. Ithaca: Cornell University Southeast Asia Program.

Hawkins, E. D. 1971. "Labor in Developing Countries: Indonesia." In *The Indonesian Economy: Selected Readings,* ed. Bruce Glassburner, 196–250. Ithaca: Cornell University Press.

Hefner, Robert W. 1993. "Islam, State, and Civil Society: ICMI and the Struggle for the Indonesian Middle Class." *Indonesia* 56:1–36.

Hein, Catherine. 1986. "The Feminisation of Industrial Employment in Mauritius: A Case of Sex Segregation." In *Sex Inequalities in Urban Employment in the Third World,* ed. Richard Anker and Catherine Hein, 277–311. Basingstoke, U.K.: Macmillan Press.

Hewison, Kevin. 1997. "Thailand: Capitalist Development and the State." In *The Political Economy of South-East Asia: An Introduction,* ed. Garry Rodan, Kevin Hewison, and Richard Robison, 93–120. New York: Oxford University Press.

Hewison, Kevin, and Andrew Brown. 1994. "Labour and Unions in an Industrialising Thailand." *Journal of Contemporary Asia* 24 (4): 483–514.

Heyzer, Noeleen, ed. 1988. *Daughters in Industry: Work, Skills, and Consciousness of Women Workers in Asia.* Kuala Lumpur: Asian and Pacific Development Center.

Hill, Hal. 1990a. "Indonesia's Industrial Transformation, Part I." *Bulletin of Indonesian Economic Studies* 26 (2): 79–120.

———. 1990b. "Indonesia's Industrial Transformation, Part II." *Bulletin of Indonesian Economic Studies* 26 (3): 75–109.

———. 1991. "The Emperor's Clothes Can Now Be Made in Indonesia." *Bulletin of Indonesian Economic Studies* 27 (3): 89–127.

———. 1992. "Manufacturing Industry." In *The Oil Boom and After: Indonesian Economic Policy and Performance in the Soeharto Era,* ed. Anne Booth, 204–257. New York: Oxford University Press.

Hirata, Helena. 1989. "Production Relocation: An Electronics Multinational in France and Brazil." In *Women's Employment and Multinationals in Europe,* ed. Diane Elson and Ruth Pearson, 129–143. London: Macmillan.

Hirsch, Susan E. 1986. "Rethinking the Sexual Division of Labor: Pullman Repair Shops, 1900–1969." *Radical History Review* 35:26–48.

Hirschman, Charles. 2002. "Fertility Transition in Southeast Asia." In *International Encyclopedia of the Social and Behavioral Sciences,* ed. Neil J. Smelser and Paul B Baltes, 8:5597–5602. Oxford: Elsevier.

Humphrey, John. 1987. *Gender and Work in the Third World: Sexual Divisions in Brazilian Industry.* London: Tavistock.

Husken, Frans. 1989. "Cycles of Commercialization and Accumulation in a Central Javanese Village." In *Agrarian Transformations: Local Processes and the State in Southeast Asia,* ed. Gillian Hart, Andrew Turton, and Benjamin White, 303–331. Berkeley: University of California Press.

Husken, Frans, and Benjamin White. 1989. "Java: Social Differentiation, Food Production, and Agrarian Control." In *Agrarian Transformations: Local Processes and the State in Southeast Asia*, ed. Gillian Hart, Andrew Turton, and Benjamin White, 235–265. Berkeley: University of California Press.

Hutchison, Jane. 1997. "Pressure on Policy in the Philippines." In *The Political Economy of Southeast Asia: An Introduction*, ed. Garry Rodan, Kevin Hewison, and Richard Robison, 64–92. New York: Oxford University Press.

INDOC (Indonesian Documentation and Information Centre). 1981–86. *Indonesian Workers and Their Right to Organise*. Leiden: INDOC.

International Labor Office. 1997. *World Labor Report: Industrial Relations, Democracy, and Social Stability*. Geneva: ILO.

Istiadah. 1995. *Muslim Women in Contemporary Indonesia: Investigating Paths to Resist the Patriarchal System*. Clayton, Victoria, Australia: Monash University, Centre for Southeast Asian Studies.

James, Daniel. 1988. *Resistance and Integration: Peronism and the Argentine Working Class, 1946–1976*. New York: Cambridge University Press.

Japanese Bureau of Statistics. 1973. *Comparison of Employed Persons in Industry in the Population Censuses, 1920–1970*. Tokyo: Japanese Bureau of Statistics.

Joekes, Susan P. 1982. *Female-Led Industrialisation: Women's Jobs in Third World Export Manufacturing: The Case of the Moroccan Clothing Industry*. Brighton, Sussex, UK: Institute of Development Studies.

——. 1987. *Women in the World Economy: An INSTRAW Study*. New York: Oxford University Press.

Jomo, K. S. 1997. *Southeast Asia's Misunderstood Miracle: Industrial Policy and Economic Development in Thailand, Malaysia, and Indonesia*. Boulder, Colo.: Westview.

Jomo, K. S., and Patricia Todd. 1994. *Trade Unions and the State in Peninsular Malaysia*. New York: Oxford University Press.

Kahin, Audrey R., and George McT. Kahin. 1995. *Subversion as Foreign Policy: The Secret Eisenhower and Dulles Debacle in Indonesia*. Seattle: University of Washington Press.

Kammen, Douglas. 1997. "A Time to Strike: Industrial Strikes and Changing Class Relations in New Order Indonesia." Ph.D. diss., Cornell University.

Kaufman, Robert R. 1979. "Industrial Change and Authoritarian Rule in Latin America: A Concrete Review of the Bureaucratic-Authoritarian Model." In *The New Authoritarianism in Latin America*, ed. David Collier, 165–253. Princeton: Princeton University Press.

Keck, Margaret E. 1992. *The Workers' Party and Democratization in Brazil*. New Haven: Yale University Press.

Kelly, Deirdre. 1986. "St. Lucia's Female Electronics Factory Workers: Key Components in an Export-Oriented Industrialization Strategy." *World Development* 14 (7): 823–838.

Kim, Mi-ju. 1994. "Gender Division of Labor and Skill as a Factor of Sex Wage Differentials." In *Gender Division of Labor in Korea*, ed. Mi-ju Kim, 106–131. Seoul: Ewha Women's University Press.

Kim, Seung-Kyung. 1997. *Class Struggle or Family Struggle? The Lives of Women Factory Workers in South Korea*. New York: Cambridge University Press.

Kinoshita, Toshihiko. 1986. "Japanese Investment in Indonesia: Problems and Prospects." *Bulletin of Indonesian Economic Studies* 22 (1): 34–56.

Koo, Hagen. 2000. "The Dilemmas of Empowered Labor in Korea: Korean Workers in the Face of Global Capitalism." *Asian Survey* 40 (2): 227–250.

——. 2001. *Korean Workers: The Culture and Politics of Class Formation.* Ithaca: Cornell University Press.

Kothari, Uma, and Vidula Nababsing. 1996. *Gender and Industrialisation: Mauritius, Bangladesh, Sri Lanka.* Stanley, Rose-Hill (Mauritius): Editions de L'Ocean Indien.

Kung, Lydia. 1994. *Factory Women in Taiwan.* New York: Columbia University Press.

Kuniko, Fujita. 1988. "Women Workers, State Policy, and the International Division of Labor: The Case of Silicon Island in Japan." *Bulletin of Concerned Asian Scholars* 20 (3): 42–53.

Kuruvilla, Sarosh. 1996. "Linkages between Industrialization Strategies and Industrial Relations/Human Resource Policies: Singapore, Malaysia, the Philippines, and India." *Industrial & Labor Relations Review* 49 (4): 635–657.

Lambert, Rob. 1990. "Kilusang Mayo Uno and the Rise of Social Movement Unionism in the Philippines." *Labour & Industry* 3 (2–3): 258–280.

——. 1997. "Authoritarian State Unionism in New Order Indonesia." In *State and Labor in New Order Indonesia,* ed. Rob Lambert, 56–82. Perth: University of Western Australia Press and Asia Research Centre.

Lee, Ching Kwan. 1998. *Gender and the South China Miracle: Two Worlds of Factory Women.* Berkeley: University of California Press.

Lee, Chung H. 1994. "Korea's Direct Foreign Investment in Southeast Asia." *ASEAN Economic Bulletin* 10 (3): 280–296.

Lee, Hyo-Chae. 1988. "The Changing Profile of Women Workers in South Korea." In *Daughters in Industry: Work, Skills, and Consciousness of Women Workers in Asia,* ed. Noeleen Heyzer, 329–355. Kuala Lumpur: Asian and Pacific Development Center.

Lee, Joseph S. 2000. "Changing Approaches to Employment Relations in Taiwan." In *Employment Relations in the Asia-Pacific: Changing Approaches,* ed. Greg J. Bamber, Funkoo Park, Changwon Lee, Peter K. Ross, and Kaye Broadbent, 100–116. London: Business Press.

Lee, William Keng Mun. 1997. "Industrial Dualism, Income, and Gender Inequality in Hong Kong." *Asian Affairs* 24 (1): 15–33.

Lev, Daniel S. 1996. "On the Other Hand?" In *Fantasizing the Feminine in Indonesia,* ed. Laurie J. Sears, 191–203. Durham, N.C.: Duke University Press.

Li, Wen L. 1973. "Temporal and Spatial Analysis of Fertility Decline in Taiwan." *Population Studies* 27 (1): 97–104.

Lie, Merete, and Ragnhild Lund. 1994. *Renegotiating Local Values: Working Women and Foreign Industry in Malaysia.* Richmond, Surrey, UK: Curzon Press.

Lim, Linda Y. C. 1978. *Women Workers in Multinational Corporations: The Case of the Electronics Industry in Malaysia and Singapore.* Michigan occasional papers in women's studies. Ann Arbor: Women's Studies Program, University of Michigan.

——. 1983. "Capitalism, Imperialism, and Patriarchy: The Dilemma of Third-World Women Workers in Multinational Factories." In *Women, Men, and the International Division of Labor,* ed. June Nash and Maria Patricia Fernandez-Kelly, 70–91. Albany: State University of New York Press.

——. 1985. *Women Workers in Multinational Enterprises.* Geneva: ILO.

——. 1990. "Women's Work in Export Factories: The Politics of a Cause." In *Persistent Inequalities: Women and World Development,* ed. Irene Tinker, 101–119. New York: Oxford University Press.

Lindblad, J. Thomas. 1997. "Foreign Investment in Southeast Asia in Historical Perspective." *Asian Economic Journal* 11 (1): 61–80.

Locher-Scholten, Elsbeth. 1987. "Female Labour in Twentieth Century Java: European Notions– Indonesian Practice." In *Indonesian Women in Focus: Past and Present Notions,* ed. Elsbeth Locher-Scholten and Anke Niehof, 77–103. Providence, R.I.: Foris.

——. N.d. "Some Remarks on the Role of Women in Indigenous Agriculture in Colonial Java (19th and 20th Century)."

Mabry, Bevars D., and Kundhol Srisermbhok. 1985. "Labor Relations under Martial Law: The Thailand Experience." *Asian Survey* 25 (6): 613–637.

Mackintosh, Maureen. 1991. "Gender and Economics: The Sexual Division of Labour and the Subordination of Women." In *Of Marriage and the Market: Women's Subordination Internationally and Its Lessons,* ed. Kate Young, Carol Wolkowitz, and Roslyn McCullagh, 3–17. London: Routledge.

Manderson, Lenore. 1980. "Right and Responsibility, Power and Privilege: Women's Roles in Contemporary Indonesia." In *Kartini Centenary: Indonesian Women Then and Now,* ed. Ailsa Gwennym Zainu'ddin, 69–92. Clayton, Victoria, Australia: Monash University.

Manning, Christopher Gibson. 1979. *Wage Differentials and Labour Market Segmentation in Indonesian Manufacturing.* Ph.D. diss., Australian National University.

——. 1993. "Structural Change and Industrial Relations during the Soeharto Period: An Approaching Crisis?" *Bulletin of Indonesian Economic Studies* 29 (2): 59–95.

——. 1998. *Indonesian Labour in Transition: An East Asian Success Story?* New York: Cambridge University Press.

Marcoes, Lies M. 1992. "The Female Preacher as a Mediator in Religion: A Case Study in Jakarta and West Java." In *Women and Mediation in Indonesia,* ed. Sita van Bemmelen, Madelon Djajadiningrat-Nieuwenhuis, Elsbeth Locher-Scholten, and Elly Touwen-Bouwsma, 203–228. Leiden: KITLV Press.

Marx, Karl. 1977. *Capital: Volume One.* New York: Vintage.

Mather, Celia. 1985. "'Rather Than Make Trouble, It's Better Just to Leave': Behind the Lack of Industrial Strife in the Tangerang Region of West Java." In *Women, Work, and Ideology in the Third World,* ed. Haleh Afshare, 153–180. New York: Tavistock.

McCall, Leslie, and Ann Orloff. 2005. Introduction to special issue, "Gender, Class, and Capitalism." *Social Politics* 12 (2): 159–169.

McGuire, James W. 1997. *Peronism without Perón: Unions, Parties, and Democracy in Argentina.* Stanford: Stanford University Press.

——. 1999. "Labor Union Strength and Human Development in East Asia and Latin America." *Studies in Comparative International Development* 33 (4): 3–34.

McVey, Ruth. 1983. "Faith as the Outsider: Islam in Indonesian Politics." In *Islam in the Political Process,* ed. James P. Piscatori, 199–225. New York: Cambridge University Press.

Mehta, Uday S. 1997. "Liberal Strategies of Exclusion." In *Tensions of Empire: Colonial Cultures in a Bourgeois World,* ed. Ann Laura Stoler and Frederick Cooper, 59–86. Berkeley: University of California Press.

Mericle, Kenneth S. 1977. "Corporatist Control of the Working Class: Authoritarian Brazil since 1964." In *Authoritarianism and Corporatism in Latin America,* ed. James M. Malloy, 303–338. Pittsburgh: University of Pittsburgh Press.

Middlebrook, Kevin J. 1995. *The Paradox of Revolution: Labor, the State, and Authoritarianism in Mexico.* Baltimore: Johns Hopkins University Press.

Miles, Angela. 1986. "Economism and Feminism: A Comment on the Domestic Labour Debate." In *The Politics of Diversity: Feminism, Marxism, and Nationalism,* ed. Roberta Hamilton and Michele Barrett, 168–179. London: Verso.

Milkman, Ruth. 1987. *Gender at Work: The Dynamics of Job Segregation by Sex during World War II.* Urbana: University of Illinois Press.

Moghadam, Valentine M. 1995. *Manufacturing and Women in the Middle East and North Africa: A Case Study of the Textiles and Garments Industry.* Durham, UK: University of Durham, Centre for Middle Eastern and Islamic Studies.

Morton, Peggy. 1971. "A Woman's Work Is Never Done." In *From Feminism to Liberation*, ed. Edith Altbach, 211–227. Cambridge, Mass.: Schenkman.

Nash, June, and Maria Patricia Fernandez-Kelly, eds. 1983. *Women, Men, and the International Division of Labor.* Albany: State University of New York Press.

O'Connell, Lesley D. 1999. "Collective Bargaining Systems in Six Latin American Countries: Degrees of Autonomy and Decentralization—Argentina, Brazil, Chile, Mexico, Peru, and Uruguay." Inter-American Development Bank, Office of the Chief Economist, Working Paper #399. Available at http://www.iadb.org/res/publications/pubfiles/pubWP-399.pdf

O'Donnell, Guillermo A. 1973. *Modernization and Bureaucratic Authoritarianism: Studies in South American Politics.* Berkeley: University of California Institute of International Studies.

Oey-Gardiner, Mayling. 1985. "Perubahan Pola Kerja Kaum Wanita di Indonesia Selama Dasawarsa 1970: Sebab dan Akibatnya." *Prisma* 10:16–40.

——. 1991. *Policies Affecting Female Employment in Indonesia.* Jakarta: ILO.

——. 1993. "A Gender Perspective in Indonesia's Labour Market." In *Indonesia Assessment—Labour: Sharing in the Benefits of Growth*, ed. Christopher Gibson Manning and Joan Hardjono, 203–213. Canberra: Australian National University.

Ong, Aihwa. 1983. "Global Industries and Malay Peasants in Peninsular Malaysia." In *Women, Men, and the International Division of Labor*, ed. June Nash and Maria Patricia Fernandez-Kelly, 426–441. Albany: State Univeristy of New York Press.

——. 1987. *Spirits of Resistance and Capitalist Discipline: Factory Women in Malaysia.* Albany: State University of New York Press.

Papanek, Hanna, and Laurel Schwede. 1988. "Women Are Good with Money: Earnings and Managing in an Indonesian City." In *A Home Divided: Women and Income in the Third World*, ed. Daisy Dwyer and Judith Bruce, 71–98. Stanford: Stanford University Press.

Pateman, Carole. 1988. *The Sexual Contract.* Stanford: Stanford University Press.

Pena, Devon G. 1997. *The Terror of the Machine: Technology, Work, Gender, and Ecology on the U.S.-Mexican Border.* Austin: CMAS, The Center for Mexican American Studies, University of Texas.

Phillips, Anne, and Barbara Taylor. 1980. "Sex and Skill: Notes towards a Feminist Economics." *Feminist Review* 6:79–88.

Phongpaichit, Pasuk. 1988. "Two Roads to the Factory: Industrialisation Strategies and Women's Employment in Southeast Asia." In *Structures of Patriarchy: State, Community, and Household in Modernizing Asia*, ed. Bina Agarwal, 151–163. London: Zed.

Pierson, Paul. 1993. "When Effect Becomes Cause: Policy Feedback and Political Change." *World Politics* 45 (4): 595–628.

——. 2004. *Politics in Time: History, Institutions, and Social Analysis.* Princeton: Princeton University Press.

Pincus, Jonathan. 1996. *Class Power and Agrarian Change: Land and Labour in Rural West Java.* New York: St. Martin's Press.

Polachek, Solomon. 1981. "Occupational Self Selection: A Human Capital Approach to

Sex Differences in Occupational Structure." *Review of Economics and Statistics* 63 (1): 60–69.

Pun, Ngai. 2005. *Made in China: Women Factory Workers in a Global Workplace.* Durham, N.C.: Duke University Press.

Pyle, Jean L. 1990. "Export-Led Development and the Underemployment of Women: The Impact of Discriminatory Development Policy in the Republic of Ireland." In *Women Workers and Global Restructuring*, ed. Kathryn Ward, 85–112. Ithaca: Cornell University Press.

Rahayu, Ruth Indiah. 1996. "Politik Gender Orde Baru: Tinjauan Organisasi Perempuan sejak 1980–an." *Prisma* 5 (May): 29–42.

Raillon, François. 1993. "The New Order and Islam, or The Imbroglio of Faith and Politics." *Indonesia* 57:197–217.

Rama, Martin, and Raquel Artecona. 2002. "A Database of Labor Market Indicators across Countries." Electronic file (computer).

Rasiah, Rajah. 1997. "Class, Ethnicity, and Economic Development in Malaysia." In *The Political Economy of South-East Asia: An Introduction*, ed. Garry Rodan, Kevin Hewison, and Richard Robison, 121–147. New York: Oxford University Press.

Republic of China National Statistics. 2005. "Table 15: Fertility Rates for Women of Childbearing Age." Available at http://eng.stat.gov.tw/public/data/dgbas03/ bs2/ yearbook_eng/y015.pdf, accessed May 11, 2006.

Riley, Denise. 1988. *Am I That Name? Feminism and the Category of "Women" in History.* Minneapolis: University of Minnesota Press.

Rios, Palmira N. 1990. "Export-Oriented Industrialization and the Demand for Female Labor: Puerto Rican Women in the Manufacturing Sector, 1952–1980." *Gender & Society* 4 (3): 321–337.

Robinson, Kathryn. 1989. "Choosing Contraception: Cultural Change and the Indonesian Family Planning Programme." In *Creating Indonesian Cultures*, ed. Paul Alexander, 21–38. Sydney: Oceania.

Rodan, Garry. 1997. "Singapore: Economic Diversification and Social Divisions." In *The Political Economy of South-East Asia: An Introduction*, ed. Garry Rodan, Kevin Hewison, and Richard Robison, 148–178. New York: Oxford University Press.

Roldan, Martha. 1996. "Women Organizing in the Process of Deindustrialization." In *Confronting State, Capital, and Patriarchy: Women Organizing in the Process of Industrialization*, ed. Amrita Chhachhi and Renee Pittin, 56–92. The Hague: Institute of Social Studies.

Rosa, Kumudhini. 1989. "Export-Oriented Industries and Women Workers in Sri Lanka." In *Women, Poverty, and Ideology in Asia: Contradictory Pressures, Uneasy Resolutions*, ed. Haleh Afshare and Bina Agarwal, 196–211. London: Macmillan.

Rose, Sonya O. 1992. *Limited Livelihoods: Gender and Class in Nineteenth-Century England.* Berkeley: University of California Press.

Ross, Michael. 2001. "Does Oil Hinder Democracy?" *World Politics* 53 (April): 325–361.

Roxborough, Ian, and Ilan Bizberg. 1983. "Union Locals in Mexico: The "New Unionism" in Steel and Automobiles." *Journal of Latin American Studies* 15 (1): 117–135.

Rudra, Nita. 2002. "Globalization and the Decline of the Welfare State in Less-Developed Countries." *International Organization* 56 (2): 411–445.

Sabel, Charles. 1982. *Work and Politics: The Division of Labor in Industry.* New York: Cambridge University Press.

Safa, Helen I. 1986. "Runaway Shops and Female Employment: The Search for Cheap Labor." In *Women's Work: Development and the Division of Labor by Gender*, ed. Eleanor Leacock and Helen Safa, 58–71. New York: Bergin & Garvey.

———. 1995. *The Myth of the Male Breadwinner: Women and Industrialization in the Caribbean.* Boulder, Colo.: Westview.

Salaff, Janet W. 1981. *Working Daughters of Hong Kong: Filial Piety or Power in the Family?* New York: Cambridge University Press.

Salih, Kamal, and Mei Ling Young. 1989. "Changing Conditions of Labour in the Semi-conductor Industry in Malaysia." *Labour and Society* 14:59–80.

Salzinger, Leslie. 1997. "From High Heels to Swathed Bodies: Gendered Meanings under Production in Mexico's Export-Processing Industry." *Feminist Studies* 23 (3): 549–574.

———. 2003. *Genders in Production: Making Workers in Mexico's Global Factories.* Berkeley: University of California Press.

———. 2004. "From Gender as Object to Gender as Verb: Rethinking how Global Restructuring Happens." *Critical Sociology* 30 (1): 43–62.

Sanderson, Warren C., and Jee-Peng Tan. 1995. *Population in Asia.* Washington, D.C.: World Bank.

Saptari, Ratna. 1995. "Rural Women to the Factories: Continuity and Change in East Java's *Kretek* Cigarette Industry." Ph.D. diss., University of Amsterdam.

Schaarschmidt-Kohl, Eva-Marie. 1988. "Indonesian Trade Unions and Hubungan Industrial Pancasila (HIP)." In *New Order Indonesia: Five Essays*, ed. B. B. Herring et al., 52–68. Clayton, Victoria, Australia: Centre for Southeast Asian Studies, Monash University.

Scott, Alison MacEwen. 1986. "Industrialization, Gender Segregation, and Stratification Theory." In *Gender and Stratification*, ed. Rosemary Crompton and Michael Mann, 154–189. New York: Blackwell.

Scott, Joan Wallach, ed. 1988a. *Gender and the Politics of History.* New York: Columbia University Press.

———. 1988b. Gender: "A Useful Category of Historical Analysis." In *Gender and the Politics of History*, ed. Joan Wallace Scott New York: Columbia University Press.

Seccombe, Wally. 1973. "The Housewife and Her Labour under Capitalism." *New Left Review* 83 (January–February): 3–24.

———. 1975. "Domestic Labour—Call and Reply to Critics." *New Left Review* 94 (November–December): 85–96.

Seguino, Stephanie. 1997a. "Export-Led Growth and the Persistence of Gender Inequality in the Newly Industrialized Countries." In *Economic Dimensions of Gender Inequality: A Global Perspective*, ed. Janet M. Rives and Mahmood Yousefi, 11–33. Westport, Conn.: Praeger.

———. 1997b. "Gender Wage Inequality and Export-Led Growth in South Korea." *Journal of Development Studies* 34 (2): 102–132.

Sen, Krishna. 1998. "Indonesian Women at Work: Reframing the Subject." In *Gender and Power in Affluent Asia*, ed. Krishna Sen and Maila Stivens, 35–62. New York: Routledge.

Sison, Carmelo V., ed. 1989. *Protection and Enhancement of Women's Rights in ASEAN Labor Law.* Manila: Friedrich Ebert-Stiftung.

Sklair, Leslie. 1993. *Assembling for Development: The Maquila Industry in Mexico and the United States.* San Diego: Center for US-Mexican Studies, University of California—San Diego.

Smith, Wendy A. 1984. "The Impact of Japanese Foreign Investment and Management Style on Female Industrial Workers in Malaysia." *Akademika* 25 (July): 7–39.

Standing, Guy. 1989. "Global Feminization through Flexible Labor." *World Development* 17 (7): 1077–1095.

———. 1996. "Cumulative Disadvantage? Women Industrial Workers in Malaysia and the Philippines." In *Patriarchy and Economic Development*, ed. Valentine M. Moghadam, 269–302. Oxford: Clarendon Press.

———. 1999. "Global Feminization through Flexible Labor: A Theme Revisited." *World Development* 27 (3): 583–602.

Stepan, Alfred. 1978. *The State and Society: Peru in Comparative Perspective*. Princeton: Princeton University Press.

Stichter, Sharon. 1990. "Women, Employment, and the Family: Current Debates." In *Women, Employment, and the Family in the International Division of Labour*, ed. Sharon Stichter and Jane Parpart, 11–72. Philadelphia: Temple University Press.

Stoler, Ann Laura. 1977. "Class Structure and Female Autonomy in Rural Java." *Signs* 3 (1): 74–89.

———. 1985. *Capitalism and Confrontation in Sumatra's Plantation Belt, 1870–1979*. New Haven: Yale University Press.

Studies in Family Planning. 1996. "Indonesia 1994: Results from the Demographic and Health Survey." *Studies in Family Planning* 27 (2): 119–123.

Sukarno. 1984. *Sarinah: Kewajiban Wanita dalam Perjuangan Republik Indonesia*. Jakarta: Gunung Agung.

Sullivan, Norma. 1991. "Gender and Politics in Indonesia." In *Why Gender Matters in Southeast Asian Politics*, ed. Maila Stivens, 61–86. Clayton, Victoria, Australia: Monash Papers on Southeast Asia, Monash University.

———. 1994. *Masters and Managers: A Study of Gender Relations in Urban Java*. Saint Leonards, New South Wales, Australia: Allen & Unwin.

Sunindyo, Saraswati. 1998. "When the Earth Is Female and the Nation Is Mother: Gender, the Armed Forces, and Nationalism in Indonesia." *Feminist Review* 58 (Spring): 1–21.

Suryakusuma, Julia I. 1987. "State Ibuism: The Social Construction of Womanhood in the Indonesian New Order." Master's thesis, Institute for Social Studies, The Hague.

Tanter, Richard. 1990. "The Totalitarian Ambition: Intelligence Organisations in the Indonesian State." In *State and Civil Society in Indonesia*, ed. Arief Budiman, 213–288. Clayton, Victoria, Australia: Centre for Southeast Asian Studies, Monash University.

Tedjasukmana, Iskandar. 1958. *The Political Character of the Indonesian Trade Union Movement*. Ithaca: Cornell University Modern Indonesia Project.

———. 1959. *The Political Character of the Indonesian Trade Union Movement*. Ithaca: Cornell University Modern Indonesia Project.

Thelen, Kathleen. 1999. "Historical Institutionalism in Comparative Politics." *Annual Review of Political Science* 2:369–404.

———. 2004. *How Institutions Evolve: The Political Economy of Skills in Germany, Britan, the United States, and Japan*. New York: Cambridge University Press.

Tiano, Susan. 1994. *Patriarchy on the Line: Labor, Gender, and Ideology in the Mexican Maquila Industry*. Philadelphia: Temple University Press.

Tiwon, Sylvia. 1996. "Models and Maniacs: Articulating the Female in Indonesia." In *Fantasizing the Feminine in Indonesia*, ed. Laurie J. Sears, 47–70. Durham, N.C.: Duke University Press.

Tjandraningsih, Indrasari. 1991. *Tenaga Kerja Pedesaan Pada Industri Besar Sepatu Olahraga Untuk Ekspor: Studi Kasus Tangerang dan Bogor.* Bandung, Indonesia: ISS-Bandung Research Project Office.

——. 2000. "Gendered Work and Labour Control: Women Factory Workers in Indonesia." *Asian Studies Review* 24 (2): 257–268.

Tomaskovic-Devey, Donald. 1993. *Gender and Racial Inequality at Work: The Sources and Consequences of Job Segregation.* Ithaca: Cornell University Press.

Tomoda, Shizue. 1995. *Women Workers in Manufacturing, 1971–91.* Geneva: ILO.

Tzannatos, Zafiris. 1997. "Growth, Adjustment and Labor Market: Effects on Women Workers." *Jurnal Perempuan* 2 (December–January): 25–36.

Vogel, Lise. 1983. *Marxism and the Oppression of Women: Toward a Unitary Theory.* New Brunswick, N.J.: Rutgers University.

——. 1995. *Woman Questions: Essays for a Materialist Feminism.* New York: Routledge.

Vreede–de Stuers, Cora. 1976. "On the Subject of the "R.U.U.": The History of a Set of Matrimonial Laws." In *Indonesian Women: Some Past and Current Perspectives,* ed. B. B. Hering, 80–114. Brussels: Centre d'Etude du Sud-Est Asiatique ed de l'Extreme Orient.

Walby, Sylvia. 1986. *Patriarchy at Work: Patriarchal and Capitalist Relations in Employment.* Minneapolis: University of Minnesota Press.

Ward, Kathryn. 1990. "Introduction and Overview." In *Women Workers and Global Restructuring,* ed. Kathryn Ward, 1–22. Ithaca: Cornell University/ILR Press.

Wells, Louis T., and V'Ella Warren. 1979. "Developing Country Investors in Indonesia." *Bulletin of Indonesian Economic Studies* 15 (1): 69–84.

Wertheim, W. F. 1986. "Indonesian Moslems under Sukarno and Suharto: Majority with Minority Mentality." In *Studies on Indonesian Islam,* ed. W. F. Wertheim, 15–36. Townsville, Queensland, Australia: Centre for Southeast Asian Studies, James Cook University.

West, Lois A. 1997. *Militant Labor in the Philippines.* Philadelphia: Temple University Press.

White, Benjamin, and Gunawan Wiradi. 1989. "Agrarian and Nonagrarian Bases of Inequality in Nine Javanese Villages." In *Agrarian Transformations: Local Processes and the State in Southeast Asia,* ed. Gillian Hart, Andrew Turton, and Benjamin White, 266–302. Berkeley: University of California Press.

Wie, Thee Kian. 1984. "Japanese Direct Investment in Indonesian Manufacturing." *Bulletin of Indonesian Economic Studies* 20 (2): 90–106.

——. 1991. "The Surge of Asian NIC Investment into Indonesia." *Bulletin of Indonesian Economic Studies* 27 (3): 55–88.

Wieringa, Saskia. 1993. "Two Indonesian Women's Organizations: Gerwani and the PKK." *Bulletin of Concerned Asian Scholars* 25 (2): 17–30.

——. 1995. "The Politicization of Gender Relations in Indonesia: The Indonesian Women's Movement and Gerwani until the New Order State." Amsterdam: University of Amsterdam, Ph.D. diss.

Willner, Ann Ruth. 1961. *From Rice-Field to Factory: The Industrialization of a Rural Labor Force in Java.* Chicago: University of Chicago, Ph.D diss.

Winters, Jeffrey A. 1996. *Power in Motion: Capital Mobility and the Indonesian State.* Ithaca: Cornell University Press.

Wolf, Diane Lauren. 1992. *Factory Daughters: Gender, Household Dynamics, and Rural Industrialization in Java.* Berkeley: University of California Press.

Wolfe, Joel. 1993. *Working Women, Working Men: São Paulo and the Rise of Brazil's Industrial Working Class, 1900–1955.* Durham, N.C.: Duke University Press.

Woo, Jung-En [Meredith Woo-Cumings]. 1991. *Race to the Swift: State and Finance in Korean Industrialization.* New York: Columbia University Press.

Wood, Adrian. 1991. "North-South Trade and Female Labour in Manufacturing." *Journal of Development Studies* 27 (2): 168–189.

Woodcroft-Lee, Carlien Patricia. 1983. "Separate but Equal: Indonesian Muslim Perceptions of the Roles of Women." In *Women's Work and Women's Roles: Economics and Everyday Life in Indonesia, Malaysia, and Singapore,* ed. Lenore Manderson, 173–192. Canberra: Australian National University.

Wu, Huoying, and Hwei-Lin Chuang 2002. *Women's Employment and First Birth Intervals in Taiwan: The Experience of a Rapidly Growing Country.* Hsinchu, Taiwan: National Tsing Hua University, Department of Economics.

Wurfel, David. 1959. "Trade Union Development and Labor Relations Policy in the Philippines." *Industrial & Labor Relations Review* 12 (4): 582–608.

Yelvington, Kevin A. 1995. *Producing Power: Ethnicity, Gender, and Class in a Caribbean Workplace.* Philadelphia: Temple University Press.

YLBHI (Yayasan Lembaga Bantuan Hukum Indonesia). 1990. *Laporan Keadaan Hak-Hak Asasi Manusia di Indonesia 1990.* Jakarta: Yayasan Lembaga Bantuan Hukum Indonesia.

——. 1991. *Demokrasi Masih Terbenam: Catatan Keadaan Hak-Hak Asasi Manusia di Indonesia 1991.* Jakarta: Yayasan Lembaga Bantuan Hukum Indonesia.

——. 1992. *Demokrasi di Balik Keranda: Catatan Keadaan Hak-Hak Asasi Manusia di Indonesia 1992.* Jakarta: Yayasan Lembaga Bantuan Hukum Indonesia.

——. 1993. *Demokrasi Antara Represi dan Resistensi: Catatan Keadaan Hak Asasi Manusia di Indonesia 1993.* Jakarta: Yayasan Lembaga Bantuan Hukum Indonesia.

——. 1997. *1996: Tahun Kekerasan: Potret Pelanggaran HAM di Indonesia.* Jakarta: Yayasan Lembaga Bantuan Hukum Indonesia.

Young, Iris. 1981. "Beyond the Unhappy Marriage: A Critique of the Dual Systems Theory." In *Women and Revolution: A Discussion of the Unhappy Marriage of Marxism and Feminism,* ed. Lydia Sargent, 43–69. Boston: South End Press.

Yusuf, Verdi. 1991. *Pembentukan Angkatan Kerja Industri Garment Untuk Ekspor: Pengalaman Dari Bandung—Jawa Barat.* Bandung, Indonesia: ISS-Bandung Research Project Office.

Zazueta, César, and Ricardo de la Peña. 1984. *La Estructura del Congreso del Trabajo: Estado, Trabajo y Capital en México, un Acercamiento al Tema.* Mexico, D.F.: Fondo de Cultura Económica, Centro Nacional de Información y Estadísticas del Trabajo.

# Index